Sunset
Menu Cook Book

Sunset
Menu Cook

LANE MAGAZINE & BOOK COMPANY,

Book

By the editors of Sunset Books and Sunset Magazine

MENLO PARK, CALIFORNIA

Contents

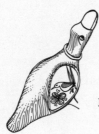

ILLUSTRATIONS BY BERNICE T. GLENN

COVER PHOTOGRAPH: Mexican Soup Supper, pages 70 and 71; photograph by Darrow Watt. PHOTOGRAPHERS: Darrow Watt, pages 11, 12, 16, 20, 27, 31, 34, 37, 41, 46, 51, 61, 63, 64, 68, 70, 71, 75, 78, 81, 83, 84, 87, 99, 100, 101, 102, 112, 115, 120, 125, 128, 142, 145, 151, 173, 175, 177, 178, 200. Glenn Christiansen, pages 19, 54, 57, 91, 109, 117, 133, 146, 156, 161, 163, 165, 166, 170, 182, 184, 187, 188, 193, 194, 197, 198. Ernest Braun, page 62. Ells Marugg, page 94.

Menus for Many Occasions

This is a book that has been written in response to many requests from *Sunset* readers. It brings together a vast collection of carefully planned and thoroughly tested menus suited to a wide variety of occasions, ranging from simple brunches and picnics to party dinners with special themes.

Although the emphasis is on informality, a few more elaborate menus are included for that very special party occasion. There are many ideas for impromptu entertaining and for the relaxed, casual kind of party that delights guests and brings compliments to the hostess. And these menus are not only for guests. There are many ideas that will make family meals memorable. Some menus are especially appropriate for special occasions such as a birthday, a holiday, or a trip to the beach or the snow country. Others may merely add a festive touch to a Sunday breakfast or a family barbecue.

The book is divided into five sections: Brunches and Lunches; Dinners and Suppers; Special Occasions and Themes; Holidays; and the Big Party. But this is a flexible book. Many of the menus are interchangeable. Most of those in the Special Occasions section can be adapted to serve a large group. Many lunches can be served as suppers or late-evening snacks. Almost any dinner can be given a theme with a little imaginative staging. And, of course, every holiday is a special occasion.

The recipes within the menus are also flexible. Almost every cook will want to make a few changes to suit her own tastes and the preferences of her family or guests. Browse through the various sections. You'll find many ways to combine recipes into a menu of your own design.

These are meals that you can serve with confidence. Every menu has been carefully planned. Every party has been carried through to the last detail and is a proven success. Every recipe has been tested in *Sunset's* kitchens.

Brunches & Lunches

A leisurely brunch or a festive luncheon offers an easy, relaxed way to entertain a few or many friends, to create happy memories in the minds of weekend guests, or to turn a family meal into a special-occasion affair. This chapter contains menus that are fancy enough to serve at a midday party, yet easy enough to prepare as a family treat. Often a few simple touches can convert family fare into a guest meal.

As a way of entertaining, the brunch or luncheon is particularly easy on the hostess. Usually only one dish requires detailed preparation, and very often it can be prepared well in advance. Since the menu is not extensive, you have more time to experiment with a new, special dish.

These are meals that can be simple or elegant. If the day is warm and sunny, present your brunch or luncheon in the garden. Or pack a picnic and head for the park or the beach. Most of these menus are convertible to indoor or outdoor service. They are ideal meals to serve before a football game or other afternoon event—and don't overlook the possibility of serving these brunch and luncheon menus as suppers or late-evening snacks.

Basque Buffet

BASQUE PIPERADE WITH HAM SLICES
SESAME CORNBREAD
BUTTER AND HONEY
GINGERED MELON BALLS

This brunch features pipérade, a dish that originated in the Basque country along the French-Spanish border. The French word *pipérade* refers to a cooked vegetable mixture of green peppers, onions, tomatoes, and garlic. But as a dish, a pipérade commonly implies an unfolded omelet or scrambled eggs garnished with the vegetable mixture. It makes an ideal breakfast, brunch, or light supper dish. Here we suggest a brunch buffet for 8 to 10 persons.

You can prepare most of this brunch a day ahead of time. Mix the fruit and chill it overnight. Bake the bread a day or so ahead, cool, and wrap in foil; cut slices, rewrap, and heat it just before serving. Have the vegetable mixture ready to cook; it can cook while you mix the eggs. You'll want to keep the pipérade warm on a serving table, so plan to use a warming tray, chafing dish, or electric frying pan for serving.

BASQUE PIPERADE

There are many versions of pipérade. Some incorporate the cooked vegetable mixture into the eggs, and some use it as a garnish as we have done here. Ham may be used merely to flavor the vegetables, or as a garnish for the eggs; our recipe includes ham slices to accompany the eggs.

    3 green peppers, thinly sliced
    1 large onion, thinly sliced
    1 clove garlic, mashed
    4 tomatoes, peeled, seeded, and chopped
 ¼ cup (⅛ lb.) butter or olive oil
 ¾ teaspoon salt
    Dash pepper
10 to 12 slices baked ham, ¼ inch thick
    3 tablespoons butter or margarine
1½ dozen eggs
 ⅔ cup whipping cream
    1 teaspoon salt
 ¼ teaspoon pepper
    2 tablespoons grated Parmesan cheese
    Parsley or chopped chives for garnish

To make the pipérade vegetable mixture, sauté the peppers, onions, garlic, and tomatoes in the butter or olive oil just until vegetables are tender

and liquid is slightly reduced. Add the ¾ teaspoon salt and dash pepper. (The classic method is to cook the vegetables to a mushy consistency, but they can be done to the texture you prefer.) Cover and keep warm, or reheat just before serving. Broil the ham slices and keep them warm.

To scramble the eggs, melt the 3 tablespoons butter or margarine in a frying pan. Beat the eggs with the cream, 1 teaspoon salt, and ¼ teaspoon pepper. Pour egg mixture into pan, and cook over low heat, stirring, until eggs are set, but moist and soft.

To serve, arrange the ham slices on a warm platter or serving dish. Spoon the pipérade mixture in a ring around the inner edges of the ham slices; then mound the eggs in the center. Sprinkle with Parmesan cheese and garnish with parsley or chopped chives. Makes 10 to 12 servings.

SESAME CORNBREAD

Toasted sesame seeds give a nutty flavor and crunchiness to this cornbread—an interesting contrast to the soft eggs. Serve with butter and honey (individual paper cups of honey make serving easier).

1½ cups unsifted all-purpose flour
½ cup sugar
1½ teaspoons salt
1¼ teaspoons soda
2 cups cornmeal
1 cup wheat germ
½ cup (2¾ oz.) sesame seed, toasted
2 cups buttermilk
¾ cup salad oil or melted butter
2 eggs, slightly beaten

Sift together the flour, sugar, salt, and soda; blend in the cornmeal, wheat germ, and sesame seed. In a separate bowl, mix together the buttermilk, salad oil or melted butter, and eggs. Blend the dry ingredients and the liquid mixture together, using a minimum number of strokes. Pour into a greased loaf pan (9 by 5 inches) and bake in a 375° oven about 55 minutes. Remove bread from pan and cool on a rack. Slice to serve. Makes 1 large loaf.

GINGERED MELON BALLS

Ginger and honey enhance the flavor of fresh melon for a refreshing fruit course. Use one type of melon or a combination of several.

6 cups melon balls (honeydew, cantaloupe, Persian, Crenshaw, casaba)
3 tablespoons honey
½ cup finely chopped crystallized ginger
Mint sprigs and chopped crystallized ginger for garnish

Combine melon balls, honey, and ginger. Spoon fruit into a large glass compote or serving dish, cover, and chill until ready to serve. Garnish the top with fresh mint leaves and a sprinkling of chopped ginger. To serve, spoon into individual serving dishes and garnish each with a sprig of mint. Makes 12 servings.

Pancake Brunch

RIBIER AND MUSCAT OR THOMPSON SEEDLESS GRAPES
APPLES ANNA   POTATO PANCAKES
OVEN-COOKED PORK SAUSAGE LINKS
MELTED BUTTER   PRESERVES

Depending upon your need and mood, this meal can answer family or company needs at any time of the day. The oven does the spattery job of browning pork sausages, and the apples cook along with them. You make the pancakes with a combination of prepared mixes. The apple dish requires the most preparation so start it first, then bake the sausages. Mix the pancake batter just before you are ready to serve the meal.

APPLES ANNA

8 to 10 medium-sized apples (any variety except Red Delicious)
½ cup (¼ lb.) butter
6 tablespoons sugar
Ground cinnamon
Cinnamon sticks

Peel, core, and thinly slice the apples; you should have 8 to 10 cups. Melt butter. In a 9-inch frying pan or a 2-quart casserole (one that you can use over direct heat), swirl around 2 tablespoons of the butter to coat pan bottom. Neatly layer the apple slices in the pan, drizzling layers occasionally with a little of the butter and a little sugar; reserve about ⅔ of the butter and sugar.

Sprinkle the reserved sugar evenly over the top of the apples and drizzle evenly with the reserved melted butter. Set pan over medium heat and cook, uncovered, for 10 minutes without stirring; apples should not brown. If edges start to darken, remove from heat. Bake, uncovered, in a 400° oven for 35 minutes.

If apples begin to look quite dry on top, baste with a little of the juices bubbling around the pan sides, or with a little more melted butter. Decorate with a dusting of cinnamon and a cinnamon stick. Makes 6 generous servings.

POTATO PANCAKES

Measure 1½ cups buttermilk pancake mix into a bowl. Add the dry measure of instant mashed potatoes as designated on the package to make 4 servings; stir together. Beat 2 eggs with 2 tablespoons salad oil and mix with 1½ cups milk. Stir into pancake mix until batter is thoroughly moistened and well blended. Bake by spoonfuls on a medium hot (350°) lightly greased electric griddle or frying pan (or in a frying pan or griddle over medium heat). Add a little more milk if batter gets thick. Serve with melted butter and a favorite fruit preserve. Makes 12 thick pancakes, each about 4 inches in diameter.

OVEN-COOKED PORK SAUSAGE LINKS

Allow 4 to 6 pork link sausages for each serving. Place sausages side by side in a shallow baking pan and pour in enough water to make a layer about ¼ inch deep. Bake sausages, uncovered, in a 400° oven for 15 minutes, then drain off the drippings and discard; return sausages to the oven to bake another 20 minutes. Do not turn the links. Drain briefly on paper towels and keep warm until ready to serve.

Patio Brunch for Four

**FRUIT-FILLED CANTALOUPE
VEAL STEAKS WITH FRIED EGGS AND ARTICHOKES
TOASTED SCONES OR ENGLISH MUFFINS**

The fruit course doubles as a centerpiece for this summery brunch for four persons. Prepare the fruit plate first but plan to serve it last. The artichokes, veal, and eggs should be cooked just before serving.

FRUIT-FILLED CANTALOUPE

Cut 4 wedges from a large cantaloupe, leaving alternate 4 wedges attached at top and bottom. Remove seeds with a spoon and place melon on serving plate. Fill center of melon with whole strawberries (you'll need about a pint basket) and arrange clusters of seedless grapes (about ½ pound) between the cut wedges of melon. Serves 4 generously.

VEAL STEAKS WITH FRIED EGGS AND ARTICHOKES

Veal cube steaks are topped with fried eggs and garnished with artichoke hearts, parsley, and lemon wedges.

  1 package (9 oz.) frozen artichoke hearts
  1 tablespoon butter
  ⅛ teaspoon whole basil
    Salt and pepper
  **4 veal cube steaks (veal that has been
    mechanically tenderized)**
    Flour
  2 tablespoons butter or margarine
  2 teaspoons lemon juice
  4 eggs
    Parsley and lemon wedges

Cook artichoke hearts according to package directions; drain. Stir in the 1 tablespoon butter, basil, and dash each of salt and pepper; cover and keep warm.

Heat the 2 tablespoons butter or margarine in a large frying pan. Dust meat lightly with flour, salt, and pepper. Sauté meat in butter over high heat until brown on both sides, about 5 minutes. Sprinkle lemon juice over each steak. Remove meat from pan and keep warm. Add a little more butter to the pan, if necessary, and fry the eggs over low heat to the doneness preferred.

Arrange meat on 4 warm plates; put an egg on top of each steak. Garnish plates with artichokes, parsley, and lemon wedges. Makes 4 servings.

Cheese-Tasting Brunch

FRESH FRUIT AMBROSIA
ASSORTED CHEESES
TOASTED PUMPERNICKEL AND RYE BREAD
HONEY PECAN COFFEE CAKE
COFFEE WITH CINNAMON

This festive breakfast is well suited to a lazy weekend when you have overnight guests. It can be set up buffet style so guests can eat when they please. Make up the fruit platter at the last minute, or make it ahead and chill until serving time. Offer cinnamon sticks for coffee stirrers. Toast pumpernickel and thin buffet rye bread, butter, and keep warm in a basket on an electric tray.

FRESH FRUIT AMBROSIA

3 oranges, peeled and sliced
2 bananas, peeled and sliced diagonally
   Lemon juice
2 cups strawberries, washed and hulled
1 papaya, peeled, seeded, and sliced (or 1 small cantaloupe)
¾ cup flaked coconut

Arrange fruits on a large platter (sprinkle bananas with the lemon juice to prevent darkening). Spoon the coconut into a small serving bowl; place on platter and let each person spoon coconut over his fruit selection. Makes 6 servings.

THE CHEESES

Buy an assortment of four or five different, fairly mild cheeses such as Kuminost, Tilsit, Gruyère, Cheddar, and smoked Edam. Arrange on a cheese board and let cheeses warm to room temperature before serving.

HONEY PECAN COFFEE CAKE

This cake keeps well—reheat to serve or toast under broiler; serve with butter.

⅔ cup shortening
¾ cup sugar
2¼ cups unsifted regular all-purpose flour
1 teaspoon cinnamon
2 teaspoons baking powder
½ teaspoon each salt and soda
½ cup honey
2 eggs
¾ cup buttermilk
⅓ cup chopped pecans

Cream together the shortening and sugar; add 1 cup of the flour and the cinnamon; blend until mixture resembles crumbs. Remove ½ cup of this mixture and set aside for topping. To remaining crumb mixture add baking powder, salt, soda, honey, and eggs; beat until blended and smooth. Add remaining 1¼ cups flour alternately with buttermilk, beating after each addition just until blended. Spread batter in a greased 9-inch square baking pan. Work reserved crumb mixture between fingers until it resembles coarse crumbs; mix in pecans. Sprinkle mixture over top of batter.
   Bake in a 375° oven for 40 minutes or until a pick inserted in the center comes out clean. Makes about 9 servings.

Snow Country Breakfast

FROZEN ORANGE JUICE

CINNAMON WAFFLES

MAPLE SYRUP   WHIPPED HONEY BUTTER

CHOPPED PECANS   CHERRY PRESERVES

CANADIAN BACON

HOT CHOCOLATE WITH MARSHMALLOWS

COFFEE

This meal adapts to tray service. You might set out the dishes buffet-style beside a blazing fire. You can prepare the syrup and honey butter in advance, although they can easily be made while you bake the waffles. Set the toppings together on a tray for easy help-yourself service. You can bake several waffles ahead and keep them warm in the oven if you wish.

Heat packaged sliced Canadian bacon in a frying pan just until hot through and crispy on the edges. Use an instant cocoa mix to make the hot chocolate, and drop in marshmallows at serving time.

CINNAMON WAFFLES

Use a pancake and waffle mix or biscuit mix and prepare waffles according to directions on the package, but add ½ teaspoon cinnamon for each cup of dry mix. Bake as usual.

MAPLE SYRUP

Place 1 package (1 lb.) light brown sugar in a saucepan; add 1 cup water and 3 tablespoons light corn syrup. Bring to a boil and let simmer, uncovered, 5 minutes. Stir in ¼ teaspoon maple flavoring. Pour into a pitcher and serve warm. Makes about 1½ cups.

WHIPPED HONEY BUTTER

Cream ½ cup (¼ lb.) butter until light, and gradually mix in, a spoonful at a time, 1 carton (12 oz.) whipped honey. (Or place ¾ cup regular honey in a mixing bowl and beat until white and fluffy; gradually beat in ½ cup soft butter.) Makes about 2 cups.

Mexican-Style Brunch

GUAVA FRUIT PUNCH

MEXICAN EGG SCRAMBLE (CHILAQUILES)

GREEN CHILE SAUCE   REFRIED BEANS

BUTTERED TOASTED FLOUR TORTILLAS

HOT CHOCOLATE   COFFEE

Electric appliances keep the food warm for serving at this Mexican-style brunch. Start the meal with the combination punch and fruit course, which might be set up on a small garden table, if weather permits. The egg dish stays creamy and fresh for about an hour held at a warm temperature in an electric frying pan. Use an electric griddle or another frying pan to heat and butter the flour tortillas at the buffet table.

GUAVA FRUIT PUNCH

3 cans (6 oz. each) frozen orange juice
   concentrate, reconstituted
3 cans (12 oz. each) guava nectar, chilled
1¼ cups light rum (optional)
2 oranges, unpeeled but thinly sliced and
   slices halved
1 fresh pineapple, peeled, cored, and cut
   in spears
1 large papaya, peeled, seeded, and sliced
2 cups whole strawberries

Combine in a punch bowl the orange juice and chilled guava nectar. Just before serving pour in the rum, if used. In a bowl arrange the orange slices, pineapple spears, papaya slices, and strawberries. Float a few pieces of fruit in the punch. To serve, spoon fruit into 12 or 14-ounce glasses, fill with punch; offer straws and spoons. Makes about 14 servings.

MEXICAN EGG SCRAMBLE
(Chilaquiles)

In Mexico this scrambled egg dish would be called *chilaquiles*. There are many versions, but all have crisp tortilla bits inside.

  6 corn tortillas
  2 tablespoons shortening or salad oil
  4 tablespoons butter or margarine
  ½ cup minced onion
  ½ to 1 can (4-oz. size) California green
       chiles, seeded and chopped
  1 cup half-and-half (light cream)
  1 can (6 oz.) white sauce
  8 eggs
  1 teaspoon salt
10 or 12 pork link sausages, cooked and drained
  3 tomatoes, peeled, seeded, and chopped
  2 cups shredded longhorn Cheddar cheese
    Pitted ripe olives for garnish
    Green or red chile sauce (optional)

Cut tortillas in matchstick-sized pieces. Heat shortening and 2 tablespoons of the butter in an electric frying pan at 350°. Sauté tortillas until crisp, about 5 minutes; push to edges of pan. Melt remaining 2 tablespoons butter in center, and sauté onion and chiles (taste for flavor, and add desired measure) about 4 minutes.

In a bowl, gradually stir cream into white sauce until smooth. With a fork, beat in eggs and salt. Reduce heat to 250°; pour in eggs; and cook, stirring, until softly scrambled, about 3 minutes—tortillas will mix into eggs.

Distribute over top the sausages, tomatoes, cheese, and olives. Cover and let stand until cheese melts, about 5 minutes. Then reduce heat of frying pan to warm until serving time. Pass the hot chile sauce. Makes 6 to 8 servings.

REFRIED BEANS

You'll need about 1 can (1 lb. 4 oz.) refried beans for each 6 to 8 servings. Heat as directed on the can—with a little butter, bacon drippings, or lard if you like more richness.

TORTILLAS

Fry the flour tortillas on a well buttered hot griddle or electric frying pan until lightly toasted, about 1 minute on each side.

Sandwich Breakfast

STRAWBERRY-PINEAPPLE JUICE
HAM-AND-EGG BREAKFAST SANDWICHES

Colorful open-faced sandwiches and chilled strawberry-pineapple juice make a cheerful way to start a day. The meat for the sandwich might be deviled ham spread, chicken spread, or one of the other sandwich meat spreads available in the market. Use your favorite melting cheese—Swiss, teleme, Cheddar, for example.

You can prepare the juice the night before, but it doesn't take long to do in the morning. Have the sandwich ingredients ready and do the cooking and assembling just before you serve.

STRAWBERRY-PINEAPPLE JUICE

2 cups (about 1 basket) fresh strawberries
3 cups canned pineapple juice
  Sugar
  Whole strawberries for garnish

Purée strawberries by whirling in a blender or pressing through a fine wire strainer; blend in pineapple juice and sweeten to taste. For garnish press a sturdy plastic drinking straw through one or several whole berries. Serve juice well chilled with a strawberry garnish in each glass. Makes 4 to 6 servings.

HAM-AND-EGG BREAKFAST SANDWICHES

4 English muffins, split and toasted
2 cans (about 4 oz. each) deviled ham (or other sandwich spread)
6 eggs
¼ cup milk or half-and-half (light cream)
¼ teaspoon salt
  Dash pepper
3 tablespoons chopped green onion (including part of the green tops)
2 tablespoons butter or margarine
8 tomato slices (about 2 large tomatoes)
8 thin slices cheese (about 8 oz.)

Spread each English muffin half with deviled ham, using about ¼ can for each. Lightly beat together the eggs, milk, salt, pepper, and green onion. Melt butter in frying pan and scramble eggs until done to stage desired. Arrange eggs over each muffin half; top each with a slice of tomato and a slice of cheese. Broil to melt cheese. Serve at once. Makes 4 servings.

Sunday Patio Brunch

EGG, ASPARAGUS, AND SALMON PLATTER
TOASTED BRIOCHE ROLLS OR ENGLISH MUFFINS
CREAM CHEESE
GINGERED STRAWBERRY SUNDAES

The simplicity of this menu has two advantages. If you have overnight guests, you can quickly prepare everything in their presence. And the food is easy to carry to a table outdoors. If possible, use a hot tray for serving.

Have all ingredients ready for quick morning preparation. Wash and hull the berries and clean and trim the asparagus the day before to save time. Make coffee, cook asparagus, scramble eggs, and toast rolls in that order. Place a chunk of cream cheese on a serving board for spreading on the hot rolls. You can assemble the sundaes just before serving.

EGG, ASPARAGUS, AND SALMON PLATTER

   1½ **pounds asparagus, washed and trimmed**
        Boiling salted water
   4 **tablespoons butter**
   8 **eggs**
   ⅓ **cup half-and-half (light cream) or**
        whipping cream
   ½ **teaspoon salt**
   ¼ **teaspoon crumbled tarragon (optional)**
        Chopped parsley
   6 **slices (about 3 oz.) smoked salmon (or**
        substitute sliced boiled ham)

Cook asparagus in boiling salted water 7 to 10 minutes, or until tender; drain. Add 2 tablespoons butter and heat, coating well.

Melt remaining 2 tablespoons of butter in a frying pan. Beat eggs lightly and mix in cream, salt, and tarragon, if desired. Pour into frying pan and cook over moderate heat, stirring lightly from the bottom until done to desired consistency.

Spoon eggs onto center of a heated platter, sprinkle with chopped parsley, and arrange asparagus spears on one side and sliced salmon on the other side. Makes 6 servings.

GINGERED STRAWBERRY SUNDAES

   3 **cups strawberries, washed, hulled, and halved**
        Sugar to taste
   1½ **pints vanilla ice cream**
   3 **tablespoons preserved ginger, finely chopped**
   1 or 2 **tablespoons syrup from preserved ginger**

Sprinkle strawberries with sugar to taste. At serving time spoon half the berries into dessert dishes, cover with a scoop of vanilla ice cream in each dish, and spoon remaining berries around sides. Sprinkle preserved ginger over sundaes along with the ginger syrup. Makes 6 servings.

Berry and Biscuit Breakfast

SUGARED RASPBERRIES   SWEET BISCUITS
SWEDISH CREAM
EDAM OR CHEDDAR CHEESE OMELETS
SHOESTRING POTATOES WITH CHIVES

Raspberry shortcakes topped with an egg-enriched whipped cream sauce can be served either to start this meal or as a dessert course. Keep the biscuits warm duing the meal in an insulated basket or on an electric warming tray. Allow ½ to ¾ cup raspberries for each serving. Save extra biscuits to toast and butter for another breakfast.

While the biscuits and the frozen shoestring potatoes bake, whip the ingredients for the Swedish Cream, arrange the berries in a serving bowl, and shred the cheese and beat the eggs for the omelets. Melt the butter for the chive potato topping in the hot omelet pan.

SWEET BISCUITS

Serve these warm, split and filled with raspberries and topped with Swedish Cream (recipe follows).

 2 cups biscuit mix
 2 tablespoons sugar
 2 tablespoons butter
 1 egg
 ½ cup half-and-half (light cream)
  Melted butter
  Sugar

Measure biscuit mix into a bowl, add the 2 tablespoons sugar, and finely cut in butter. Beat egg with half-and-half and stir into the biscuit mix until thoroughly moistened. Turn dough out onto a board dusted with some of the biscuit mix and knead 8 to 10 turns. Pat or roll out ½ inch thick and cut in 2½-inch rounds. Place slightly apart on an ungreased baking sheet, brush tops with melted butter, and sprinkle with sugar. Bake in a 450° oven for 8 to 10 minutes or until golden brown. Makes 8 to 10 biscuits.

SWEDISH CREAM

 1 egg, separated
 ¾ cup sifted powdered sugar
 ½ cup whipping cream
 ½ teaspoon vanilla

Beat egg white until frothy, then gradually beat in the powdered sugar and continue to whip until white holds shiny, soft peaks. Set aside, and with the same beaters whip the cream with the egg yolk until mixture is stiff. Add vanilla and fold in the beaten egg white. Makes about 1½ cups, enough for 6 to 8 shortcakes.

EDAM OR CHEDDAR CHEESE OMELETS

For each person, make a 2-egg omelet as described on page 53. Before folding, fill with about 2 tablespoons shredded Edam or Cheddar cheese. Turn out, and top with more shredded cheese, if desired.

SHOESTRING POTATOES WITH CHIVES

Bake 1 package (12 oz.) frozen shoestring potatoes according to package directions (in same oven with the biscuits, but potatoes may take longer). Dress with 2 or 3 tablespoons melted butter mixed with 2 or 3 tablespoons chopped fresh, frozen, or freeze-dried chives. Makes 4 servings.

Brunch for Four

PINEAPPLE-OLIVE SKEWERS WITH CHUTNEY DIP
SHRIMP SCRAMBLED EGGS ON
TOASTED ENGLISH MUFFINS
SALTED NUTS   FRESH FRUITS   COOKIES
MILK PUNCH   COFFEE

Planned around a scrambled-at-the-table egg dish, this meal opens with a fresh pineapple appetizer. Serve milk punch while your guests dip the fruit into a piquant chutney dip. Following the egg course, provide an assortment of salted almonds and walnuts, fresh fruits, and favorite cookies to go with coffee and conversation.

Both the pineapple and the dip can be made ahead and kept in the refrigerator. Prepare the milk punch quickly in a blender. Sauté mushrooms and shrimp in butter in an electric frying pan or chafing dish at the table; beat together the eggs and seasonings and bring to the table in a pitcher. Toast and butter the muffins ahead and keep them warm in the oven.

PINEAPPLE-OLIVE SKEWERS WITH CHUTNEY DIP

1 medium-sized pineapple, pared, cored, and cut
    into 1-inch cubes
    Stuffed Spanish-style green or pitted ripe olives
1 small package (3 oz.) cream cheese, softened
2 to 3 tablespoons finely chopped chutney
½ teaspoon each curry powder and grated onion
1 teaspoon lemon juice
    About 3 tablespoons light cream

Skewer pineapple cubes with olives on wooden picks. Serve with a chutney dip made by combining cream cheese with chutney, curry powder, onion, and lemon juice; beat until soft and fluffy. Add cream to bring the mixture to a good dipping consistency. Makes about ¾ cup of dip.

SHRIMP SCRAMBLED EGGS

¼ cup (⅛ lb.) butter
1 cup sliced fresh mushrooms
½ pound small, whole cooked shrimp (shelled
    and deveined)
8 eggs
¼ cup half-and-half (light cream)
½ teaspoon salt
    Dill weed
1 tablespoon dry Sherry
4 English muffins, split, toasted, and buttered

Melt butter in an electric frying pan or chafing dish; add mushrooms and shrimp and cook until mushrooms are soft. Beat eggs with cream, salt, ⅛ teaspoon dill weed, and Sherry. Add egg mixture to the pan and stir gently until eggs are set. Serve over muffins; sprinkle with additional dill weed. Makes 4 servings.

MILK PUNCH

1 cup brandy
2 cups cold milk
6 tablespoons powdered sugar
½ teaspoon vanilla
6 to 8 ice cubes, coarsely crushed
    Nutmeg

Pour brandy into blender with milk, sugar, vanilla, and ice cubes. Whirl until mixture is frothy and well blended. Pour into glasses or punch cups; sprinkle with nutmeg. Makes about 5½ cups, 4 to 6 servings.

Special-Occasion Brunch

CRANBERRY-ORANGE JUICE COCKTAIL
EGGS A LA CREME
BUTTERED TOAST WEDGES   CHERRY JAM

For some special morning—perhaps a birthday, or a Sunday when you have house guests—this menu provides for a meal that is elegant yet very easy to prepare.

Mix the fruit juices and refrigerate them while you prepare the rest of the meal. Set the table and make the coffee before you begin the Eggs à la Crème and the toast.

CRANBERRY-ORANGE JUICE COCKTAIL

Prepare 1 can (6 oz.) frozen orange juice concentrate according to directions on the can. In a large pitcher, mix orange juice with 1 cup cranberry juice cocktail; chill. Just before serving, mix in 1 bottle (10 oz.) well chilled ginger ale. Makes 6 to 8 servings.

EGGS A LA CREME

    1 can (10½ oz.) white sauce
    ½ cup sour cream or whipping cream
    2 tablespoons grated Parmesan cheese
    ¼ teaspoon each dry mustard and salt
    6 eggs
    1½ cups croutons
    3 to 4 tablespoons butter
      Stuffed Spanish-style green olives

Make sauce by mixing in a saucepan the white sauce, sour cream or whipping cream, cheese, mustard, and salt. Heat over a very low heat or in a double boiler.

Meanwhile, poach the eggs and heat the croutons (you can make croutons in advance or buy them) in the butter, tossing so butter is evenly distributed. For each serving, arrange about ¼ cup buttered croutons in a custard cup or similar small dish. Top with a poached egg, spoon over about 3 tablespoons cream sauce, and garnish with several olive slices. Makes 6 servings.

Hearty Swiss-Style Breakfast

SAUTEED APPLE SLICES
PORK LINK SAUSAGES
SWISS-STYLE CEREAL

"Nourishing" may seem an old-fashioned claim, but it suits this hearty, wholesome breakfast that features a flavorful version of the Swiss oat cereal called *Müsli (mewz-*lee), a blend of quick-cooking rolled oats and wheat germ crowded with toasted nuts and dried fruit. The dish was developed more than 50 years ago by a doctor named Bircher. In Switzerland, breakfast is often a one-dish meal called *Birchermüsli.*

If you wish, omit the sautéed apples from this menu and instead top the cereal with fruit—almost any kind is good, including sliced bananas, apples, pears, or papayas, sliced or halved strawberries, halved seeded grapes, or halved orange slices.

SAUTEED APPLE SLICES

3 tablespoons butter
3 large unpeeled Golden Delicious apples, cored and thickly sliced
1 teaspoon sugar
1½ pounds cooked pork link sausages

Melt butter in a wide frying pan; add apples, and cook over moderately high heat, turning gently from time to time with a wide spatula until fruit begins to soften, looks translucent, and browns lightly. Sprinkle with the sugar; cook 1 more minute. Serve hot with pork link sausages, cooked according to directions on the package. Makes 6 servings.

SWISS-STYLE CEREAL

This recipe makes enough cereal for about 16 servings; prepare it ahead and store it in the cupboard to serve as you would any uncooked cereal.

1 cup each whole filberts and whole blanched almonds
3 cups quick-cooking rolled oats
¾ cup sweetened wheat germ
1 cup dried currants
⅔ cup finely chopped dried apricots
¾ cup firmly packed brown sugar
Milk or cream
Fresh fruit (optional)

Spread filberts on a rimmed baking sheet, and the almonds on another one. Bake in a 350° oven for 5 to 8 minutes or until very lightly browned; shake pans occasionally. Let nuts cool; rub filberts in your hands to loosen as much of the brown exterior as possible, then blow or fan off this chaff. Chop filberts and almonds coarsely.

Blend nuts with oats, wheat germ, currants, apricots, and sugar. Store in a tightly closed container at room temperature. Serve in bowls with milk or cream; top with fruit, if you like. Makes 8 cups or about 16 servings of ½-cup size.

Swedish Pancake Breakfast

PINK GRAPEFRUIT IN SHELLS
SWEDISH OVEN PANCAKE (FLASKPANNKAKA)
BUTTERED FRESH ASPARAGUS
LINGONBERRY PRESERVES

A baked pancake filled with tender bits of pork makes a light and delicate main dish for a brunch or breakfast. Tart preserves complement the pancake; if lingonberry preserves are not available, use any other tart jelly or jam, or cranberry preserves.

Brown the diced pork in a frying pan, then pour in the thin egg batter and bake; the pancake puffs and billows like a popover as it browns. Cook the asparagus while the pancake bakes.

SWEDISH OVEN PANCAKE

Serve this puffy baked pancake as soon as you take it from the oven; it collapses as it cools.

½ pound boneless pork butt, cut into
    ½-inch squares
    Salt
3 eggs
½ cup milk
½ cup unsifted regular all-purpose flour
    Lingonberry preserves

Sprinkle pork squares lightly with salt. Brown in a 9-inch frying pan over moderate heat. Meanwhile, beat eggs with milk and gradually beat in flour until smoothly blended.

Pour batter over pork in pan (if you do not have a frying pan that can go into the oven, distribute meat and drippings in a 9-inch pie pan; pour batter over). Bake in a 400° oven for 25 minutes, or until puffed and well browned. Cut in wedges and serve at once with lingonberry preserves. Makes 4 to 5 servings.

Chilly-Morning Breakfast

HOT TOMATO BOUILLON
EGGS IN TOAST RINGS
PORK SAUSAGE PATTIES
COFFEE   INSTANT MOCHA

A warm breakfast will raise spirits on a cold or foggy morning and provide a nourishing way to start the day. Serve the hot tomato drink first, to be sipped while you are preparing the eggs and sausage patties. Instant coffee powder and instant cocoa mix make a quickly prepared hot mocha drink.

HOT TOMATO BOUILLON

Heat together 1 can (10½ oz.) condensed beef broth and 1 can (1 pt. 2 oz.) tomato juice; add a dash *each* of liquid hot-pepper seasoning and lemon juice, if you wish. Makes 3½ cups; any left over can be reheated later.

EGGS IN TOAST RINGS

For each serving:

1 slice of white, oatmeal, or whole wheat bread
  Butter
1 egg

Cut a circle about 3 inches in diameter from the center of each slice of bread (use a jar top if you don't have a cutter this size). Butter the bread "frames" on both sides, reserving bread rounds cut from center for toast. Place frame in a frying pan over medium heat and cook until the bread is toasted on one side; turn, add a little butter to the frying pan, and break an egg into the center of each. Cook until egg is set and toast is browned on underside.

With a wide spatula, carefully remove each egg-and-bread combination. Serve at once.

INSTANT MOCHA

For each cup, place 2 teaspoons *each* instant coffee powder and instant cocoa mix in a mug. Fill with hot milk; stir to blend. Serve immediately.

Oven-Fried Fish Breakfast

OVEN-CRUSTED HALIBUT
SOFT-COOKED EGGS   WHOLE WHEAT TOAST
FRESH PINEAPPLE WITH BROWN SUGAR
CUSTARD SAUCE

Your oven does the job of butter-browning the fish for this breakfast or brunch. Make the custard sauce for the pineapple while the oven preheats for the fish; the sauce should be almost cooled to room temperature when you serve it with the fruit.

OVEN-CRUSTED HALIBUT

6 halibut steaks, 1 inch thick (about 2 lbs.)
  Salt
  Yellow cornmeal
  Flour
2 to 3 tablespoons butter

Sprinkle halibut steaks with salt. Turn fish in a mixture of equal portions cornmeal and flour. Melt butter in a shallow baking pan over direct heat or in the preheating oven). Coat fish on all sides in butter and arrange, without crowding, in the pan.

Bake in a 500° oven for 8 to 12 minutes or until fish breaks easily when a fork or knife tip is inserted in the center or thickest part; turn fish after the first 5 minutes. Makes 6 servings.

PINEAPPLE WITH BROWN SUGAR AND CUSTARD SAUCE

1 egg
1 cup milk
2 tablespoons sugar
¼ teaspoon rum flavoring
1 medium-sized pineapple
  Brown sugar

In the top of a double boiler beat the egg with milk and sugar. Cook, stirring, over gently simmering water until custard is thick enough to coat the back of a metal spoon with a smooth, opaque film—this takes about 5 to 8 minutes. Remove from heat at once and stir in rum flavoring. Let stand, uncovered, until lukewarm; to hasten cooling, set pan in cold water.

Cut the fruit from the pineapple into bite-sized pieces and place in a serving bowl. To serve, spoon into individual dishes, top with brown sugar to taste, and drizzle with some of the lukewarm custard sauce. Makes 4 to 6 servings.

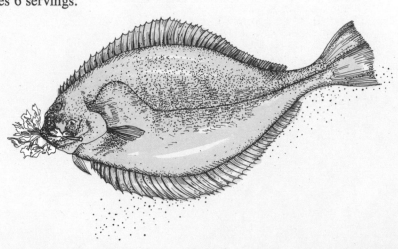

Hot or Cold Lunch

CORNED BEEF BRISKET
SOUR CREAM SPINACH SOUP
DARK BREAD
BUTTER   MUSTARD
DILL PICKLES   RADISHES
ORANGES

This is an integrated soup-and-sandwich meal that is just as good cold as it is freshly prepared and served hot. Allow ample time for the corned beef to cook; if it is ready early, just keep it warm in the broth. The soup can be made early, too, if you like, but you can also wait until the last minute to prepare it.

CORNED BEEF BRISKET

Each person makes his own sandwich from slices of freshly cooked corned beef, served hot or cold.

4 pounds corned beef brisket
Water
1 bay leaf
3 or 4-inch cinnamon stick
1 small, hot, red chile
½ teaspoon each whole coriander, allspice, and mustard seed
1 onion, sliced

Wash corned beef well under cold running water, then place meat in a deep pan. Cover with 2 quarts water and bring to boiling; drain and cover again with 2 quarts hot water. Bring to boiling, reduce heat to simmer, add bay leaf, cinnamon stick, chile, coriander, allspice, mustard seed, and sliced onion. Cover pan and simmer gently for about 4 hours or until meat is very tender when pierced with a fork.

Dip out 4 cups of the cooking liquid; strain and set aside for the soup (recipe follows). (Strain remaining brisket broth and reserve to thin the chilled soup, if desired, or for use in making other soups.) Serve the meat hot or cold to slice for sandwiches. Makes 6 to 8 servings.

SOUR CREAM SPINACH SOUP

Taste the brisket broth; if quite salty, as occasionally happens if the corned beef has been prepared in a particularly strong brine, use canned, regular-strength chicken broth instead of brisket broth to make the soup.

In a pan combine 4 cups broth with 2 packages (10 oz. *each*) frozen chopped spinach and bring to boiling, breaking the spinach apart as quickly as possible. Whirl spinach mixture, a portion at a time, in a blender until puréed, or rub through a wire strainer or a food mill. Add 2 cups sour cream to one portion while blending. Blend the soup and serve (reheat, if needed, but do not boil), or chill. Makes 2½ quarts.

Soup and Salad Luncheon

CHILLED POTATO SOUP
CRESCENT ROLLS
CRAB AND EGG SALADS
LEMON CUSTARD ICE CREAM

This party luncheon is quick to assemble. The menu offers flexibility. You have a choice of making and chilling the soup and salads early in the morning or doing them just before serving. Place ice cream balls in dessert bowls and, if you wish, pass an orange-flavored liqueur.

CHILLED POTATO SOUP

1 can (10¼ oz.) frozen potato soup, thawed
1 soup can milk
1 tablespoon minced parsley
  Chopped chives

In a blender purée soup, milk, and parsley. Chill. Serve in small bowls, sprinkled with chopped chives. Makes 4 servings.

CRAB AND EGG SALADS

Make the dressing for the salads ahead and chill until serving time.

1 large head iceberg lettuce
2 cups (about 1 lb.) crab meat, fresh, frozen, or canned
1 cup chopped celery
2 tablespoons capers
  Salad Dressing (recipe follows)
  Cherry tomatoes, dill pickles, and lemon wedges for garnish
2 hard-cooked eggs

Line 4 salad plates with lettuce; shred 2 cups lettuce and mound on each plate. Reserve several large pieces of crab meat for garnish. Mix remaining crab meat with celery and capers. Spoon on lettuce-lined plates. Spoon dressing over each salad. Garnish with reserved crab pieces, cherry tomatoes, dill pickles, and lemon wedges, and grate hard-cooked eggs on top. Chill until serving time. Makes 4 servings.

Salad Dressing. Mix together ⅓ cup *each* mayonnaise and sour cream, 2 tablespoons chile sauce, 1 tablespoon lemon juice, and a few drops aromatic bitters (optional).

Make-Ahead Party Luncheon

PIQUANT CRAB SALAD
HOT BUTTERED ROLLS
PECAN TASSELS

Molded main dish salads are a boon to the hostess who's looking for a luncheon menu with a minimum of last-minute preparation. This crab salad, molded in a tangy dressing, can be made early in the day or a day ahead.

PIQUANT CRAB SALAD

Avocado, tomatoes, and ripe olives accompany this party-size molded crab salad. You can use Dungeness or King crab, fresh, canned, or frozen (thawed).

  2 envelopes unflavored gelatin
1½ cups water
  ⅔ cup chile sauce
  ½ cup mayonnaise
  1 cup sour cream
  ½ teaspoon salt
  ¼ cup each lemon juice and chopped green
       onion (including part of the tops)
  4 hard-cooked eggs, chopped
  1 cup finely chopped celery
  3 cups (about 1½ lbs.) crab meat,
       fresh, frozen, or canned
  2 medium-sized ripe avocados, peeled and sliced
  2 tablespoons lemon juice
  1 basket (about 1½ cups) cherry tomatoes
    Parsley for garnish

Soften gelatin in water; set over simmering water and heat, stirring, to dissolve gelatin. Blend in chile sauce, mayonnaise, sour cream, salt, and lemon juice. Refrigerate until mixture is slightly thickened, stirring occasionally. In another bowl, combine onion, eggs, celery, and crab meat. When gelatin mixture is slightly thickened, gently stir in crab mixture. Pour into an 8-cup mold, cover, and chill until set, 3 to 4 hours. To serve, dip mold in hottest tap water for a few seconds to loosen edges, place a flat serving dish over salad, and invert to unmold. Garnish with avocado slices, sprinkled with lemon juice to retard discoloration, cherry tomatoes, and parsley. Serves 6 to 8.

PECAN TASSELS

  2 eggs
1½ cups brown sugar, firmly packed
  2 tablespoons melted butter
    Dash salt
  ¼ teaspoon vanilla
  ¾ cup finely chopped pecans
1¾ cups regular all-purpose flour
  ¾ cup (⅜ lb.) butter
1½ small packages (3-oz. size) cream cheese

Beat eggs with brown sugar, melted butter, salt, vanilla, and pecans; set mixture aside while making crust.

Sift and measure flour into a bowl. Add butter and cream cheese and cut into flour with a pastry blender (or rub between your fingers) until no particles are larger than small peas. Pat dough into a flat round cake and divide equally into 16 portions. Press each portion, with your fingers, into a standard-size muffin cup (about 2½-inch size); bring dough flush with, but not over, top edge. Take care to have no holes or thin spots in dough.

Put an equal amount of the pecan filling into each cup. Bake in a 350° oven for 15 minutes, then reduce temperature to 250° and continue baking for 10 minutes. Remove from oven and set pans on wire racks to cool for about 10 minutes. Tarts should come out when pans are inverted; if not, gently pry free with a fork. Serve warm or cold. (To reheat, place in a 350° oven for 10 minutes.) Makes 16 tarts.

Salmon Salad Luncheon

SWEDISH SALMON PLATE

SOUR CREAM DRESSING

HOT ROLLS

LIME SHERBET

COOKIES

You can arrange this handsome, serve-yourself salad plate in advance, then chill it, ready to serve to luncheon guests. Serve it with hot rolls. Lime sherbet makes a refreshing dessert.

SWEDISH SALMON PLATE

Crisp vegetables surround the fish in this attractive luncheon dish. You can substitute poached or baked fresh salmon for the canned salmon, if you wish.

  1 can (1 lb.) salmon
  ½ pound asparagus, cooked and chilled
  ⅓ pound raw mushrooms, sliced
  ⅓ cup olive oil or salad oil
2½ tablespoons white wine vinegar
  ¼ teaspoon each salt and dry mustard
     Salad greens
  1 cucumber
  2 tomatoes
     Sour Cream Dressing (recipe follows)

Drain salmon and remove bones, leaving fish in large fillets. Place fish, asparagus, and mushrooms separately in a shallow dish. Mix together the oil, vinegar, salt, and mustard. Spoon over salad; cover, and chill 1 hour. Arrange greens on an oval platter, place fish fillets in the center, and radiate spokes of asparagus from the fish. Place mushrooms at either end. Slice cucumber thinly and arrange on the sides, flanked by tomato wedges. Accompany with a bowl of Sour Cream Dressing. Makes 6 servings.

Sour Cream Dressing. Mix together ½ cup *each* mayonnaise and sour cream, 1 tablespoon anchovy paste, 2 tablespoons *each* chopped parsley and capers, and salt and pepper to taste. Makes 1¼ cups.

Crab Salad Luncheon

VINTNERS' CONSOMME
GRAPEFRUIT AND CRAB SALAD
SOUR CREAM MAYONNAISE
CRESCENT ROLLS   BUTTER
HOT BRAZIL NUT SUNDAES

This soup and salad meal is well suited to serving last-minute guests. It has plenty of eye appeal, yet it goes together quickly.

Make the salad dressing, assemble the salad plates, and chill both. Heat bakery or frozen rolls. Prepare the first-course soup. Put together the sundae sauce and reheat it at dessert time.

VINTNERS' CONSOMME

1 can (10½ oz.) condensed consommé
1 soup can water
2 tablespoons golden raisins
2 tablespoons Madeira or pale dry Sherry

Heat consommé with water and raisins just until steaming. Stir in Madeira or Sherry. Serve in small teacups. Makes 4 servings.

GRAPEFRUIT AND CRAB SALAD

Butter lettuce leaves
2 cups (about 1 lb.) crab meat, fresh, frozen, or canned
2 pink grapefruit
1 avocado
Lemon juice
½ cup pomegranate seeds (optional)
Sour Cream Mayonnaise (recipe follows)

Arrange a bed of butter lettuce leaves on four salad plates. Place a mound of crab meat in center of each plate. Peel grapefruit and cut into sections, discarding white membrane. Peel and slice avocado; dip slices in lemon juice to prevent darkening. Arrange grapefruit and avocado in radiating spokes from the crab. If desired, sprinkle salads with pomegranate seeds. Top each salad with a spoonful of Sour Cream Mayonnaise and pass additional dressing. Makes 4 servings.

Sour Cream Mayonnaise. Beat 2 egg yolks with 1 teaspoon dry mustard and ½ teaspoon salt using a wire whip or an electric mixer; then gradually beat in 1 cup salad oil, adding it drop by drop. When all the oil is incorporated, mix in 2 tablespoons lemon juice. Stir in ½ cup sour cream. Makes about 1½ cups.

HOT BRAZIL NUT SUNDAES

2 teaspoons butter
¾ cup coarsely chopped Brazil nuts, cashews, or filberts
½ cup whipping cream
½ cup brown sugar, firmly packed
1 pint vanilla or coffee ice cream

Melt butter in a small frying pan. Add chopped nuts and heat until lightly toasted. Add whipping cream and brown sugar. Bring to a boil and simmer just until blended, stirring constantly. Spoon warm sauce over individual servings of ice cream. Makes 4 servings.

Dutch Broodje Lunch

BROODJES WITH ASSORTED FILLINGS

HARD-COOKED EGGS

DILL PICKLES

APPLES AND PEARS

JAN HAGEL COOKIES

MILK   DUTCH BEER

This menu is inspired by the *broodjeswinkels,* or sandwich shops, of Amsterdam. A *broodje* (pronounced *broh*-ja) is a sandwich consisting of a small, soft roll, generously buttered and filled with a thick layer of meat, cheese, fish, or a salad mixture. Assembled, the sandwich is almost as tall as it is wide. *Winkels* are the impeccable restaurants where the sandwiches are served.

Although the bill of fare of an Amsterdam broodje shop may offer 30 or more varieties, we recommend that you limit the choices of fillings to from four to six. Milk is the customary beverage accompaniment, but adults might prefer a full-bodied Dutch beer.

For dessert, serve fresh fruit and cookies. Bake those we suggest here, or select packaged or bakery spice cookies.

BROODJES

As fillings for the broodjes, you might offer several cold meats and cheeses from the delicatessen: ham, mortadella, and liver sausage; Edam, Gouda, or Swiss cheese. Have all of these sliced as thinly as possible when you buy them; broodje fillings typically consist of many thin layers. You can arrange the meats and cheese on a platter, cover it with clear plastic film, and refrigerate it several hours before serving.

Either of the salad fillings can be made two to three hours before serving and refrigerated. To serve the fillings, mound sandwich-sized portions (about ¼ cup each) on leaves of butter lettuce (an ice cream scoop works well for making the

mounds); guests pick up the filling, lettuce and all, and transfer it to a buttered roll. Thinly sliced cold roast beef might be an alternative to the tartare filling for those who don't care for this classic raw meat mixture.

For the rolls, look for packaged small, soft dinner rolls. Resembling small hamburger buns, about 3 inches in diameter, they are usually sold in plastic bags of 12, plain or with sesame seeds. Have them split and well buttered for guests to use in making their own broodjes. You can expect each diner to eat about three.

Salmon Salad Filling. Drain and flake 1 large can (1 lb.) red sockeye salmon; remove bones and skin. Blend ½ cup mayonnaise, 2 teaspoons lemon juice, 1 teaspoon prepared mustard, ¼ teaspoon dill weed, and ⅛ teaspoon nutmeg. Lightly blend mayonnaise mixture, salmon, ½ cup finely chopped celery, and 2 hard-cooked eggs, chopped. Makes about 2½ cups, enough for 10 to 12 sandwiches.

Beef Tartare Filling. The day of your party, purchase 1½ pounds freshly ground round steak. Mix in 2 eggs, slightly beaten; 1 teaspoon *each* salt, dry mustard, and Worcestershire; ¼ teaspoon pepper; 2 tablespoons *each* grated onion and drained capers; and ¼ cup finely chopped dill pickle, blending lightly but thoroughly. Serve with lemon wedges to squeeze over each portion. Makes about 3½ cups, enough for 14 to 18 sandwiches.

JAN HAGEL COOKIES

These spice cookies were named after a renowned nineteenth-century baker.

1¾ **cups unsifted regular all-purpose flour**
 ½ **cup sugar**
 ½ **cup sliced almonds**
 ¾ **teaspoon cinnamon**
 ½ **teaspoon vanilla**
 ¾ **cup (⅜ lb.) firm butter or margarine**
  Sugar

Mix flour, the ½ cup sugar, almonds, and cinnamon thoroughly. Stir in vanilla. Cut in butter to form particles the size of dried peas. Work mixture with your hands until you can shape it into a smooth ball.

Divide dough into 2 equal parts; roll out one portion at a time about ⅛ inch thick on a floured board. Cut into 2-inch rounds. (Or shape dough into two rolls, each about 2 inches in diameter. Wrap dough well and refrigerate it for 1 to 2 hours or until you are ready to bake. Then slice dough ⅛ inch thick and continue as for rolled cookies.)

Sprinkle cookies lightly with sugar. Bake in a 400° oven for 8 to 10 minutes or until lightly browned. Makes about 3½ dozen cookies, 2½ inches in diameter.

Chicken Soufflé Luncheon

CHILLED FRESH FRUIT CUPS
INDIVIDUAL CHICKEN SOUFFLES
TARRAGON-FLAVORED ARTICHOKE HEARTS
CHERRY TOMATOES
TOAST ROUNDS OR CRACKERS
ICED COFFEE AND TEA

For lunch to be served away from the main dining area, food prepared in individual dishes and served on trays is convenient. Here is a menu that fits this situation and is especially appropriate for a ladies' lucheon or a light supper in the living room or on the patio. For the fruit cup, use a combination of melons and fresh fruit in season. Chicken soufflé bakes in individual dishes; and marinated artichoke hearts are served on crisp lettuce with cherry tomatoes.

The artichoke hearts should be prepared the day before or early the day they are to be served, so they can marinate in the flavorful dressing. (You can buy marinated artichoke hearts, although not tarragon-flavored ones.) Prepare the fruit cup early enough in the day so that it chills thoroughly. As the soufflés must be timed to finish just at serving time, you'll need to have the trays, dishes, and other food ready then.

INDIVIDUAL CHICKEN SOUFFLES

⅓ cup chopped mushrooms
2 tablespoons chopped green onion
5 tablespoons butter or margarine
3 tablespoons flour
½ teaspoon salt
½ teaspoon chicken stock base
1 cup warm milk
4 egg yolks
2 cups finely diced cooked chicken
5 egg whites

Sauté the mushrooms and onion in 2 tablespoons of the butter or margarine; set aside. Melt remaining 3 tablespoons butter in a small pan; stir in flour and salt until thoroughly blended. Dissolve chicken stock base in milk; gradually blend into flour and butter; cook about 3 minutes.

Beat egg yolks together slightly; stir a little of the warm sauce into the yolks, then stir all the yolks into the warm mixture. Cook, stirring, until the mixture is smooth and slightly thickened. Remove from heat and blend in chicken and the sautéed mushrooms and onion. Beat egg whites until stiff but not dry; gently fold the chicken mixture into the egg whites.

Turn into well buttered individual soufflé dishes (1-cup size) or 8-ounce custard cups, filling each about ¾ full. Set on a baking sheet and bake in a 350° oven 25 minutes or until golden brown. Serve immediately. Makes 8 servings.

ARTICHOKE HEARTS IN TARRAGON DRESSING

½ cup olive oil or salad oil
¼ cup tarragon vinegar
⅛ teaspoon salt
Dash each pepper and tarragon
2 packages (9 oz. size) frozen artichoke hearts, thawed
Crisp lettuce
Cherry tomatoes
Pitted ripe olives

Combine olive oil or salad oil with vinegar, salt, pepper, and tarragon. Pour over the artichoke hearts and refrigerate, covered, for several hours or overnight. Drain the artichokes and serve on a bed of lettuce along with several cherry tomatoes and olives. Makes 8 servings.

Seafood Luncheon

SHELLFISH RAMEKINS
CRESCENT ROLLS
BUTTER LETTUCE SALAD
CASABA MELON   FONTINA CHEESE

Clams, scallops, and shrimp in a cheese sauce can be made up early in the morning of this luncheon if you want to avoid last-minute preparation. Bake the shellfish in individual dishes while you heat crescent rolls purchased from the bakery or the supermarket's frozen foods section.

For the salad, dress butter lettuce with oil, vinegar, and seasonings of your choice. Melon wedges and cheese make a light, refreshing finish to the meal.

SHELLFISH RAMEKINS

    1 can (7½ oz.) minced clams
⅓ cup dry white wine
    1 pound scallops
    2 tablespoons each butter and flour
    1 cup half-and-half (light cream)
    2 egg yolks
    6 tablespoons shredded Parmesan cheese
½ pound small cooked shrimp

Drain liquid from clams into a saucepan and set clams aside. Add wine and scallops to saucepan, bring to a boil, cover, and simmer 5 minutes or just until scallops turn white; lift out scallops with slotted spoon to a bowl. Measure liquid; you should have ¾ cup—otherwise cook down to make that amount. Turn into a measuring cup. Melt butter in saucepan and blend in flour; cook stirring, until bubbling. Stir in half-and-half and cooking liquid and let sauce cook 5 minutes.

Beat eggs yolks until light and stir in cream sauce. Return to saucepan, add 4 tablespoons Parmesan cheese, and cook 2 minutes over moderate heat. Add scallops, shrimps, and clams. Spoon into buttered scallop shells or individual ovenproof dishes and sprinkle tops with remaining cheese. Bake in a 375° oven for 15 minutes or until cheese melts and shellfish is hot through. Makes 4 servings.

Broiled Lobster Luncheon

BROILED LOBSTER TAILS
COLD ASPARAGUS WITH YOGURT DRESSING
BROILED TOMATOES WITH PARMESAN
RYE QUARTERS
ORANGE SOUFFLE

Many people appreciate luncheons that stay well within a modest calorie count. This menu is planned for a maximum of good flavors and a minimum of calories—well under 400 per person. Contrary to popular belief, lobster is extremely low in calories. Many lobster dishes *do* have a high calorie count, but only because of the large portions of cream, cheese, and butter included. Here the lobster is lightly brushed with a lemon-butter baste.

A few hours before the luncheon, split the lobster tails, mix the butter baste, and prepare the tomatoes for broiling; cover and refrigerate to have ready to slip under the broiler just before serving. Cook and cool the asparagus, and make salad dressing. Cut and toast bread. Just before guests arrive, mix the simple soufflé; let it cook in a double boiler while you serve the main course.

BROILED LOBSTER TAILS

2 large cooked lobster tails, split lengthwise
2 tablespoons melted butter
2 tablespoons lemon juice
1 teaspoon minced parsley
½ teaspoon salt
Dash pepper
Lemon wedges

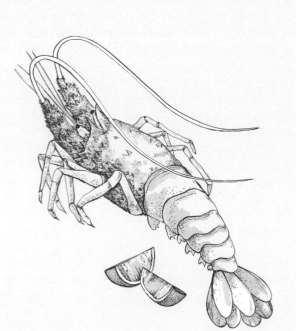

Place split lobster tails on broiler pan, shell side down, and baste with a mixture of the butter, lemon juice, parsley, salt, and pepper. Broil about 4 inches from heat for 4 minutes, just to heat through. Garnish with lemon wedges. Makes 4 servings of a half tail each.

RYE QUARTERS

Remove crusts from 4 square slices of rye bread. Butter lightly; cut diagonally in quarters. Toast under broiler. Serve warm or cold. Makes 4 servings of 4 quarters each.

COLD ASPARAGUS WITH
YOGURT DRESSING

2 pounds asparagus, washed and trimmed
Salted water
½ cup plain yogurt
2 tablespoons catsup
½ teaspoon salt
Dash Worcestershire

Cook asparagus, uncovered, in salted water until
tender. Drain, cover, and cool in refrigerator.
Make dressing by combining yogurt with catsup,
salt, and Worcestershire. Blend well and chill;
serve over asparagus. Makes 4 servings.

BROILED TOMATOES
WITH PARMESAN

4 medium-sized firm tomatoes
2 teaspoons butter
4 teaspoons grated Parmesan cheese
Salt and pepper

Halve the tomatoes, dot each half with about ¼
teaspoon butter, and sprinkle each with ½ teaspoon cheese and a dash of salt and pepper. Broil
4 inches below heat for 4 minutes. Serve hot.
Makes 4 servings of 2 halves each.

ORANGE SOUFFLE

This soufflé cooks in a double boiler on top of
your range rather than in the oven.

4 egg whites
¼ teaspoon salt
About 3 tablespoons powdered sugar
⅓ cup orange marmalade

Beat egg whites until they are stiff, gradually
adding salt and 3 tablespoons powdered sugar;
beat until satiny. Fold marmalade into the egg
white mixture and turn into a well buttered, 2-
quart double boiler. Cover and cook over simmering water for about 1 hour and 20 minutes.
Do not remove lid while cooking.

Turn out cooked soufflé on a plate and dust
lightly with powdered sugar. Serve immediately,
dividing soufflé with an angel cake slicer or two
forks. Serves 4 to 6.

Winter Lunch

MEXICAN CHILE CON CARNE
MIXED VEGETABLE SALAD
BUTTERED HOT FRENCH BREAD
ICE CREAM

A meaty Mexican chile is the basis for this hearty lunch. Salad and hot bread are the only main-course accompaniments needed to make a perfect cold-weather meal.

Since the chile requires a long simmering period, you may want to make a large quantity and freeze some of it, ready for a quick meal another day. Once the chile is cooked, you only need to make the salad and heat the bread.

To make the ice cream festive, you might serve it in a fancy shape—pack it into a mold ahead of time and refreeze.

MEXICAN CHILE CON CARNE

Instead of the dry beans this recipe calls for, you could use 5 cans (15 oz. each) red kidney beans, drained. Add them after the meat has simmered about 1 hour, then simmer 30 minutes more.

   1 pound dry pink or red beans
   4 pounds beef stew meat, cubed
   3 tablespoons salad oil
   1 large onion, sliced
   1 clove garlic, mashed
   1 can (1 lb. 12 oz.) whole tomatoes
2½ teaspoons salt
   2 teaspoons each chile powder and oregano
   ½ teaspoon ground cumin

Soak the beans overnight in water to cover, or cover them with water, bring to a boil, simmer 2 minutes, and let soak for 1 hour. Drain beans, reserving the liquid.

Brown the meat in the oil; then add the soaked beans, the onion, garlic, tomatoes, salt, chile powder, oregano, cumin, and about 3 cups of the bean liquid. Cover, bring to a boil, and simmer gently about 1½ hours, adding more liquid as needed. Makes 12 to 16 servings.

Casserole Picnic

BAKED MEATBALLS AND RICE WITH MUSTARD SAUCE

GREEN CABBAGE SLAW

FRENCH BREAD

WATERMELON   BIG SUGAR COOKIES

If your picnic destination is not more than about an hour's drive from home, there's no reason why you can't carry a hot main dish—in this case, meatballs baked with rice and a tangy mustard sauce. The casserole can be prepared ahead and refrigerated; about an hour before you leave on your picnic, reheat it in the oven and add the hot sauce. Cover the casserole, wrap it in several layers of newspaper and then a heavy cloth. Place it in an insulated bag or styrene foam chest.

Pack French bread, cookies, and eating utensils and linens around the casserole, filling the carrying container as full as possible to help keep the heat in. Cold drinks, watermelon, the mixed salad greens, and a container of dressing can go into a second container to keep cool.

BAKED MEATBALLS AND RICE WITH MUSTARD SAUCE

    1 package (7 oz.) Italian-style rice mix
    2 pounds ground beef chuck
    1 large can (4½ oz.) deviled ham
    ½ cup each fine dry bread crumbs and milk
    2 eggs
    ¼ teaspoon garlic or onion salt
    36 Spanish-style green olives, drained
        Mustard Sauce (recipe follows)
        Sliced olives for garnish

Prepare rice mix according to package directions. Spread in a buttered 2½-quart casserole or baking pan; set aside.

Combine ground beef, deviled ham, crumbs, milk, eggs, and garlic or onion salt. Mix lightly to blend. Shape around olives to form 36 meatballs the size of golf balls. Place in an ungreased shallow baking pan; bake uncovered in a 500°

oven for 12 to 15 minutes or until well browned and cooked to stage desired (cut into a center meatball to test). Pour off and reserve 1 tablespoon of the pan drippings for Mustard Sauce.

Arrange meatballs over rice. Cover and refrigerate. Then bake, covered, in a 350° oven until meat and rice are heated through, 45 minutes to 1 hour. Pour hot sauce over all. Garnish with sliced olives to serve. Makes 6 to 8 servings.

Mustard Sauce. Heat reserved 1 tablespoon drippings with 2 tablespoons butter until bubbly. Stir in 1 medium-sized onion, finely chopped, and sauté until onion is soft and translucent. Stir in 2 tablespoons prepared mustard, ⅛ teaspoon nutmeg, dash cayenne, and 3 tablespoons flour; cook, stirring occasionally, until bubbly. Gradually add 1 can (about 14 oz.) regular-strength chicken broth; cook until thickened, stirring constantly. Blend in 1 cup shredded Cheddar cheese, stirring until it is melted and smooth.

GREEN CABBAGE SLAW

    8 cups finely shredded cabbage
    1 cup each finely chopped parsley and thinly
        sliced green onions (including part of
        green tops)
    2 tablespoons sugar
    1½ teaspoons salt
    ½ cup white vinegar
    ⅓ cup salad oil

Lightly mix together the cabbage, parsley, and onions. Cover and chill. To serve, lightly mix in a dressing made by combining in a jar or blender the sugar, salt, vinegar, and oil. Makes 6 to 8 servings.

Dinners & Suppers

The dinner or supper that is prepared with careful attention to detail and served in an exciting, imaginative way need not be complicated in order to impress. Most of the menus featured in this chapter stress informality and ease of service; but the dishes they present are attractive, flavorful, and fun to serve.

Sometimes the meal is planned around one substantial main dish. For a small group, consider a pasta and sausage supper and mix the fettucine in a chafing dish in front of your guests. For a larger group, you might try a soup buffet. The busy hostess will find dinners that can be made ahead and dinners that can be whipped up in a matter of minutes. Many of the menus take advantage of packaged or frozen foods and suggest new ways to turn them into party fare.

There is versatility in this chapter: meals that can be served hot or cold, indoors or out-of-doors, at home or away from home. And there is variety: picnic suppers and soup suppers, garden barbecues and meals cooked at the table, buffet meals and sit-down dinners.

Lamb Fondue Party

LAMB FONDUE
GOLDEN ONION PILAF
CHUTNEY SAUCES
FLOUR TORTILLA CRACKER BREAD
CHOCOLATE MALLOW MOUSSE

Few cooking tools have been accepted so enthusiastically in recent years as the metal fondue set (not to be confused with the ceramic dish used for cheese fondue). Its classic function is the service of fondue bourguignonne (beef fondue), with lavish sauces such as Béarnaise. Here it is used for preparing a lighter entrée—lamb fondue, served with piquant sauces that are reassuringly lean in calories.

All the preparation can be done as much as a day ahead. The actual cooking is done by the guests, seated in groups of six (or fewer) around small tables. For each group of six, prepare the amounts listed.

Mound the onion pilaf on individual plates. With a fork, guests push cooked meat from skewers onto the pilaf. If you like, arrange citrus leaves on each plate to hold the sauces (the mustard sauce needs a cup). Pass crisp toasted flour tortillas.

LAMB FONDUE

Have your meatman bone a leg of lamb for the fondue. To serve, arrange the prepared meat in a basket lined with green leaves.

1 leg of lamb (about 5 lbs.), boned
1 cup each salad oil and butter or margarine

Trim off and discard fat and connective tissue from meat; cut meat in bite-sized pieces (you can do this a day ahead). Cover and chill until ready to serve.

To prepare the cooking fat, combine salad oil and butter or margarine in a 7 to 8-cup fondue pot. If you have a larger or smaller pot, fill to no more than ¼ the depth. (The mixture foams vigorously at times and can be dangerous if it flows over pan sides into flame. For additional safety place the fondue set on a small tray when in use; some sets have a liner.) Heat fat on a range over direct heat until bubbling, then place over denatured alcohol flame on the fondue stand; adjust heat to keep fat bubbling.

Invite guests to spear 2 or 3 pieces of lamb on each of several bamboo skewers, immerse in the hot fat, and cook until meat is as done as desired. Repeat procedure as often as needed. Serve with pilaf and chutney sauces. Makes 4 to 6 servings.

GOLDEN ONION PILAF

3 medium-sized onions, finely chopped
6 tablespoons butter or margarine
1⅓ cups uncooked long grain rice
2⅔ cups regular-strength chicken broth
(½ cup additional broth if pilaf is reheated)
Salt to taste

Cook onions in 4 tablespoons of the butter or margarine in a wide frying pan or Dutch oven, stirring occasionally, for about 15 minutes or until lightly browned. Remove from pan and add remaining 2 tablespoons butter and the rice. Cook, stirring, over high heat until rice becomes opaque and lightly browned. Add onions and the 2⅔ cups broth; bring to a boil, cover, and cook over low heat for 20 minutes or until rice is tender and liquid absorbed. Salt to taste. Serve hot or let cool. To reheat, add ½ cup broth, cover, and heat in 375° oven for 40 minutes. Serves 6.

(continued)

ZUCCHINI YOGURT CHUTNEY

1 small zucchini, grated (⅓ to ½ cup)
1 cup unflavored yogurt
2 tablespoons minced green onions
    (including some of the green tops)
½ teaspoon cumin seed
    Salt to taste

Blend all ingredients. Cover and chill as long as overnight. Makes 1⅓ cups.

SOUR CREAM MINT CHUTNEY

1 cup sour cream
1 tablespoon crushed dried mint leaves
½ teaspoon dry mustard
2 tablespoons minced parsley
1 small clove garlic, minced
¼ teaspoon grated lemon peel
1 tablespoon lemon juice.

Blend all ingredients. Cover and chill as long as overnight. Makes 1⅓ cups.

BANANA YOGURT CHUTNEY

1 small ripe banana
1 cup unflavored yogurt
¼ cup minced red onion
3 tablespoons minced green pepper
    Salt to taste

Finely chop the banana and blend with yogurt. Add onion, green pepper, and salt. Cover and chill as long as overnight. Makes about 1½ cups.

MUSTARD DILL CHUTNEY

2 tablespoons Dijon-style mustard
½ teaspoon sugar
2 tablespoons red wine vinegar
½ teaspoon dill weed
⅓ cup salad oil

Stir together the mustard, sugar, vinegar, and dill weed. With a fork, beat in salad oil. Cover and keep at room temperature as long as overnight; serve in tiny dishes. Makes ⅔ cup.

TOMATO LEMON CHUTNEY

1 tablespoon salad oil
1 small whole dried hot red chile
½ teaspoon cumin seed
½ teaspoon mustard seed
¼ teaspoon nutmeg
1 can (1 lb.) whole tomatoes and juices
½ cup currants
½ cup sugar
½ lemon, finely chopped (including peel)

In a saucepan combine salad oil, chile, cumin seed, mustard seed, and nutmeg. Heat, stirring, until seeds start to pop and jump, then stir in tomatoes and juices, currants, sugar, and lemon. Boil rapidly, stirring frequently to break up tomato, until very thick. Cover and chill; this sauce is best made 3 or 4 days before use. Makes 1⅓ cups.

FLOUR TORTILLA CRACKER BREAD

Arrange oven rack in the top position. Heat oven to 350°, then spread 8 to 12 flour tortillas in single layer directly on rack. Bake 4 or 5 minutes or until crisp. Serve hot or cold, breaking to eat.

CHOCOLATE MALLOW MOUSSE

4 ounces semisweet chocolate
3 tablespoons hot water
1 teaspoon instant coffee powder
4 egg whites
1 cup marshmallow cream
1½ cups whipping cream

Place chocolate, water, and coffee powder in top of a double boiler; heat over hot water until chocolate is melted. Stir to blend. Let cool.

Beat egg whites until soft peaks form. Add marshmallow cream, a large spoonful at a time beating until meringue holds stiff peaks. Fold the chocolate mixture into the meringue. Beat whipping cream until stiff and fold into the chocolate mixture. Spoon into 8 small soufflé dishes or other small bowls, swirling the tops. Cover and freeze until firm. Place in refrigerator for 15 minutes to soften slightly before serving. Serves 8.

Tostada Supper

A Mexican-style tostada is a meal in itself, with its crispy tortilla base, meat sauce, shredded cheese, and assortment of relishes for guests to pile on top. Rum stirred into soft coffee ice cream contrasts pleasantly as a cool finish to the meal.

Fry the tortillas and keep them warm in a low oven while simmering the meat sauce and assembling the relishes in small bowls. For 6 to 8 servings, offer several or all of the following: 2 cups shredded iceberg lettuce; 1 cup shredded jack cheese; 1 small avocado, diced, or 1 can (7¾ oz.) guacamole sauce; 1 large tomato, chopped; and 1 can (2 oz.) sliced ripe olives.

CALIFORNIA TOSTADAS

Guests assemble their own tostadas, topping them off with the condiments of their choice.

½ cup salad oil
12 corn tortillas (1 package)
 2 medium-sized onions, finely chopped
 1 tablespoon butter
 2 pounds ground beef
 1 teaspoon salt
½ teaspoon garlic salt
¼ teaspoon ground cumin
 2 cans (8 oz. each) tomato sauce

Heat salad oil in a large frying pan over moderate heat. Slip one tortilla at a time into the hot oil and cook for about 30 seconds on a side (until it bubbles and browns slightly); turn with a fork or tongs and cook until crisp; remove to paper towels to drain. Wrap loosely in foil and keep warm in a low oven. Offer extra tortillas as a bread.

For the meat sauce, sauté onions in butter until golden brown; turn out of the pan and reserve. Brown ground beef in pan, stirring with a fork to crumble. Season with salt, garlic salt, and cumin. Add sautéed onion and tomato sauce. Cover and simmer 20 minutes. Makes enough sauce for 8 servings.

To assemble tostadas, each guest places a crisp tortilla on his plate, spoons over the meat sauce, and sprinkles on the condiments of his choice.

Hungarian Soup Supper

GOULASH SOUP (GULYAS)

BUTTER LETTUCE SALAD   CHIVE DRESSING

RYE BREAD

ALMOND STRUDEL

WHIPPED CREAM

A simple meal planned around just one substantial main dish can create a relaxed atmosphere which will be enjoyed by both hostess and guests. Here the main dish of goulash soup is what the Hungarians call *gulyás* (pronounced goo-*yahsh*). If you have the time, it's best to make this soup a day or two ahead and refrigerate, skim, then reheat it.

Serve tart butter lettuce salad as a first course or, in the more characteristically eastern European fashion, with the hot soup. To make the salad, add fresh or freeze-dried chopped chives to your favorite oil-and-vinegar dressing.

GOULASH SOUP
(Gulyás)

Sweet Hungarian paprika is the principal seasoning in this soup; you'll find it in delicatessens and in the food sections of many import stores. You could use regular paprika instead.

3 pounds boneless beef chuck, cubed
2 tablespoons each salad oil and butter or
    margarine
2 large onions, chopped
1 small clove garlic, minced or mashed
1 tablespoon sweet Hungarian paprika or
    regular paprika
5 cups water
1 large green pepper, seeded and cut in strips
2 teaspoons salt
⅛ teaspoon pepper
1 teaspoon caraway seed
2 tomatoes, peeled, seeded, and coarsely
    chopped
1 small dried hot red chile, crushed (optional)
2 medium-sized potatoes, cut in eighths

Brown meat, about a fourth at a time, in heated oil in a large deep pan (at least 4-quart size); remove and reserve meat as it browns. When all is browned, pour off any pan drippings and discard them; melt butter in the same pan over medium heat. Add onions and garlic, and cook until onions are soft and golden (do not brown); blend in paprika. Stir in browned meat and its juices, water, green pepper, salt, pepper, caraway seed, chopped tomatoes, and chile (if used).

Bring soup to a boil, reduce heat, cover, and simmer for about 2 hours, or until meat is almost tender. If possible at this point, cool the soup slightly, cover, and refrigerate for several hours or overnight; skim off fat and discard it, then bring soup to a simmer again. Add potatoes and cook for 20 to 30 minutes more, until both potatoes and meat are tender. Serve steaming hot. Makes 6 servings.

ALMOND STRUDEL

Sumptuous Hungarian pastry rolls with almond soufflé filling are easy to create when you use commercial fila dough for a foundation. Also called strudel dough, this remarkable pastry dough is stretched almost as thin as onionskin; it is increasingly available in 1-pound packages (12 by 18-inch sheets) in delicatessens and Near East bakeries.

You can use a small amount of dough at one time, then wrap the remainder well and freeze. To use later, let it thaw completely before unwrapping. Keep the dough dry as you work with it, but cover dough you're not actually working with plastic film to keep it from getting too dry.

1¼ cups finely ground unblanched almonds
  2 egg yolks
  2 whole eggs, separated
  1 teaspoon grated lemon peel
  1 cup sugar
  1 teaspoon vanilla
  ½ teaspoon almond extract
  18 to 20 sheets fila
  ½ cup (¼ lb.) sweet (unsalted) butter, melted
    Powdered sugar
  1 cup whipping cream

Spread ground almonds (finely ground to a coarse powder in a blender) in a shallow baking pan and toast in a 350° oven 5 to 10 minutes, or until lightly browned. Beat the 4 egg yolks until light and thick. Combine lemon peel and sugar and gradually add, a tablespoon at a time, to the egg yolks; beat after each addition. Mix in the toasted ground nuts, vanilla, and almond flavoring. Beat the 2 egg whites until soft peaks form and fold into the nut mixture.

Lay out 1 sheet fila and brush half of it with melted butter. Fold over the second half and brush it with melted butter. Spoon a heaping tablespoon of nut batter over the narrow end of the dough, allowing a 1-inch margin around edges and base. Fold over the two long sides 1 inch. Fold up the bottom 1 inch. Then roll up the pastry loosely so filling can expand without bursting through the thin dough; place seam side down on a buttered baking sheet. Repeat process for each pastry roll.

Bake in a 375° oven for 15 to 20 minutes, or until nicely browned. Dust tops while hot with powdered sugar. Place on rack. Serve warm or cool with sweetened whipped cream. Makes 18 to 20 pastries.

Swiss Cheese Supper

JACK CHEESE, RACLETTE STYLE
BAKED POTATOES
MARINATED ONIONS
CALIFORNIA GREEN CHILES   DILL PICKLES
ICED APPLE CIDER
FRUIT BASKET   BUTTER COOKIES

The famous Swiss dish, Raclette, is made of cheese melted in a special way and served with potatoes. It's ideal for an informal party after a football game or other event. In the hour it takes the potatoes to bake, you have ample time to organize the rest of the meal—and to enjoy conversation with your guests.

If you have time, marinate the onions for several hours; otherwise, chill them in the dressing just while the potatoes bake. If you want a meat with the meal, cook a pound of bacon until crisp.

JACK CHEESE, RACLETTE STYLE

Scrub 4 to 6 medium-large baking potatoes, dry, and rub with salad oil. Bake in a 400° oven about 1 hour, or until potato gives easily when pressed (protect your fingers when testing).

Allow 1½ pounds jack cheese for 4 servings or 2 pounds for 6 servings. Cut in slices about ¼ inch thick. Arrange in overlapping slices in two shallow bake-and-serve pans about 9 inches in diameter, or equivalent; pie pans will do if you have nothing else suitable.

During the last 10 minutes the potatoes bake, put one cheese-filled pan in the oven. Then remove potatoes and broil melted cheese about 4 inches from heat for about 5 minutes, until a lightly browned crust forms. Serve at once, ladling generous spoonfuls into each split baked potato. Eat each bite of potato and cheese with a portion or combination of the marinated onions, green chiles, and pickles.

As you serve the first pan of cheese, the remaining one should go into the 400° oven for 10 minutes; then broil it for about 5 minutes. Keep this pan warm—on an electric warming tray, if you have one—to provide second helpings for the remainder of the potatoes. Makes 4 to 6 hearty servings.

MARINATED ONIONS

Thinly slice 3 to 4 cups mild red or white onions and separate into rings. Mix with ½ cup tarragon wine vinegar, 1 teaspoon sugar, and ½ teaspoon salt. Cover and chill; you can serve when just cold, but flavor is best after several hours. Makes 4 to 6 servings.

CALIFORNIA GREEN CHILES

Remove seeds and pith from 1 can (4 oz.) California green chiles. Chop chiles finely. Warn guests to test-taste cautiously, as these chiles range in flavor from mild to quite lively. Makes enough for 4 to 6 servings.

An Omelet Supper

TWO-EGG OMELETS

SOUR CREAM   CAVIAR   CHERRY PRESERVES

ASPARAGUS SPEARS

GINGERED PINEAPPLE HALF SHELLS

CRESCENT ROLLS

Individual omelets with assorted toppings are welcome fare for an impromptu supper party—after the theater, following a ball game, or just to wind up an evening with friends.

Fresh pineapple in its shell makes a handsome dessert, but you can substitute canned pineapple (which you're more likely to have on hand if it's an unplanned event), perhaps served in a footed compote. Prepare the dessert, cover, and refrigerate. Put rolls in to heat, and cook fresh or frozen asparagus spears. Fill condiment dishes with sour cream, lumpfish caviar, and cherry preserves; pass to spoon over omelets.

Then assemble the omelet ingredients so you can make the omelets one right after another. As each is made, turn it out on a warm plate and keep it warm in a low oven until all are made. Since the omelets must be made singly, the menu is appropriate only for a small group, say four to six.

TWO-EGG OMELETS

For each omelet:

  2 eggs
¼ teaspoon salt
  1 tablespoon water
  1 tablespoon butter

For each omelet, break eggs into a bowl, add salt and water, and beat with fork or wire whisk just enough to mix yolks and whites. Heat butter in a 7 or 8-inch omelet pan or frying pan over medium heat until the butter sizzles. Tilt pan so butter coats bottom evenly, then pour in beaten eggs. As the eggs start to set, lift edges with a fork so that the liquid on top can run under. Repeat until liquid is gone but eggs are still moist and soft.

Remove pan from heat and with a spatula flip over a third of the omelet toward the center. Fold over the other third and turn out of pan on hot plate. Repeat, allowing 1 omelet per person. Keep plates hot in low oven until all are ready to serve.

GINGERED PINEAPPLE HALF SHELLS

Cut 1 large fresh pineapple in half lengthwise, leaving leaves on; use a grapefruit knife to scoop out fruit. Cut out core; dice fruit and return to the half shells along with 1 can (11 oz.) mandarin oranges, drained. (Or mix canned pineapple with mandarin oranges in attractive serving dish.) Sprinkle with 1 tablespoon finely chopped ginger, if desired. Serves 6 to 8.

Cook-at-the-Table Barbecue

HOT BEEF OR CHICKEN BROTH

FRIED RICE WITH VEGETABLES

SKEWERED MEATS: BEEF SIRLOIN WITH GREEN PEPPER;

LAMB KEBAB WITH EGGPLANT; SWORDFISH WITH SHRIMP;

BONED CHICKEN BREAST WITH CHICKEN LIVERS

CUCUMBER SLICES   RADISHES   CELERY FANS

RICE COOKIES   HOT TEA

The Japanese method of cooking right at the table was the inspiration for this menu. Each guest has a glass or mug of soy-seasoned sauce for dipping and glazing skewered meats before cooking them on table barbecues. Start the charcoal fire in a large barbecue nearby and use tongs to transfer hot coals to tables as needed. Table barbecues should be large enough to hold several skewers for each guest—have only a small group using each barbecue. Keep fires hot enough to cook foods quickly.

Broth is passed in mugs to guests before they are seated. Serve other items on the menu, including the selection of filled skewers, from a buffet table. Rice can be kept warm in an electric frying pan.

FRIED RICE WITH VEGETABLES

4 tablespoons (⅛ lb.) butter or margarine
6 cups cooked rice (hot or cold)
  About 3 green onions, sliced
1 small can (5 oz.) water chestnuts, drained
    and sliced
2 carrots, shredded
  About ½ cup regular-strength chicken broth
    (more if needed)
3 teaspoons soy sauce

In an electric frying pan or other pan, heat butter or margarine. Sauté rice until golden. Add onions, water chestnuts, carrots, chicken broth, and soy sauce. Cook, stirring, until heated, adding more broth if needed. Reduce heat to warm; cover. Keeps well up to about 1 hour. Makes about 8 servings.

SKEWERED MEATS

Allow about ½ pound meat and fish for each guest. For each 8 servings, allow about 4 green peppers and 1 medium-sized eggplant. Meat and vegetables should be cut in bite-sized pieces. Arrange together on skewers the foods that cook in same time; string 4 or 5 pieces close together at the end of each skewer.

Glazing Sauce. Combine 4 cups soy sauce, 2 cups sweet Sherry or apple juice, 1 cup salad oil, ½ cup sugar, and 1 teaspoon ground ginger; heat. Makes enough to fill 8 mugs.

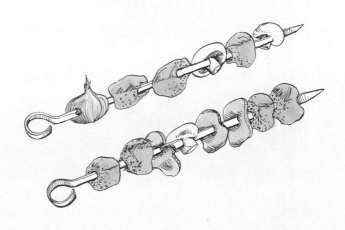

Small Sit-Down Dinner

ICED BROCCOLI SOUP   BREAD STICKS
GLAZED ROAST ROCK CORNISH GAME HENS
FILBERT WILD RICE STUFFING
ARTICHOKES PARMESAN
WATERCRESS SALAD   HOT ROLLS
FLAMING PEARS IN RUM BUTTER SAUCE
VANILLA ICE CREAM

You can't escape the fact that cooking and entertaining take time, but you can split that time into convenient parcels. That's the philosophy behind this distinguished dinner menu. The day before, set out Rock Cornish game hens to thaw, make and chill soup, and prepare rice stuffing, salad dressing, and artichokes. In the morning on the day of the dinner, you can peel fruit for salad and chill it in the dressing, and poach pears in rum sauce for dessert. That afternoon, stuff the birds and prepare garnish for soup.

With so much of the preparation completed well ahead of time, you can be relaxed to enjoy your role as hostess as you invite guests to sit down to soup. For the main course, the host can serve the birds, stuffing, and artichokes, and the hostess the salad. Flame the pears at the table.

ICED BROCCOLI SOUP

Except for the garnishing, the soup can be completed the day before.

1½ pounds broccoli, washed and trimmed
   4 cups boiling regular-strength chicken broth
   2 egg yolks
   1 cup half-and-half (light cream)
   Salt to taste
   Thin slices of lemon
½ cup heavy cream, whipped and salted
      to taste

Cook broccoli until tender in the broth; cool in broth. Whirl smooth in a blender; add cooking liquid as needed (or rub broccoli through a fine wire strainer). Beat egg yolks with half-and-half; combine with broccoli and all remaining hot broth. Salt to taste.

Cover and chill until serving time. Pour soup into chilled bowls and garnish each dish with a lemon slice topped with a puff of salted whipped cream. Makes 6 servings.

GLAZED ROAST ROCK CORNISH GAME HENS

**4 to 6 Rock Cornish game hens
    (14 to 20 oz. each)
    Salt
    Filbert Wild Rice Stuffing (recipe follows)
½ cup (¼ lb.) butter
2 tablespoons currant jelly
    Artichokes Parmesan for garnish
        (recipe follows)**

Thaw game hens. Remove giblets and save for stuffing. Rinse birds in cold water, drain thoroughly, and pat dry. Sprinkle neck and body cavity with salt and fill (do not pack tightly) with stuffing. Close cavities securely with small metal or wooden skewers. Place birds breast side up with a small space between each on a rimmed baking sheet. Bake in a 350° oven for 60 to 70 minutes or until leg joint moves easily.

Baste occasionally with glaze made by melting butter and blending with currant jelly. (If the oven is filled by the birds and the artichokes, exchange contents of upper and lower racks halfway through baking time to assure more even browning.)

Serve on a large heated platter garnished with some of the wild rice stuffing and a few of the artichokes. Makes 4 to 6 servings.

FILBERT WILD RICE STUFFING

You can make the stuffing a day ahead and refrigerate it, but don't stuff the birds before the afternoon of the party.

**1½ cups uncooked wild rice
    Water
1½ teaspoons salt
½ pound bulk pork sausage
1 cup chopped filberts
1 medium-sized onion, chopped
2 tablespoons butter or margarine
¼ cup brandy
    Salt and pepper to taste
    Livers, gizzards, and hearts from game
        hens, chopped
3 tablespoons butter or margarine**

Cover rice with cold water and let stand several hours. Drain, rinse thoroughly, and drain again. Add rice to 3 cups boiling water seasoned with the 1½ teaspoons salt. Return to boil, reduce to simmer, and cook, covered, for 40 minutes or until rice is tender; stir if necessary. Remove from heat and let cool slightly.

Meanwhile, break apart sausage in a frying pan. Add filberts and cook, stirring, until meat is browned. In another pan cook onion in 2 tablespoons butter until soft. Combine onion with pork mixture; add brandy and cook rapidly, stirring, for about 2 minutes. Mix with the rice. Season to taste with salt and pepper.

After stuffing the birds, you should have about 2 cups of rice mixture left over; reserve this extra portion. Just before serving time, cook the giblets in 3 tablespoons butter; stir in the extra stuffing and heat through. Spoon around the roast birds on the serving tray; top with artichokes.

(continued)

ARTICHOKES PARMESAN

2 cans (1 lb. each) artichoke bottoms, 12
    to 14 cooked and chilled frozen
    artichoke bottoms, or 12 to 14
    trimmed, cooked, and chilled fresh
    large artichoke bottoms
About 2 tablespoons minced chives
About 1½ teaspoons pepper
2 packages (3 oz. each) cream cheese,
    softened
Melted butter
1½ cups shredded Parmesan cheese

Drain and rinse canned artichoke bottoms, if used. Pat dry. Into the hollow of each sprinkle about ½ teaspoon minced chives and ⅛ teaspoon pepper; fill with softened cream cheese and spread smooth, even with rim of artichoke bottom. Dip in melted butter and coat with Parmesan cheese (put cheese in paper bag and shake artichoke bottoms in it, one at a time).

Place in a baking pan; sprinkle with a little more Parmesan. Cover and chill overnight, if desired, until ready to cook. Bake in a 350° oven for about 40 minutes. Makes 6 servings.

WATERCRESS SALAD

½ cup salad oil
⅓ cup tarragon vinegar
1 tablespoon orange marmalade
1 teaspoon salt
2 grapefruit, peeled and cut in sections
    Hearts from 2 heads butter lettuce
3 cups chopped watercress

Mix oil, vinegar, marmalade, and salt. Pour over grapefruit and chill several hours. Break 1 lettuce heart into small pieces and toss with watercress. Line salad bowl with leaves from the other lettuce heart; add watercress mixture. Cover and chill until serving time. Pour fruit and dressing over greens; toss and serve on chilled salad plates. Makes 6 servings.

HOT ROLLS

Shape 2 packages (8 oz. *each*) refrigerated crescent rolls as directed on package; arrange on a baking sheet. Let stand at room temperature about an hour. Bake in a 375° oven for 12 minutes or until browned. (Unless you have an extra oven, slip rolls in to bake when you remove the birds, increasing temperature to 375°.)

FLAMING PEARS IN RUM BUTTER SAUCE

Poach the pears several hours ahead, if you like, then reheat and flame with rum to serve with ice cream balls.

1½ cups brown sugar, firmly packed
1 cup water
¼ cup (⅛ lb.) butter or margarine
4 large ripe pears, peeled, cored, and
    sliced
About ½ cup rum
Ice cream balls (about 1 quart ice cream)

In a narrow, deep saucepan, combine the sugar, water, and butter; bring to a boil, and let simmer 10 minutes. Add pears and 3 tablespoons of the rum; simmer until fruit is cooked, about 5 minutes. Keep fruit immersed by frequently pushing down with slotted spoon. Lift pears from syrup and place in a bowl.

Boil syrup rapidly until reduced about half. Add to pears and let stand, covered, at room temperature until serving time. To serve, heat in a chafing dish over direct heat until boiling (or bring hot fruit to table in a heatproof serving bowl); add about ¼ cup warmed rum and flame immediately. Serve ice cream from a large chilled bowl; spoon pears and sauce over ice cream balls in individual serving bowls. Makes 6 servings.

One-Hour Oven Supper

SAUSAGE AND MUSHROOM QUICHE
AVOCADO AND GRAPEFRUIT SALAD
CROISSANTS
APPLE CRISPY   WHIPPED CREAM

Sausage-mushroom quiche and apple dessert bake together for a party supper that's ready to serve about an hour after you begin preparing it. If you prefer, assemble the dessert and pastry shell in advance. Then about 40 minutes before dinner fill the pastry with the quiche ingredients and bake it and the dessert simultaneously. Meanwhile dress a mixed green salad with oil and vinegar and garnish with a pinwheel of sliced avocado and pink grapefruit segments.

SAUSAGE AND MUSHROOM QUICHE

½ pound mushrooms
1 tablespoon butter or margarine
4 eggs
1½ cups half-and-half (light cream)
¼ teaspoon salt
1½ cups shredded Cheddar cheese
1 tablespoon flour
1 can (4 oz.) Danish cocktail sausages
    or 16 small cocktail sausages
9-inch unbaked pastry shell
2 tablespoons finely chopped parsley

Wash and slice mushrooms and sauté in butter just until tender; set aside. Beat eggs until blended and stir in half-and-half and salt; set aside. Dust the cheese with flour. Alternate layers of sausages, cheese, and mushrooms in the pastry shell, arranging the top layer of sausages in an attractive pinwheel pattern. Pour over the custard and sprinkle with parsley. Bake in a 375° oven for 35 minutes or until set. Makes 6 servings.

APPLE CRISPY

5 large cooking apples (Winesap, Golden
    Delicious, or Pippin)
1 tablespoon lemon juice
1 teaspoon cinnamon
4 tablespoons (⅛ lb.) butter or margarine
6 tablespoons unsifted all-purpose flour
⅔ cup light brown sugar, firmly packed
    Whipped cream

Peel, quarter, and core apples, then arrange in a buttered 9-inch square (or similar size) baking pan. Sprinkle with lemon juice and dust with cinnamon. For topping, mix with a pastry blender until crumbly the butter, flour, and brown sugar; sprinkle evenly over the apple slices.

    Bake in a 375° oven for 35 to 40 minutes, or until the apples are tender. Serve while still warm, topped with whipped cream. Makes 6 servings.

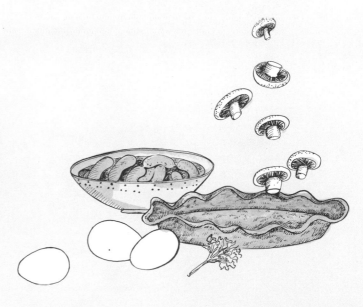

Economical Dinner for Guests

GREEN SALAD WITH SHRIMP AND SLICED CUCUMBER

OVEN RUMP ROAST

SOUR CREAM MUSHROOM SAUCE

SWEDISH BROWNED POTATOES

PARSLEY-BUTTERED CARROTS

BUTTERFLAKE ROLLS

CHERRY ANGEL PIE

The special advantage of this oven meal is that it can wait unspoiled if dinnertime is delayed. The entrée is a rump roast, a fairly economical cut of beef that is usually pot roasted. You'll find it is just as succulent when roasted uncovered in the oven as suggested here.

The roast, potatoes, and mushroom casserole all bake at the same temperature. If your dinner guests are tardy, you can lower the oven temperature to 200° to hold the foods. For the salad, mix assorted greens, small shrimp, and sliced cucumber with a plain French dressing. Cook carrots whole, then roll them in parsley-seasoned melted butter.

You can make the meringue shell for the dessert a day in advance, if you wish, then fill it several hours before serving. Or you can complete the pie and freeze it further ahead of time; let it thaw in the refrigerator for 6 to 8 hours before serving.

OVEN RUMP ROAST

> **6-pound boneless rump roast**
> **2 teaspoons salt**
> **1 teaspoon dry mustard**
> **¼ teaspoon each garlic salt and pepper**
>   **Unseasoned meat tenderizer (optional)**
> **1 tablespoon catsup**
> **1 teaspoon Worcestershire**
> **½ cup dry red wine (or ½ cup water and**
>   **1 tablespoon lemon juice)**

Rub roast with salt, mustard, garlic salt, and pepper. If you wish, use meat tenderizer, following directions on package. Insert a meat thermometer into the center of the thickest part of the roast, and place meat on a rack in a shallow baking pan.

Mix together catsup, Worcestershire, and wine; brush meat with this basting sauce. Roast in a 325° oven until the meat thermometer registers 130° for rare meat, or about 1 hour 45 minutes. (Figure on about 18 minutes per pound for rare meat.) Baste with the wine sauce several times during roasting.

Let the meat stand at room temperature 10 minutes to set the juices, then slice and serve with the mushroom sauce (recipe follows). Makes 10 to 12 servings.

Note: Because the rump is a very lean beef roast, it should be removed from the oven before the meat thermometer registers the usual temperature of 140° for rare beef. If temperature is allowed to go to 140°, meat will be past the prime pink and juicy stage.

SOUR CREAM MUSHROOM SAUCE

2 pounds mushrooms
6 tablespoons butter or margarine
3 tablespoons instant-type all-purpose flour
2 teaspoons each salt and prepared mustard
¼ teaspoon each nutmeg and pepper
2 cups (1 pint) sour cream
¼ cup each minced parsley and instant minced onions

Wash and slice mushrooms. Cream together the butter or margarine, flour, salt, mustard, nutmeg, pepper, sour cream, parsley, and onions. Alternate layers of sliced mushrooms and sour cream sauce in a buttered 2½-quart casserole. Bake uncovered in a 325° oven for 1 hour, stirring once or twice. (If you wish, stir some of the juices from the roast into the sauce.) Serves 8 to 10.

SWEDISH BROWNED POTATOES

Peel medium-sized baking potatoes, allowing 1 per serving, and cut almost through the potatoes, crosswise, making the slices about ⅛ inch thick. Brush with melted butter. Place in a shallow baking pan and bake in a 325° oven for 1½ hours or until tender.

CHERRY ANGEL PIE

6 egg whites
¼ teaspoon each salt and cream of tartar
1½ cups sugar
2 teaspoons vanilla
1½ cups whipping cream
1½ teaspoons vanilla
2 tablespoons powdered sugar
2 teaspoons lemon juice
1 can (1 lb. 5 oz.) prepared cherry pie filling

For the meringue shell, beat egg whites until foamy, add salt and cream of tartar, and beat until soft peaks form. Gradually beat in sugar, 1 tablespoon at a time, until stiff peaks form when beater is withdrawn. Beat in the 2 teaspoons vanilla. Spread meringue on the bottom and sides of a buttered 10-inch cheesecake pan or deep baking pan with removable bottom. Bake in a 300° oven for about 1 hour, or until pie is lightly browned and dry on the outside. Let cool (it settles as it cools).

Several hours before serving, whip the cream until stiff and flavor with the 1½ teaspoons vanilla and the powdered sugar. Spread in the bottom of the meringue shell. Blend lemon juice into cherry pie filling and carefully spoon filling over the cream. Chill. Makes 8 to 10 servings.

Beach Cabin Dinner

SKEWER FOODS
BUTTERED PARSLEY RICE
GREEN SALAD
HOT FLAT BREAD
ASSORTED FRUITS

When you get away to a weekend cabin in the mountains or at the beach, you can't leave meal preparations behind; but the situation permits a flexibility in food choice, style of service, and cooking methods that is in pleasant contrast to home routine.

For this meal, guests choose and skewer meats, vegetables, and fruits from a selection arranged on a tray. The host then barbecues the skewered entrées on two hibachis or a large barbecue brazier, basting those that require it. For the rice, use the quick-cooking kind and add freeze-dried parsley. The bread, made from a loaf of commercial frozen bread dough, is similar to the *focaccia* of San Francisco's North Beach section.

SKEWER FOODS

Offer as many of these foods as you wish: cubed lamb, steak, or ham; bacon, chicken livers, cocktail frankfurters or smoky links; onions, green peppers, mushroom caps, canned artichoke hearts, tomato wedges or cherry tomatoes; pineapple chunks, apple wedges, preserved kumquats, pitted apricots.

Lamb and less tender cuts of steak should be marinated for several hours before cooking. Use a prepared marinade, if you wish. Add oil or melted butter to the marinade later, heat, and use for basting while cooking.

HOT FLAT BREAD

Thaw 1 loaf commercial frozen bread dough. Roll out to fit a greased 10½ by 15½-inch baking pan. Using index finger, poke holes in the dough at 1-inch intervals; sprinkle with 1 teaspoon salt and drizzle with 3 tablespoons olive oil. (For additional flavor, mix 1 tablespoon grated Parmesan cheese or ¼ teaspoon garlic salt, basil, or oregano with the oil.) Let rise in a warm place about 30 minutes or until almost doubled. Bake in a 425° oven 12 to 15 minutes or until well browned. Cut in strips and serve hot. Makes 15 pieces, 2 by 5 inches.

Picnic Supper Salad

BEEF AND MUSHROOMS VINAIGRETTE
BUTTERED, SLICED FRENCH ROLLS
CANTALOUPE   FRESH STRAWBERRIES

Marinated salad entrées are the summer cook's friend. They can be completely made ahead, and they travel easily to almost any picnic spot. To transport the beef and mushroom salad, cover it securely and pack it in an ice cooler. Or, for short trips, wrap the chilled salad container in several thicknesses of newspaper to insulate against heat.

Take along buttered, sliced French rolls and a cantaloupe to cut in wedges and serve with fresh strawberries.

BEEF AND MUSHROOMS VINAIGRETTE

You can use leftover beef roast, extra barbecued steak, or broiled flank steak to make this entrée.

    1 pound mushrooms
    3 tablespoons olive oil
      Juice of 1 lemon
    2 teaspoons chicken stock base
1½ pounds sirloin or flank steak, broiled and
        chilled, or leftover beef roast
    4 tablespoons cup olive oil
¼ cup dry red wine
    3 tablespoons red wine vinegar
¼ teaspoon each chervil, thyme, basil, and
        marjoram
      Salt and pepper to taste
    1 tomato
    4 canned or cooked artichoke hearts

Wash and slice mushrooms, then sauté in 3 tablespoons of the oil along with lemon juice and chicken stock base, cooking just until barely tender; let cool. Slice meat into ⅜-inch-thick strips. For the salad dressing, mix together the 4 tablespoons oil, red wine, wine vinegar, cher-

vil, thyme, basil, and marjoram; stir in the juices drained from the mushrooms. Add salt and pepper to taste.

Arrange meat strips in a shallow serving dish and spoon mushrooms down the center. Peel tomato, cut in wedges, and place around the sides along with artichoke hearts. Pour over the dressing. Cover and chill at least 3 hours, basting several times with dressing. Serves 4 to 6.

Sausage Roast for Teen-Agers

ASSORTED SAUSAGES

FRANKFURTER BUNS   CRUSTY FRENCH ROLLS

ASSORTED MUSTARDS

CATSUP   PICKLE RELISH

SLICED ONIONS   DILL PICKLES   RIPE OLIVES

ITALIAN-STYLE CHEF'S SALAD

ICE CREAM   COOKIES

Whatever the season, indoors or out, hungry young people find it hard to resist a frankfurter roast. Any other sausage that fits on a stick will qualify, too. Possible choices for roasting at the fireplace, in addition to the traditional frankfurters, include fat Italian and German garlic sausages, slender smoked link sausages, long smoked Polish sausages, pale veal bockwurst. Plan to have at least 1 frankfurter and 1 or 2 other sausages for each person.

Some of the sausages may require thorough cooking; you can do this early in the day and chill meat until ready to use. For example, simmer Italian garlic sausage in water to cover for 20 minutes; cover veal bockwurst with boiling water and let stand 30 minutes. Ask your meatman how to cook varieties with which you are not familiar.

You can set out several types of rolls: regular soft frankfurter buns, crusty French rolls, perhaps some boat-shaped rolls. And with so many kinds of mustards available, it's easy to offer a range of flavors and degrees of heat. A potato salad abounding in good Italian ingredients provides a new taste in the salad course.

ITALIAN-STYLE CHEF'S SALAD

The salad chills for two to four hours before final ingredients are added.

6 cups boiled, peeled, and sliced potatoes
½ cup each diced celery and chopped
    green onions
1 small green pepper, seeded and
    thinly sliced
6 peperoncini (Italian-style pickled
    peppers), drained and chopped
    Oil Dressing (recipe follows)
    About 12 cherry tomatoes, halved
    Lettuce leaves
½ cup each thinly sliced dry salami and
    Provolone or Swiss cheese, cut in
    thin strips

In a large bowl gently toss potatoes, celery, green onions, green pepper, pickled peppers, and oil dressing until well mixed. Cover and chill for 2 to 4 hours. Mix lightly again, adding tomatoes, and spoon into a serving bowl lined with lettuce. Garnish with salami and cheese. Serves 8 to 10.

Oil Dressing. Combine ½ cup olive oil or salad oil with ¼ cup red wine vinegar, ¾ teaspoon salt, and ⅛ teaspoon pepper.

Beef and Bread Barbecue Dinner

SESAME-MARINATED BEEF ROAST

BARBECUE-BAKED ONION BREAD

BARBECUED CORN   MIXED GREEN SALAD

ICED MELON

A savory beef roast and fresh onion yeast bread bake together in a covered barbecue for this dinner.

Make marinade and refrigerate meat in it, covered, for about 24 hours. Start bread about 3 hours before you plan to serve dinner. Start barbecue fire 2 to 2½ hours before dinner; this allows at least 30 minutes for it to reach the proper temperature. Use about 25 long-burning briquets and follow directions for your barbecue to regulate heat.

When a thermometer inside (or in the lid of the barbecue) registers between 350° and 375°, put in bread and meat. Bread will bake in about 45 minutes; meat will be roasted to rare stage (130°) in about 1½ hours. Allow about 30 minutes longer for well done meat.

Strip the corn down to the last 3 or 4 layers of husk and place in cold water for about 30 minutes. Drain well; place on grill for 10 to 15 minutes. Remove husks and silk before serving. (If barbecue won't hold corn, husk it and cook it in boiling salted water on your range.)

BARBECUE-BAKED ONION BREAD

Prepare 1 package (about 14 oz.) hot roll mix as directed on package, except increase warm water in which you dissolve yeast to 1 cup. Stir in with the egg and flour mixture 3 tablespoons instant toasted onion and ¼ teaspoon *each* celery seed and whole thyme, crushed; blend in well. Cover and let rise in a warm place until doubled in volume, about 45 minutes.

Stir dough down; spoon into a well greased, 9 by 5-inch loaf pan. Cover and let rise in a warm place until doubled, about 30 minutes. Bake in a barbecue that has a hood, at 375°. Don't open barbecue during the first 20 minutes. The bread should be well browned and done in about 45 minutes. Turn loaf out of the pan; keep warm. Serve with butter. Makes 1 loaf.

SESAME-MARINATED BEEF ROAST

⅓ cup (2¼-oz. package) sesame seed
½ cup salad oil
½ cup soy sauce
⅓ cup lemon juice
2 tablespoons white wine vinegar
1 tablespoon sugar
2 cloves garlic, mashed
1 medium-sized onion, sliced
4-pound boneless beef roast such as cross rib (shoulder clod) or sirloin tip

For the marinade, heat sesame seed in salad oil just long enough to brown the seeds slightly. Combine with soy sauce, lemon juice, vinegar, sugar, garlic, and onion. Pour over meat, cover, and marinate in refrigerator about 24 hours, turning meat occasionally.

To barbecue, drain roast, saving the marinade. Arrange glowing coals in a ring around the perimeter of the fire grate in your barbecue and place a foil drip pan in the center. Insert meat thermometer into center of roast and place on grill over drip pan. Cover barbecue and regulate dampers to maintain a temperature of 350° to 375°. You may need a few additional burning briquets during last part of cooking. It will take about 1½ hours for meat to reach 130° (rare). Baste occasionally with marinade. Serves 6.

Delicatessen Buffet

SLICED CORNED BEEF, PASTRAMI, COOKED HAM OR PROSCIUTTO

SLICED SWISS CHEESE

ONION ROLLS, BAGELS, AND CRUSTY ROLLS

CREAM CHEESE   SWEET BUTTER   MUSTARD

BUTTER LETTUCE

SEEDED GREEN PEPPERS   CHERRY TOMATOES

COARSE (KOSHER-STYLE) SALT

RIPE WINTER PEARS   GRAPES

DANISH CAMEMBERT, SMALL WHOLE CHEDDAR CHEESE

A meal ideally suited to impromptu entertaining, this buffet literally comes out of the shopping bag. You can buy the ingredients on the way home from a football game or have them on hand and ready to serve after the theater. The foods are agreeable for any hour of the day.

You begin with a tray of sandwich makings, offering a choice of meats, cheeses, rolls, and spreads. For six people allow a total of 1½ pounds sliced meats, about ½ pound sliced Swiss cheese, and at least 2 rolls apiece. Split rolls before serving. Also have a 3-ounce package of cream cheese, ¼ pound sweet butter, and a jar of mustard such as Dijon or English style.

Accompany sandwich makings with a basket of handsome vegetables: lettuce (broken up for sandwiches), cherry tomatoes (one basket should

be enough), and green peppers. Choose 2 large, shiny peppers and, leaving them whole, cut out core and seeds and pull out pith; gash peppers so they will break apart easily. Dip tomatoes and pepper sections in salt to eat.

For dessert, group fruit and whole cheeses on a board, to be sampled at leisure. Offer 3 to 6 pears and a large bunch of grapes with a Danish Camembert (tinned ones are often available in supermarkets) and a small Cheddar cheese.

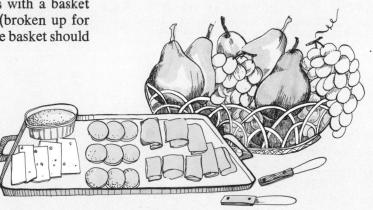

Pasta and Sausage Supper

ANTIPASTO PLATTER   BREAD STICKS
FETTUCINI ALFREDO
BROWNED ITALIAN SAUSAGES
WINTER PEARS

A delicious pasta dish, drenched in a creamy cheese sauce which you blend in just before serving, is the star of this Italian-inspired supper. The simplicity of the meal makes it well suited for a late night supper party. Mixing the fettucini in a chafing dish in front of your guests will add to the fun.

First start the sausages. Then make up an antipasto platter, including such ingredients as canned white albacore tuna in a round chunk, pitted ripe olives, marinated artichoke hearts, celery sticks, cherry tomatoes, and canned pickled red hot chiles.

Then concentrate on the fettucini, which you can complete either in a chafing dish at the table or in the kitchen.

FETTUCINI ALFREDO

1 package (12 oz.) tagliarini (fine egg noodles)
  Boiling salted water
6 tablespoons butter
1 cup whipping cream
2 cups shredded Parmesan cheese
  Freshly ground pepper

Cook tagliarini in boiling salted water for 6 minutes, or until barely tender; drain thoroughly. In a large frying pan or chafing dish, melt butter, add noodles, and pour over whipping cream. Sprinkle with cheese; using two forks, mix lightly over moderate heat until sauce blends together and coats pasta thoroughly. Sprinkle with pepper and serve immediately. Serves 6.

BROWNED ITALIAN SAUSAGE

Place 6 to 8 Italian garlic sausages (about 2 pounds) in a pan with water to cover; simmer 20 minutes; drain and sauté until browned. Arrange around fettucini.

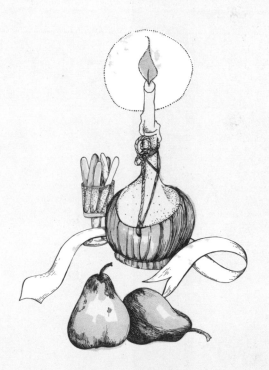

Mexican Soup Supper

AZTEC SOUP

MEAT SANDWICHES

SPICED MEXICAN CUSTARD

(JERICALLA)

The menu pictured on the cover of this book is based on Mexican flavors. The soup recipe is from Guadalajara. The vegetable condiments, to be spooned into individual servings, are typically Mexican. The dessert is a Mexican specialty —a golden custard with the distinctive spicy flavor of cinnamon.

You can make the soup ahead and reheat it, but prepare the condiments just before serving. You heat the milk mixture for the custard the night before and chill it in the refrigerator overnight; bake the custards early on the day of the party.

AZTEC SOUP

1 chile ancho (a mild dried chile available in Mexican markets or delicatessens)
  Boiling water
6 cups brown stock (or regular-strength chicken broth)
  Salt
2 tablespoons uncooked rice
⅓ cup drained canned garbanzos
1 medium-sized onion, chopped
1 medium-sized tomato, peeled and chopped
1 canned green California chile (seeds and pith removed), **chopped**
  Salt
1 ripe avocado
  Lime juice
½ cup chopped, lightly packed cilantro (also called Chinese parsley or fresh coriander; available in Mexican or Oriental markets)
2 or 3 limes, cut in wedges

Remove stem and seeds from the chile ancho; cover chile with boiling water, and let stand 10 minutes. Drain, and cut in small pieces. Heat stock and salt to taste. Add chile pieces, rice, and garbanzos. Bring to a boil, cover, and simmer about 15 minutes or until rice is tender.

Combine ¼ cup of the chopped onion with the tomato, green chile, and salt to taste. Peel and dice the avocado, and moisten with a little lime juice to prevent darkening. Place the remainder of the onion, the tomato-onion-chile mixture, and the avocado in individual dishes. Remove soup from heat, and stir in the cilantro. Ladle into bowls, adding onion, tomato, and avocado as you like. Serve with lime wedges, to be squeezed into the soup. Makes 4 to 5 main dish servings.

MEAT SANDWICHES

Slice a slender loaf of French bread in half lengthwise (or use split French rolls). Spread the bottom half with sweet butter, then cover with a layer of thinly sliced baked ham, roast beef, corned beef, or turkey. Add lettuce leaves, if desired. Put top back on the loaf, and slice crosswise into sandwich-size lengths.

SPICED MEXICAN CUSTARD
(Jericalla)

To develop the spicy cinnamon flavor yet preserve the pale gold tones of this custard, you heat the milk and sugar with cinnamon sticks and let this mixture chill overnight. Then set the cinnamon sticks aside (to use later as a garnish), and bake the custards.

2 cups milk
2 sticks whole cinnamon, each 3 or 4
    inches long
½ cup sugar
 3 eggs, beaten

Combine milk, cinnamon sticks, and sugar in a saucepan and, stirring, bring to a boil. Cover and chill overnight.

Set 4 small baking dishes (each at least ⅔-cup size) in a baking pan and surround with hottest tap water to about half the depth of the dishes. Remove dishes, set the pan of water in the oven,

and set heat at 350°. When oven has reached that temperature, again heat the milk mixture to scalding, stirring. Set cinnamon aside and beat hot milk into the eggs with a fork. Pour an equal portion of mixture into each baking dish and set the dishes in the hot water bath.

Bake at 350° for 25 to 30 minutes, or until the centers of the custards jiggle only slightly when a dish is shaken gently. At once remove custards from water, using a wide spatula or kitchen tongs. Chill custards and serve in the baking dishes. (If you like, rinse cinnamon sticks, drain, break in half. Set a piece atop each jericalla.) Makes 4 servings.

Dinner in a Hurry

SALAD NORWEGIAN

STEAKS ROQUEFORT WITH ONION RINGS

SHERRIED PEAS AND MUSHROOMS

HOT CROISSANTS

PETITE CHOCOLATE MOUSSES WITH ALMONDS

It's always good to have ample time to plan a special meal for company, but for occasions when you don't know until the last minute that people are coming, changes in routine are essential. You can put together this dinner by shopping for specific quick-to-cook foods and literally prepare the meal for six guests as you open the containers.

Make the dessert first and put it in to chill. Leave the peas and frozen croissants (or buy croissants from the bakery) out to thaw and start the mushroom seasonings for the peas. Mix up the Roquefort sauce for the steaks, and put together the salads while the oven heats for the onion rings and croissants.

Shortly before you are ready to serve, bake 2 packages (7 oz. *each*) frozen French-fried onion rings according to package directions. Warm croissants in same oven for about 5 minutes. Sauté steaks in butter, then broil them with their topping while onions and rolls keep warm in lower section of oven and the peas heat on top of the range.

SALAD NORWEGIAN

3 tomatoes, cut into thin wedges
**1 can (about 3¾ oz.) small sardines packed
    in mustard sauce**
1 tablespoon salad oil
2 teaspoons vinegar
  Salt and pepper
  Parsley or watercress sprigs for garnish.

On each of six individual salad plates arrange the wedges of a half tomato. Open can of sardines and gently lift out the sardines, placing one or two alongside the tomatoes on each plate (using all). Blend salad oil and vinegar with the sauce left in the sardine can, and drizzle evenly over salads. Salt and pepper, and garnish liberally with parsley or watercress sprigs. Chill until ready to serve. Serves 6.

STEAKS ROQUEFORT

Garnish these steaks with some of the French fried onion rings to serve.

   1 small package (1¼ oz.) Roquefort cheese
½ can (6-oz. size) white sauce
   1 egg yolk
¼ teaspoon Worcestershire
   2 tablespoons chopped fresh, frozen, or
      freeze-dried chives
   6 individual serving-size steaks (about 2 to
      2½ pounds beef) such as top round,
      cube steaks, or sirloin
   Salt and pepper
   3 tablespoons melted butter

Mash cheese with a fork and blend in white sauce, egg yolk, Worcestershire, and chives.

About 10 minutes before you are ready to serve, sprinkle steaks with salt and pepper and brown in the butter over high heat until meat is as done as you like. Transfer to a broiler rack (or serving dish that can be put under the broiler) and divide Roquefort sauce evenly among the steaks, spreading over the surface of the meat. Broil close to the heat just until topping browns lightly, 1 to 2 minutes. Makes 6 servings.

SHERRIED PEAS AND MUSHROOMS

   2 cans (3 or 4-oz. size) sliced mushrooms
   2 tablespoons melted butter
¼ teaspoon marjoram
⅛ teaspoon nutmeg
   2 tablespoons Sherry
   2 packages (10 oz. each) frozen petite peas

Drain mushrooms, reserving liquid. In a wide pan heat mushrooms in butter until sizzling, then stir in marjoram, nutmeg, and Sherry. Bang each package of peas against a hard surface to break peas apart, then pour into pan with mushrooms, turn off heat, and let stand. Just before you are ready to serve, add 2 tablespoons of the reserved mushroom liquid and bring to boiling, stirring occasionally. Makes 6 generous servings.

PETITE CHOCOLATE MOUSSES WITH ALMONDS

   1 package (6 oz.) semisweet chocolate pieces
   1 teaspoon each sugar and vanilla
⅓ cup boiling water
   4 eggs, separated
      Whole almonds for garnish

In an electric blender whirl chocolate pieces until powdery; stir to free from corners of blender. Add sugar, vanilla, and boiling water, and whirl until chocolate is smooth (or combine ingredients over hot water and stir until blended).

Add the egg yolks to the blending chocolate; beat the egg whites until they hold short distinct peaks. Fold the chocolate into the whites, then pour mixture into six individual serving dishes or cups. Cover lightly and chill at least an hour. Top each mousse with a few whole almonds for decoration and serve. Makes 6 servings.

Cook-Ahead Party Dinner

SHRIMP-STUFFED WHOLE ARTICHOKES

BEEF EN DAUBE

FRENCH BREAD

STRAWBERRIES JUBILEE

This three-course party menu can be prepared a day in advance. Chilled stuffed artichokes are the first course, followed by beef stew in individual ramekins or casseroles. Serve the fruit sauce flambé over ice cream as the finale.

If you choose to prepare the meal the day before, cook and chill the artichokes and mix the dressing for them, but wait until just before serving to fill them. Completely prepare stew, cool, and chill; reheat, covered, in a 350° oven until hot through, about 30 minutes. Mold the ice cream in a fancy mold or scoop it into balls and refreeze. Since the fruit sauce can be assembled quickly, make it the day you serve the meal.

SHRIMP-STUFFED WHOLE ARTICHOKES

    6 medium-sized artichokes
      Boiling salted water
    1 tablespoon each salad oil and lemon juice
    ⅓ cup mayonnaise
    ¼ cup sour cream
    1½ tablespoons lemon juice
    ½ teaspoon grated lemon peel
    ¼ teaspoon each salt, tarragon, and
      Dijon-style mustard
    ½ pound small cooked shrimp
      Lemon wedges for garnish

Slice stem ends and about a third of each top from artichokes. Drop into a large amount of boiling salted water seasoned with the salad oil and 1 tablespoon lemon juice and simmer, covered, until tender, about 40 minutes; drain and cool. Then use a teaspoon to scoop out the center choke (fuzzy part) in each artichoke; turn upside-down to drain. Cover and chill.

For dressing, mix together the mayonnaise, sour cream, 1½ tablespoons lemon juice, lemon peel, salt, tarragon, and mustard. Just before serving, spoon 2 tablespoons dressing into the center of each artichoke and distribute shrimp on top of the dressing. Garnish with lemon wedges. Serves 6.

BEEF EN DAUBE

French-style beef stew, complete with mushroom caps, braised onions, peas, and ripe olives, cooks in a Dutch oven, but for a festive presentation serve it in individual ramekins.

3 strips bacon, cut in 1-inch pieces
2 pounds beef stew meat
½ cup regular strength beef broth
1 cup dry red wine
1 teaspoon salt
¼ teaspoon crumbled dried thyme
2 cloves garlic, minced
1 tablespoon instant minced onion
2 strips orange peel (cut from fruit with
    a vegetable peeler)
2 tablespoons cornstarch
2 tablespoons brandy or water
1 pound small whole onions
    Boiling salted water
¾ pound small mushrooms (about 1 inch in
    diameter)
3 tablespoons butter or margarine
1 teaspoon sugar
½ cup pitted ripe olives
1 package (10 oz.) frozen peas, thawed

In a large Dutch oven, sauté bacon until crisp, remove from pan, and set aside; pour off all but 1 tablespoon of the drippings. Add meat to pan and brown on all sides. Pour in beef broth and wine and season with salt, thyme, garlic, minced onion, and orange peel. Cover and simmer until tender, about 1 to 1¼ hours. Blend cornstarch with brandy or water and stir into the juices in the pan; bring to a boil and cook until thickened, stirring constantly.

Meanwhile, peel onions and cook in boiling salted water until barely tender, about 15 minutes, and drain. Cut stems from mushrooms, slice, and sauté with the whole caps in 2 tablespoons of the butter until slightly browned, then add (with juices) to the meat.

In the same pan sauté onions in remaining butter until lightly browned, sprinkle with sugar, and heat until glazed; add to the meat. Mix in olives and peas and simmer for 1 minute, and then remove from heat. Serves 6.

STRAWBERRIES JUBILEE

1 quart vanilla ice cream
1 large navel orange
1 can (6 oz.) frozen orange juice
    concentrate (undiluted)
1½ cups whole strawberries, washed
    and hulled
3 tablespoons brandy

Scoop ice cream into balls and refreeze, covered. (Or pack ice cream into a fancy mold and refreeze.) Peel and thinly slice the orange; cut each slice in half.

Just before serving, heat orange juice concentrate and add orange slices and strawberries. Warm the brandy, ignite, and spoon flaming over the fruit sauce. Spoon sauce over the ice cream balls, placed in dessert bowls, or around the ice cream mold, unmolded on a rimmed platter. Serves 6.

Lamb Dinner for Guests

HERBED LEG OF LAMB
BAKED ORANGES
GREEN BEAN-CAULIFLOWER PLATTER   MUSTARD SAUCE
BAKED POTATOES WITH SOUR CREAM AND CHIVES
CRISP GREEN SALAD   CREAMY FRENCH DRESSING
CREAM HEARTS WITH CHERRY SAUCE

A colorful meal that is particularly pleasing to the eye, this dinner features roast leg of lamb and a dessert of cream hearts with cherry sauce. It is easy to prepare and serve. The dessert can be made the day before. You may wish to serve the dinner buffet style.

Start the lamb about 2½ hours before you plan to eat. Scrub large baking potatoes, dry them, rub with salad oil to coat evenly, and put into the oven about 1½ hours before serving time. Cut and trim the oranges; bake during the last 15 minutes the meat roasts.

Prepare salad greens and place them in the refrigerator to crisp. Make the dressing a few hours ahead so the flavors will combine. Cook the vegetables and keep them hot; arrange together on a platter just before serving.

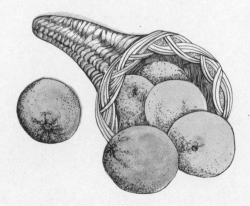

HERBED LEG OF LAMB

1 tablespoon salad oil
6-pound leg of lamb
1 clove garlic, peeled and mashed
1 teaspoon salt
½ teaspoon each powdered ginger, thyme,
    sage, and marjoram
½ cup each dry white wine and water (or
    ¼ cup lemon juice and ¾ cup water)
Baked Oranges (recipe follows)

Rub salad oil evenly over leg of lamb. Combine garlic, salt, ginger, thyme, sage, and marjoram; crumble evenly over the meat. Place in a roasting pan and insert a meat thermometer into the thickest portion of the meat.

Add wine and water to the roasting pan. Roast, uncovered, in a 350° oven for 2½ hours or until the thermometer registers 170° to 180°; baste occasionally with pan juices. Garnish with Baked Oranges. Serves about 8.

BAKED ORANGES

Cut 4 large oranges in halves (if you wish, make a zigzag design with a pencil and cut along line with a sharply pointed knife). Cut out white membrane from each center with scissors. Dot each half with 1 teaspoon honey. Bake in a 350° oven for 10 to 15 minutes or until heated through. Put a parsley sprig in the center of each orange half. Makes 8.

GREEN BEAN-CAULIFLOWER PLATTER

1 medium-sized head of cauliflower
¾ cup water
  About ¼ teaspoon salt
  Dash pepper
2 packages (10 oz. each) frozen whole
    green beans
  Salt, pepper, and butter to taste
  Mustard Sauce (recipe follows)
  Chopped chives

Place whole cauliflower in a pan and add the water; season with about ¼ teaspoon salt and a dash of pepper. Cover, bring to boil over medium heat, and cook for 10 to 15 minutes or until tender-crisp. In another pan, cook the beans according to package directions. Season to taste with salt, pepper, and butter.

Just before serving, place hot cooked cauliflower in center of a platter and arrange the hot cooked beans around it. Cover the cauliflower with Mustard Sauce and sprinkle with chopped chives. Serves 8.

Mustard Sauce. Combine 1 cup sour cream (at room temperature) with 1 tablespoon lemon juice, 2 teaspoons prepared mustard, and ¼ teaspoon salt.

CREAMY FRENCH DRESSING

Make this dressing several hours ahead, and then serve it over crisp salad greens.

1 can (10½ oz.) tomato soup
¾ cup red wine vinegar
1 cup salad oil
½ cup sugar
½ teaspoon white pepper
2 teaspoons salt
1 teaspoon each dry mustard, prepared
    horseradish, and paprika
1 clove garlic, mashed

Combine ingredients in a quart jar; shake until well combined. Or combine the ingredients in an electric blender; whirl at low speed until dressing is smooth and well blended. Store in a cool place. Makes about 3 cups dressing.

CREAM HEARTS WITH CHERRY SAUCE

To facilitate unmolding, line bottoms of molds with waxed paper cut to fit before filling with cream mixture.

1 cup creamed cottage cheese
1 large package (8 oz.) cream cheese,
    softened
1½ teaspoons vanilla
  3 tablespoons sugar
  1 cup whipping cream
  1 envelope unflavored gelatin
½ cup milk
  Cherry Sauce (recipe follows)

Press cottage cheese through a wire strainer or whirl in blender until smooth. Turn into the small bowl of electric mixer. With mixer at low speed, combine with cream cheese, vanilla, and sugar, mixing until smooth and well blended.

Beat in cream. Soften gelatin in milk and dissolve over hot water. Turn mixer to high speed and pour dissolved gelatin into the creamy mixture in a thin stream, mixing until well blended. Turn mixture into 8 individual cheesecake molds, heart-shaped molds, or custard cups and chill until set. To unmold, loosen edges with a knife; turn out onto dessert dish. Serve with Cherry Sauce. Makes 8 servings.

Cherry Sauce. Combine 1 can (1 lb. 5 oz.) cherry pie filling with 2 tablespoons kirsch *or* 1 teaspoon almond extract. Spoon over individual cream hearts.

Guest Dinner Italian Style

ANTIPASTO SALAD
VEAL WITH ARTICHOKES
POTATO PUFFS PARMESAN
BREAD STICKS
VENETIAN CHOCOLATE TORTE   GRAPES

This menu quickly transforms a bag full of groceries into an imaginative dinner. Convenience foods speed the dinner preparation.

First start the dessert; then arrange and chill the salads. Proceed to potato puffs, and sauté veal last. Less than 30 minutes after you start, the meal is ready for your guests.

ANTIPASTO SALAD

Arrange 4 lettuce cups on a platter. Open 1 jar (3 oz.) marinated mushrooms and 1 can (4¾ oz.) Portuguese sardines and spoon some on each lettuce cup. Place 2 pickled sweet red peppers on each salad. Cover and chill. Serves 4.

VEAL WITH ARTICHOKES

   1 package (8 oz.) frozen artichoke hearts
      Boiling salted water
   1 package (15 oz.) frozen buttered veal
      steaks, thawed
   ½ teaspoon salt
   ¼ teaspoon garlic salt
   1 lemon
   ¼ cup dry white wine or Vermouth

Place artichoke hearts in boiling salted water; simmer 3 minutes and drain. Quickly sauté veal steaks in the butter packaged with the meat; turn to brown both sides. Season with salt and garlic salt and remove to a hot platter. Add drained artichoke hearts to pan drippings and heat just until lightly browned; spoon along one side of the veal steaks. Halve lemon lengthwise; cut one half into 4 wedges to garnish platter; squeeze juice from other half into pan. Pour wine or Vermouth into pan and let cook over high heat until reduced by half. Spoon over veal. Garnish with lemon wedges. Serves 4.

POTATO PUFFS PARMESAN

Prepare instant mashed potatoes as directed on the package for 4 servings. Drop mashed potatoes from a spoon into 4 mounds on a sheet of buttered foil. Sprinkle 1½ teaspoons grated Parmesan cheese over each mound and dot with butter. Place in a 450° oven for 10 minutes, or until lightly browned. Makes 4 servings.

VENETIAN CHOCOLATE TORTE

      12-ounce frozen pound cake
      4 ounces semisweet baking chocolate
   3½ tablespoons hot water
   ½ teaspoon instant coffee powder
   ½ teaspoon vanilla
   1 cup (½ pint) whipping cream
      Chocolate shot or chopped nuts

Remove cake from its package and slice into 4 horizontal layers while still frozen. Melt baking chocolate over hot water with the 3½ tablespoons hot water and the coffee powder. Remove from heat and stir in vanilla; let cool to room temperature. Whip cream until stiff and fold into the cool chocolate. Spread between cake layers and on top. Sprinkle top with chocolate shot or chopped nuts. Chill. Makes 6 to 8 servings.

Garden Barbecue

MIXED SALAD WITH CHEESE DRESSING
BARBECUED SIRLOIN TIP ROAST WITH ANCHOVY BUTTER
POTATO PUFFS
HOT CHIVE AND BUTTER BREAD
QUICK ALMOND CAKE
VANILLA ICE CREAM (OPTIONAL)   BERRIES

Guests will enjoy relaxing out-of-doors—perhaps on a Sunday afternoon—as meat, potatoes, and bread aromatically come to perfection on the barbecue. A barbecue with a hood or spit is ideal.

Prepare a package mix for yellow or pound cake; coat the buttered sides of the pan with sliced almonds, pour batter into pan, and bake. Have a basket of berries ready for eating as they are or making into sundaes for those who wish.

MIXED SALAD WITH CHEESE DRESSING

3 quarts torn mixed greens (butter, red, and iceberg lettuce)
¼ pound raw mushrooms, sliced
  Cheese Dressing (recipe follows)
1 cucumber, thinly sliced
1 avocado, peeled and sliced

Place greens and sliced mushrooms in a salad bowl. Pour over Cheese Dressing and mix well. Garnish with the cucumber and avocado slices. Serves 8 to 10.

Cheese Dressing. Mash 3 ounces blue or Roquefort cheese with 3 tablespoons white wine vinegar, 1 tablespoon lemon juice, 1 teaspoon anchovy paste, and ½ teaspoon Dijon-style mustard. Blend in ½ cup olive or salad oil, ½ teaspoon *each* salt and garlic salt, and pepper to taste. Shake well and chill. Makes 1 cup.

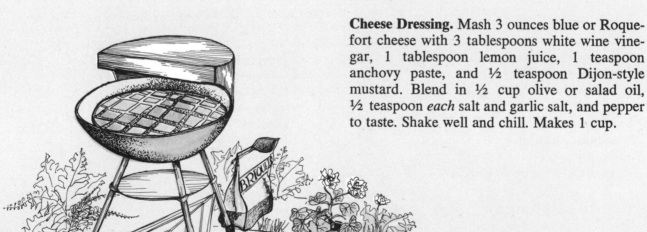

BARBECUED SIRLOIN TIP ROAST WITH ANCHOVY BUTTER

4 or 5-pound sirloin tip roast
3 or 4 cloves garlic, split
2 teaspoons salt
½ teaspoon pepper
2 teaspoons whole thyme, crumbled
  Unseasoned meat tenderizer (optional)
  Anchovy Butter (recipe follows)

Make several incisions in the roast and insert the garlic cloves. Rub the outside of the meat with the salt, pepper, and thyme. If desired, treat the meat with unseasoned meat tenderizer as directed on the package. Insert a meat thermometer in the center of the roast.

Place on a barbecue grill over medium coals, cover with a hood, and barbecue until the meat thermometer registers 130° for rare meat, about 1½ hours. (Or impale the meat on a revolving spit and cook.) Place on a carving board and spread the Anchovy Butter over the top of the roast; or, if you prefer, serve the Anchovy Butter alongside. Carve in thin slices to serve. Makes 10 to 12 servings.

Anchovy Butter. Cream ½ cup butter with 2 tablespoons anchovy paste. Blend in 2 tablespoons finely chopped parsley and 1 clove garlic, minced.

POTATO PUFFS

Place contents of 1 large package (2 lbs.) frozen potato puffs in a large, heavy cast iron frying pan. Heat over the barbecue and shake frequently for 15 minutes, or until potatoes are hot through and crisp. Makes 8 to 10 servings.

HOT CHIVE AND BUTTER BREAD

Spread 1 loaf sliced rich white bread with softened butter. Sprinkle one side of each slice with finely chopped chives. Reassemble the loaf and wrap in heavy foil. Place on the barbecue and heat for 10 to 15 minutes, or until hot through.

Two-Family Barbecue

CHILLED APPLE JUICE OR HOT CONSOMME

SMOKED CHEDDAR CHEESE   SESAME CRACKERS

MAKE-YOUR-OWN SALAD

ROQUEFORT SOUR CREAM DRESSING

STEAK KEBABS

BARBECUED CORN   ONIONS IN FOIL

SOUR CREAM · CHOCOLATE BIT CAKE

Two families might collaborate on a jaunt to a nearby park for this barbecue. The food preparation is easily divisible between two cooks.

If the day is warm, bring iced apple juice in a spigot-type vacuum jug; otherwise, provide steaming consommé. Cheese and crackers will tide over young children—and the rest of the group—while the meat barbecues. Offer such salad makings as crisp torn greens, whole cherry tomatoes, and canned garbanzos to be mixed and dressed by each picnicker.

The meat should be marinated several hours ahead of time; carry it to the picnic in a plastic container, ready to thread on skewers. Wrap the ears of corn and the onions in foil at home.

A large terrycloth beach towel is an easy-to-launder tablecloth, and terry fingertip towels can double as napkins.

ROQUEFORT SOUR CREAM DRESSING

Place in a blender (or use an electric mixer) 1 cup sour cream, ⅓ cup mayonnaise, 3 tablespoons lemon juice, 1 package (4 oz.) Roquefort cheese, 1 clove garlic, and ½ teaspoon salt. Blend or mix until smooth. Makes about 1 pint.

STEAK KEBABS

¾ cup dry red wine
3 tablespoons olive oil
3 tablespoons lemon juice
2 cloves garlic, minced
½ teaspoon salt
¼ teaspoon each whole rosemary and whole thyme
3 pounds top sirloin steak, cut in 1½-inch
    cubes

Mix the wine, olive oil, lemon juice, garlic, salt, rosemary, and thyme. Marinate steak, covered, in the mixture for several hours or overnight. At the picnic site skewer the meat and barbecue over moderately hot coals for about 8 minutes, turning once, for rare meat. Makes 8 servings.

BARBECUED CORN

Husk and remove silk from 12 ears of corn. Place each ear on a separate sheet of heavy foil. Mix ½ cup melted butter and 3 tablespoons soy sauce, and pour about a tablespoon of the mixture over each ear of corn. Wrap securely, using a freezer-style wrap. To cook, place in the barbecue coals for 15 minutes, turning several times. Makes 8 ample servings.

ONIONS IN FOIL

For each serving, peel 2 small white onions and cut a cross in the stem ends. Place on a small sheet of heavy foil, dot with butter, and season with salt and pepper. Wrap securely, using a freezer wrap. Place directly in the barbecue coals for 30 minutes, turning several times.

SOUR CREAM - CHOCOLATE BIT CAKE

This self-frosted, one-layer cake is an ideal dessert for toting to a picnic ground. It's both attractive and easy to put together. You sprinkle semisweet chocolate bits over the lightly spiced sour cream batter. Even after the baking, the chocolate stays slightly soft and creamy.

> 6 tablespoons soft butter or margarine
> 1 cup plus 1 tablespoon sugar
> 2 eggs
> 1⅓ cups unsifted all-purpose flour
> 1½ teaspoons baking powder
> 1 teaspoon each soda and cinnamon
> 1 cup sour cream
> 1 package (6 oz.) semisweet chocolate bits

Mix butter with the 1 cup sugar until blended, then beat in eggs, one at a time. Stir flour with baking powder, soda, and cinnamon, then blend with creamed mixture. Mix in the sour cream.

Pour batter into a greased and flour-dusted 9 by 13-inch baking pan. Scatter the chocolate bits evenly over the batter, then sprinkle with the 1 remaining tablespoon of sugar.

Bake in a 350° oven for 35 minutes or until cake just begins to pull away from sides of pan. Serve warm or cooled (do not refrigerate), cut in rectangles. Makes 10 to 12 servings.

Cheese Fondue Supper

SWISS BEER FONDUE
BARBECUED MINIATURE FRANKFURTERS
FRENCH BREAD
MIXED GREEN SALAD
WINTER PEARS AND GRAPES
TOASTED POUND CAKE

Having guests help cook their own meal always seems to set a festively informal mood. Part of this menu is cooked over a log fire—another guest-pleasing feature.

Each person spears barbecued frankfurters and French bread cubes to dip into a beer-flavored cheese fondue. The franks are pre-cooked in a hinged wire broiler over coals in a fireplace. You might delegate a guest to blend the fondue ingredients over an alcohol burner while you dress a mixed green salad with oil and vinegar and garnish with cherry tomatoes and avocado slices.

rise to the surface, add cheese mixture, a spoonful at a time, and stir slowly in a figure-8 pattern with a wooden spoon until all the cheese is blended to a smooth sauce. If the cheese and liquid do not blend, increase heat. If that fails, mix the 1 tablespoon cornstarch and cold water and stir into the hot mixture; keep stirring until it is blended.

Cut the French bread into 1-inch cubes with some crust on each; pile into a basket. Skewer French bread or barbecued frankfurters with a fork and dip into the cheese mixture. Serves about 4.

SWISS BEER FONDUE

½ pound each Swiss Gruyère or Danish Samsoe
    cheese and Swiss Emmanthaler,
    coarsely shredded
1½ tablespoons cornstarch
1 teaspoon dry mustard
½ teaspoon garlic salt
    Dash pepper
1 can (12 oz.) beer
1 tablespoon lemon juice
1 tablespoon each cornstarch and cold
    water (if needed)
1 small loaf French bread
    Barbecued miniature frankfurters
    (directions follow)

Mix cheeses with the 1½ tablespoons cornstarch, dry mustard, garlic salt, and pepper. Heat beer and lemon juice in a fondue pot over moderate heat of an alcohol burner. When bubbles start to

BARBECUED MINIATURE FRANKFURTERS

Place 1 pound small cocktail frankfurters in a wire broiler and heat over coals just until they are hot through and start to toast. Place in a heated serving dish and keep warm over hot water or on an electric warming tray.

TOASTED POUND CAKE

Slice a fresh or thawed, frozen pound cake into ¾-inch-thick slices. Place the slices in a wire basket or hinged wire broiler and toast over coals.

Soup Buffet

SEAFOOD BISQUE   CONDIMENTS

CHILLED RELISHES   HOT PARSLEY BREAD

ASSORTED COLD MEATS: MORTADELLA,

RUSSIAN BOLOGNA, METTWURST, DUTCH LOAF

WINTER PEARS AND TANGERINES

FLUFFY LEMON CHEESECAKE

A wine-flavored bisque laden with fresh seafood is the basis for this menu. The easily-prepared accompaniments are an assortment of cold cuts from the delicatessen and parsley bread you make from a bakery loaf.

Provide card tables or other arrangements for sit-down dining. Though you serve buffet-style, if you wish you can have the soup and garnishes as a separate course before the relishes, hot bread, and cold meats.

SEAFOOD BISQUE

This soup is best if freshly made the day of the party. It doesn't tolerate freezing.

1¼ cups butter or margarine
  1 cup instant-type all-purpose flour
  4 cans (7½ oz. each) minced clams or
    4 cups fresh minced clams
½ gallon (8 cups) milk
  1 pint (2 cups) half-and-half (light cream)
  6 to 8 green onions
  2 pounds (about 4 cups) crab meat,
    fresh, frozen, or canned
  1 pound shelled, cooked, small shrimp
  1 cup dry white wine
⅓ cup dry Sherry
  Parsley sprig for garnish
  Assorted condiments: sieved hard-cooked
    egg yolks and egg whites (about 8
    eggs), ¾ cup chopped chives, and
    ¾ cup chopped macadamia nuts

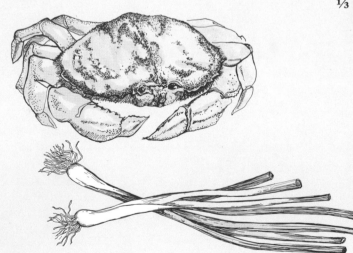

Melt ¾ cup of the butter in a 6-quart heavy-bottomed pan. Blend in flour and cook until bubbling. Drain liquid from clams and stir in the liquid, stirring until blended (reserve clams). Slowly stir in the milk and half-and-half, and cook until sauce is thickened.

Chop the onions finely, discarding half the green part. In a large frying pan, sauté onions in the remaining ½ cup butter until limp. Add the crab, shrimp, and clams, and cook in the butter, stirring lightly, until seafood is hot through. Add to the soup mixture and stir in the white wine and Sherry. Heat just until hot through. Turn into a heated tureen or other large serving bowl or casserole. Garnish with a parsley sprig. Surround with small bowls of condiments. Makes 5 quarts or about 16 generous servings.

HOT PARSLEY BREAD

Buy a good bakery egg bread and have it thin-sliced. Mix together ¾ cup softened butter or margarine, ¼ cup finely chopped parsley, and ½ teaspoon crumbled dried tarragon. Spread herb butter on each slice of bread and reassemble loaf. Wrap in foil and heat in a 375° oven for 15 to 20 minutes.

FLUFFY LEMON CHEESECAKE

Yogurt and cottage cheese are blended to make this tangy, smooth dessert that is low in calories.

    1 package (6 oz.) zweiback, finely crushed
⅓ cup brown sugar (firmly packed)
⅓ cup melted butter
    1 pound (2 cups) small curd cottage cheese
¼ cup mild honey
    4 eggs, separated
¼ teaspoon salt
    1 teaspoon grated lemon peel
    2 tablespoons lemon juice
    1 teaspoon vanilla
    1 cup unflavored yogurt
½ cup granulated sugar

Combine zweiback crumbs, brown sugar, and butter and mix until crumbly; reserve ¾ cup. Pat remaining crumbs evenly over bottom of a 9-inch cheesecake pan. Bake in a 350° oven for 10 minutes. Cool.

Combine in a blender the cottage cheese, honey, egg yolks, salt, lemon peel and juice, vanilla, and yogurt; blend smooth. Beat egg whites until soft peaks form; gradually add sugar, beating until stiff. Fold in cheese mixture until blended. Turn into prepared pan. Sprinkle with reserved crumbs.

Bake in a 250° oven for 1 hour. Turn off heat, leave cake in oven 1 hour more. Cool thoroughly, then chill. Serves 8 to 10.

Company Casserole Dinner

FRESH SPINACH SALAD
CHOPS AND SAFFRON SPAGHETTI
WHOLE KERNEL CORN WITH
SAUTEED GREEN PEPPER STRIPS
PARSLEY-BUTTERED FRENCH BREAD
CREME DE MENTHE ICE   CHOCOLATE WAFERS

A Mexican influence is evident in the seasonings for the pork chop casserole featured in this colorful meal. Both the casserole and the dessert can be made ahead of time. If you prepare the casserole ahead, refrigerate it and bake just before serving, increasing baking time to 1 hour if taken directly from refrigerator. You can make and freeze the sherbet up to a week ahead.

Use a blue cheese dressing for the salad; you might combine spinach with other salad greens. Heat the bread while the casserole bakes. Sauté green pepper in butter just until tender, then mix it lightly with hot cooked corn.

CHOPS AND SAFFRON SPAGHETTI

2 medium-sized onions, chopped
2 cloves garlic, crushed
¼ cup olive oil or salad oil
3 medium-sized tomatoes, peeled, seeded, and
    coarsely chopped
1 canned California green chile, seeded
    and chopped
1 tablespoon chopped parsley
2 beef bouillon cubes
¾ teaspoon salt
½ teaspoon saffron
1 quart boiling water
12 ounces spaghetti, broken in half
6 garlic sausages (about 1¾ lbs.), sliced
6 loin pork chops (about 2 lbs.), ¾ inch thick
½ cup shredded Cheddar cheese
¼ cup toasted, slivered blanched
    almonds (optional)

In a deep 4-quart pan that has a cover, sauté onions and garlic in 3 tablespoons of the oil until soft and golden. Stir in tomatoes, chile, parsley, bouillon cubes, salt, saffron, and water; bring to a boil. Add spaghetti and sausage slices; cover and simmer about 30 minutes or until most of liquid has been absorbed, stirring occasionally.

Meanwhile, brown chops well on both sides in remaining 1 tablespoon of oil. Turn spaghetti mixture into a greased shallow casserole (about 3-quart size); top with chops, cover, and bake in a 350° oven about 45 minutes or until chops are tender. Remove cover, sprinkle with cheese and almonds, and return to oven for a few minutes longer or until cheese melts. Makes 6 servings.

CREME DE MENTHE ICE

2 cups sugar
4 cups water
¾ cup lemon juice
    Dash salt
1 egg white
3 tablespoons green crème de menthe

Combine sugar and water; boil for 5 minutes. Cool to room temperature. Stir in lemon juice and salt. Cover and freeze until firm, several hours or overnight. In a large mixer bowl, beat egg white until foamy; add crème de menthe and the frozen mixture in large spoonfuls, beating well until the mixture is very smooth. Cover and freeze again until firm, at least 8 hours. Makes about 2 quarts.

Do-Ahead Guest Dinner

ONION SOUP WITH HOT GARLIC CROUTONS
BAKED STUFFED CHICKEN BREASTS
WHOLE GREEN BEANS
FLAKY YEAST ROLLS
MELBA ICE CREAM PIE

An almond and mushroom stuffing fills chicken rolls which can be assembled ahead, refrigerated, and then baked just before mealtime. To start the meal, you might serve the onion soup informally outside or in another room.

Use a dry mix for the soup, substituting ½ cup dry Sherry for an equal amount of the water used in reconstituting it, if you wish. Sauté bread cubes in garlic butter for the croutons.

Heat the yeast rolls along with the chicken. Let the frozen pie mellow in the refrigerator for about 15 minutes so that it will be soft enough to cut and serve.

BAKED STUFFED CHICKEN BREASTS

4 whole chicken breasts, boned and halved
Mushroom Filling (recipe follows)
¼ cup (⅛ lb.) butter or margarine, melted
1¼ cups finely crushed potato chips
Sautéed whole mushrooms for garnish

Remove skin from boned and halved chicken breasts. Pound chicken halves between sheets of waxed paper to flatten to about ⅜ inch thick. Place a spoonful of Mushroom Filling on each piece; roll, tucking in edges, and fasten with skewers or wooden picks.

Coat chicken rolls evenly with butter, then with potato chips. Place in a greased baking dish, skewer sides down. Cover and bake in a 350° oven for 45 minutes (if taken directly from refrigerator, increase time to 1 hour); uncover and bake 15 minutes longer or until crumbs are browned. Serve on warm platter garnished with sautéed whole mushrooms. Makes 4 servings.

Mushroom Filling. Sauté 2 tablespoons *each* finely chopped onion and celery and ¼ pound mushrooms, sliced, in 2 tablespoons butter until soft; blend in ¼ teaspoon salt, a dash pepper, 1 tablespoon lemon juice, and ⅓ cup toasted, slivered blanched almonds. Stir in 1 teaspoon flour; continue cooking until thickened.

MELBA ICE CREAM PIE

Let this pie thaw in the refrigerator for about 15 minutes so you can cut it easily.

Vanilla Wafer Crust (recipe follows)
1 quart peach ice cream, softened
2 packages (10 oz. each) frozen raspberries, thawed
1 tablespoon each cornstarch and sugar
2 teaspoons lemon juice

Firmly press the crumb crust around bottom and sides of a 9-inch pan. Bake in a 400° oven for 6 to 8 minutes or until rim browns. Chill. Scoop the ice cream into cooled crust. Freeze until firm (at least 8 hours).

Meanwhile, drain the thawed raspberries well, saving syrup. Gradually blend syrup with mixture of cornstarch and sugar until smooth. Heat, stirring constantly, until thickened and clear; cool slightly. Stir in drained raspberries and the lemon juice. Chill.

To serve, cut pie and spoon raspberry sauce over each wedge. Makes 6 to 8 servings.

Vanilla Wafer Crust. Crush about 35 packaged vanilla wafers to make 1 cup fine crumbs; blend with 3 tablespoons sugar and ¼ cup butter, melted.

An Elegant Picnic

CHICKEN LIVER-MUSHROOM PATE
SESAME WATER CRACKERS
WINE-POACHED TROUT
SALAD RELISH SKEWERS
ASPARAGUS TIPS MARINATED IN FRENCH DRESSING
RUSSIAN RYE BREAD
BABA AU RHUM

With no more effort than you usually expend in getting together an ordinary picnic, you can prepare the elegant picnic suggested here. This is a picnic for adults. It features epicurean foods, but the dishes are simple to make, and they transport easily. Use crystal, silver, and china to emphasize the elegance of the menu.

CHICKEN LIVER-MUSHROOM PATE

Make the creamy paté the day before your picnic so it can chill overnight.

   1 pound chicken livers
½ pound fresh mushrooms
   1 teaspoon each garlic salt and paprika
⅓ cup finely chopped green onions
   4 tablespoons (⅛ lb.) butter
⅓ cup dry white wine
⅛ teaspoon dill weed
   3 drops liquid hot-pepper seasoning
½ cup (¼ lb.) soft butter
   Salt

Combine in a frying pan the chicken livers, mushrooms, garlic salt, paprika, and green onion, and simmer over moderate heat for 5 minutes in the 4 tablespoons butter. Add wine, dill weed, and liquid hot-pepper seasoning; cover and cook slowly 5 to 10 minutes longer. Cool, and sieve or whirl smooth in a blender. Blend in the ½ cup butter and salt to taste. Pack in jar; chill overnight. Makes about 3 cups. Carry to picnic in an insulated bag.

WINE-POACHED TROUT

Chilled glazed trout are easy to prepare and are impressive contributions to an outdoor meal.

1¼ cups rosé or Chablis wine
1¼ cups regular-strength chicken broth
  1 teaspoon chicken stock concentrate
  2 tablespoons lemon juice
  1 teaspoon salt
  1 small sprig fresh rosemary
  4 to 6 medium-sized trout (heads removed)
1½ envelopes unflavored gelatin
  3 tablespoons dry white wine
    Sliced stuffed green olives

In a pan that will hold the trout flat on the bottom, bring to a boil the 1¼ cups wine, chicken broth, chicken stock concentrate, lemon juice, salt, and rosemary. Place trout in stock and poach gently for 5 to 10 minutes, or until fish flakes. Remove herb sprig; let trout cool in liquid. Carefully lift trout from stock and place on a wire rack on a tray; cover and chill thoroughly.

Meanwhile prepare glaze: Soften gelatin in the 3 tablespoons wine. Strain stock; add gelatin, and heat until dissolved. Chill until syrupy. Arrange slices of stuffed green olives in a row alongside the neck of each fish. Spoon aspic over all; coat 2 or 3 times, chilling between (and re-using aspic that drips on tray). Makes 4 to 6 servings. Carry trout to picnic on a chilled tray, wrapped in foil.

SALAD RELISH SKEWERS

On silver skewers, place cherry tomatoes, pickled artichoke hearts, hors d'oeuvre pickled onions, and jumbo ripe olives stuffed with Cheddar cheese spread put through a pastry tube. Wrap in foil and carry to picnic in an insulated container. To serve, plunge skewers into a melon (or grapefruit) placed in the center of a small tray or serving plate (cut a small slice from one side of melon to keep it steady). Surround melon with bunches of grapes.

BABA AU RHUM

Drain and save syrup from 1 or 2 cans (12-oz. size) rum cakes. Arrange cakes in a basket lined with clear plastic wrap, then wrap all in foil. (You might like to tuck in a few blossoms and leaves.) For each can of rum cakes, whip ½ cup cream and fold in rum syrup. Carry cream in a covered container in an insulated bag. Spoon on when ready to serve. Each 12-ounce can of rum cakes serves 4.

Sunday Roast Dinner

GREEN SALAD WITH PAPAYA

MUSTARD-COATED LAMB ROLL

PARSLEY-BUTTERED NEW POTATOES

ZUCCHINI FANS

HOT BUTTERFLAKE ROLLS

ORANGE-FILLED COCONUT CREAM CAKE

Since the succulent lamb roast and main-course accompaniments are simple to prepare, you can devote your efforts to putting together a fancy dessert. A cake mix provides a short-cut for an impressive torte; make the cake and filling a day ahead, if you wish, and fill the cake layers, but wait to frost the cake with whipped cream the day you serve it.

The boned, rolled, and tied leg of lamb is a cut that carves easily. You can coat it with its mustard glaze early in the day so it will absorb the seasonings. Try to time its roasting precisely to meet the dinner schedule, as lamb is at its best served piping hot. Cook the vegetables the last 15 minutes, and serve the roast on a board surrounded with the hot vegetables. Embellish your favorite green salad with slices of peeled papaya.

MUSTARD-COATED LAMB ROLL

Have your meatman bone, roll, and tie a leg of lamb for this company roast.

    5 to 6-pound leg of lamb, boned, rolled, and tied
⅓ **cup Dijon-style mustard**
  1 **tablespoon soy sauce**
¼ **teaspoon each garlic salt and ground ginger**
  1 **teaspoon crumbled dried rosemary**
  1 **tablespoon salad oil**

Place the meat on a rack on a roasting pan. For coating, mix the mustard, soy sauce, garlic salt, ginger, rosemary, and salad oil. Spread over roast, coating completely, and let stand at least 1 hour.

Insert a meat thermometer and roast in a 300° oven until the thermometer registers 150° for pinkish rare meat (about 1½ hours) or 160° for medium well done meat. Remove to a platter and carve. Makes 10 to 12 servings.

PARSLEY-BUTTERED NEW POTATOES

Cook 2 pounds small new potatoes (unpeeled) in boiling salted water to cover for 15 minutes, or until tender. Drain and dress with 2 tablespoons *each* melted butter and finely chopped parsley. Serves 8.

ZUCCHINI FANS

8 medium-sized zucchini
2 small tomatoes
¼ cup water
2 tablespoons olive oil
¼ teaspoon each salt and garlic salt

Cut the ends off the zucchini and make three lengthwise cuts in each to within an inch of one end, forming a fan. Core tomatoes, cut in ⅓-inch-thick wedges, and insert a wedge in each cut in the zucchini. Place in a single layer in a large frying pan and add the water, olive oil, salt, and garlic salt. Simmer, uncovered, for 15 minutes, or until tender. Lift out carefully with a wide spatula and arrange on serving platter. Makes 8 servings.

ORANGE-FILLED COCONUT CREAM CAKE

A cake mix simplifies the preparation of this dessert, but if you wish to simplify the procedure even further, you could buy two plain sponge cake layers from a bakery instead.

1 package orange chiffon cake mix
    Orange Filling (recipe follows)
1½ cups whipping cream
1 teaspoon vanilla
1 tablespoon sugar
⅓ cup grated coconut or toasted sliced almonds

Bake cake mix in three 9-inch round layer cake pans. Cool; freeze one layer to use another time. Split the two remaining layers horizontally to make four layers and spread Orange Filling between the layers.

Whip the cream until stiff and flavor with vanilla and sugar. Spread on top and sides of the cake and sprinkle top with coconut or almonds. Chill until serving time. Makes about 12 servings.

Orange Filling. Combine in a small pan ¾ cup sugar, 5 tablespoons cornstarch, and ¼ teaspoon salt. Stir in 2 cups orange juice and 1 teaspoon grated orange peel. Stirring constantly, bring to a boil and cook until thickened. Stir into 2 slightly beaten eggs, return to pan, and cook 2 minutes more, stirring constantly. Remove from heat; stir in 2 tablespoons lemon juice and 1 tablespoon butter. Cool to room temperature before using.

Baked Steak Dinner

BAKED STEAK WITH GLAZED VEGETABLES
BULGUR PILAF
GREEN SALAD WITH ORANGE DRESSING
CRUSTY SOURDOUGH ROLLS
CHOCOLATE-CHERRY ROLL

One large steak bakes in a very hot oven while you finish the rest of this meal. The vegetables in the menu garnish the steak.

Do-ahead tasks include making the cake for the dessert, preparing and refrigerating the salad dressing, and slicing the vegetables. Assemble the dessert about an hour ahead and refrigerate until served. In the 30 minutes before dinner, bake the steak, cook quick-cooking cracked wheat (bulgur) using your favorite recipe or one suggested on package, make the salad, and heat rolls.

BAKED STEAK

1½ to 2-inch-thick piece of boneless top sirloin (about 3 lbs.) or first cut of top round or equally thick rib or Porterhouse steak (about 2½ lbs.)
Melted butter
Garlic salt
Pepper
Glazed Vegetables (recipe follows)
Chopped parsley (optional)

Place meat on broiler pan; brush with melted butter and sprinkle with garlic salt and pepper. Bake in a preheated 500° oven for 10 minutes. Turn steak and insert a meat thermometer horizontally into center. Brush second side with butter and sprinkle with garlic salt and pepper. Basting once with butter, bake 10 to 20 minutes, or until thermometer registers degree of doneness you prefer; a 2-inch-thick top sirloin will reach 130° (rare) in about 15 minutes.

Remove steak to warm serving platter and spoon Glazed Vegetables over it. Sprinkle with chopped parsley, if you wish. Makes about 6 servings.

GLAZED VEGETABLES

½ pound mushrooms, sliced ⅛ inch thick
3 large carrots, sliced ⅛ inch thick
1 large onion, sliced ⅛ inch thick
3 tablespoons butter or margarine
½ teaspoon sugar
¼ teaspoon each salt and whole thyme
   Dash pepper
2 tablespoons lemon juice or dry white wine

Sauté the mushrooms, carrots, and onion slices in a large frying pan with butter, sugar, salt, thyme, pepper, and lemon juice or wine. Cook, stirring occasionally, over high heat about 10 minutes, or until pan juices are reduced and vegetables tender. Spoon over steak. Makes 4 to 6 servings.

GREEN SALAD WITH ORANGE DRESSING

Combine and refrigerate the dressing at least an hour ahead of time so that the flavors blend.

2 quarts mixed salad greens
1 can (11 oz.) mandarin orange sections, well drained

Wash, dry, and tear salad greens. Refrigerate in a plastic bag until needed. Just before serving, combine the greens with the mandarin orange sections and green onions. Toss with enough dressing to coat greens; refrigerate remaining dressing. Makes 6 servings.

Orange Dressing. Combine in blender or jar ⅔ cup salad oil; ⅓ cup orange juice; 1½ tablespoons grated orange peel; 3 tablespoons white wine vinegar; 1 small clove garlic; 1 green onion, cut up (including part of the tops); 1½ teaspoons tarragon; ½ teaspoon sugar; ¼ teaspoon salt; dash pepper. Whirl smooth or shake until blended. Refrigerate at least 1 hour. Makes about 1½ cups.

CHOCOLATE-CHERRY ROLL

3 eggs
⅔ cup sugar
⅓ cup unsifted regular all-purpose flour
3 tablespoons sweet ground chocolate or cocoa
1 teaspoon baking powder
   Sifted powdered sugar
½ cup cherry preserves
¾ cup whipping cream
   Fresh cherries with stems

Prepare an 11 by 15-inch shallow baking pan by fitting waxed paper over bottom; lightly grease paper and sides of pan. Beat eggs with sugar until thick and pale yellow, about 5 minutes on high speed of electric mixer. Sift together the flour, chocolate or cocoa, and baking powder. Sift again over the well beaten eggs; fold gently together. Spread in pan and bake in a 350° oven 15 to 18 minutes, or until cake springs back when lightly pressed.

Dust a clean, smooth towel with sifted powdered sugar. Turn cake out onto towel immediately, remove paper, and roll up towel and cake together so that cloth finally covers cake. Cool thoroughly.

To assemble dessert, carefully unroll cake and remove towel. Spread preserves over inside surface of cake. Whip cream and spread evenly over preserves. Carefully reroll cake and place on serving plate. Dust top with sifted powdered sugar and garnish with fresh cherries with stems. Serve slices of cake roll with fresh cherries. Makes 6 to 8 servings.

Patio Buffet

CUCUMBER STICKS   CARROT SLICES   RADISHES
ITALIAN GREEN BEANS
SOURDOUGH FRENCH BREAD   SWEET BUTTER
VEAL LOAF WITH TUNA SAUCE
FRESH PEACH MELBAS GALLIANO

Here's a menu that can change with the weather —if it's chilly, serve the veal loaf hot rather than cold. It's an excellent dish either way.

Much of the preparation can be done ahead. Mix, bake, and chill the veal loaf. Whirl the tuna sauce in a blender and chill. Purée the raspberry sauce for the dessert and chill. If you wish, cook the green beans ahead, then chill in a French dressing; or serve them hot with butter, if you prefer.

VEAL LOAF WITH TUNA SAUCE

If you have leftovers of this dish, you'll find they make excellent cold sandwiches.

  2 pounds ground veal
  ¾ pound ground beef chuck
  ½ cup crushed soda crackers
  ¾ cup milk
1½ teaspoons salt
  1 teaspoon Worcestershire
  1 tablespoon instant minced onion
  1 teaspoon grated lemon peel
  ½ teaspoon garlic salt
  ⅛ teaspoon nutmeg
1½ tablespoons lemon juice
  2 eggs
    Tuna Sauce (recipe follows), chilled
  6 rolled anchovies with capers
    Lemon wedges and parsley sprigs

Place ground veal and ground beef in a large bowl. In a blender, mix until smooth (or beat with a rotary beater) the soda crackers, milk, salt, Worcestershire, onion, lemon peel, garlic salt, nutmeg, lemon juice, and eggs. Pour mixture over the meat and mix with your hands until well blended.

Pat into an oval loaf shape and place on a buttered rimmed baking pan. Bake in a 375° oven for 50 to 55 minutes. Cool and chill. At serving time, spoon Tuna Sauce over the top of the loaf and garnish with anchovies with capers. Place lemon wedges and parsley sprigs around the platter. Makes 10 to 12 servings.

Tuna Sauce. Place in a blender 6 tablespoons *each* mayonnaise and sour cream, 3 tablespoons lemon juice, 1 can (6½ or 7 oz.) tuna, and 6 rolled anchovies with capers. Purée until smooth. Cover and chill.

FRESH PEACH MELBAS GALLIANO

1 package (10 oz.) frozen raspberries (or 1¼ cups fresh raspberries, sugared to taste)
1 quart vanilla ice cream
3 peaches, sliced and sugared
  Galliano liqueur (optional)

Make a raspberry sauce by puréeing the raspberries in a blender; push through wire strainer to remove seeds. Scoop ice cream into balls and place in six dessert bowls. Top with peach slices and pour over the sauce. If you wish, pass a pitcher of Galliano liqueur. Makes 6 servings.

Turkey Supper

TURKEY DIVAN SOUFFLE
ORANGE AND AVOCADO SALAD WITH
FRENCH DRESSING
BREADSTICKS OR SESAME CRACKERS
CRANBERRY-MINCEMEAT TARTS
ICE CREAM OR WHIPPED CREAM

The flavors associated with the classic Turkey Divan are combined to make the hearty soufflé in this menu. Here's a good way to use leftover cooked turkey you may have in your freezer.

During the 30 minutes the soufflé takes to bake, you can prepare all the rest of the meal. For the dessert tarts you can use the ready-to-eat tart shells available in most grocery stores. To make the salad, arrange slices of orange and avocado in lettuce leaves on individual salad plates. Just before serving, pour on a tart French dressing. If you wish to serve the breadsticks or crackers hot, place them in a shallow pan and heat during the last 10 minutes that the soufflé bakes.

TURKEY DIVAN SOUFFLE

If you don't have the turkey or chicken for this soufflé, you can substitute one can (7½ oz.) tuna, drained.

  1 can (10 oz.) condensed cream of chicken soup
¼ cup each shredded Swiss cheese and grated
      Parmesan cheese
  1 green onion, chopped
  1 teaspoon minced parsley
½ teaspoon salt
¼ teaspoon dry mustard
⅛ teaspoon nutmeg
    Dash pepper
  6 eggs, separated
  1 package (10 oz.) frozen chopped
      broccoli, thawed
  1 cup diced cooked turkey or chicken
  2 tablespoons grated Parmesan cheese for top

Pour soup into top of double boiler and add the Swiss cheese and ¼ cup Parmesan, onion, parsley, salt, mustard, nutmeg, and pepper. Stir over simmering water until cheeses melt and ingredients are blended. Remove from heat; beat in the egg yolks, one at a time. Stir in the broccoli and turkey or chicken. Beat egg whites until stiff but not dry; fold into the creamed mixture.

Pour into a well buttered, 2-quart soufflé dish and sprinkle with the 2 tablespoons Parmesan cheese. Bake in a 375° oven about 30 minutes or just until set. Serve immediately. Makes about 6 servings.

CRANBERRY-MINCEMEAT TARTS

2 cups well drained prepared mincemeat
1 cup drained whole cranberry sauce
2 teaspoons quick-cooking tapioca
1 teaspoon grated orange or lemon peel
6 baked tart shells
    Vanilla ice cream or sweetened whipped cream

In a pan stir together the mincemeat and cranberry sauce. Stir in the tapioca and orange or lemon peel. Heat until mixture bubbles, then cook about 5 minutes, stirring constantly. Spoon filling into baked tart shells; cool. Serve warm or cooled with vanilla ice cream or whipped cream. Makes 6 individual tarts.

Chicken-on-Skewers Supper

BROCHETTE OF CHICKEN AND PINEAPPLE ON RICE
PEAS WITH ONIONS IN ARTICHOKE BOTTOMS
SAUTEED CARROTS
VEGETABLE-FRUIT SALAD WITH BLUE CHEESE DRESSING
HOT ROLLS
PUMPKIN CAKE

Broiled chicken and pineapple are featured in this easy-to-serve meal. Most of the preparations for the dinner can be done early in the day: Bone the chicken and let it marinate several hours; slice the carrots, wrap in plastic film, and refrigerate; prepare salad ingredients (avocado slices may be covered with lemon juice and refrigerated several hours). Bake the cake as much as a day ahead.

Just before dinner time, cook the rice and vegetables, broil the chicken and pineapple, and arrange the salads.

BROCHETTE OF CHICKEN AND PINEAPPLE

1 can (8¾ oz.) pineapple spears
Orange Glaze (recipe follows)
2 whole chicken breasts, boned and cut into bite-size pieces
White or brown rice or wild rice

Drain pineapple spears and use the syrup for the Orange Glaze; marinate chicken in the glaze for several hours. On skewers, alternate chicken and pineapple spears (cut in half); place about 5 inches from the heat source and broil about 8 minutes, turning once and basting several times with the marinade. Serve on rice. Makes 4 servings.

Orange Glaze. Combine ¼ cup (⅛ lb.) melted butter, ⅔ cup orange juice, 1 teaspoon dry mustard, 1½ teaspoons grated orange peel, ⅓ cup syrup drained from the pineapple, and 1 tablespoon dry white wine.

PEAS WITH ONIONS IN ARTICHOKE BOTTOMS

1 package (10 oz.) frozen peas and onions
8 canned artichoke bottoms
2 teaspoon butter or margarine

Cook the peas and onions as package directs. Drain artichoke bottoms and put ¼ teaspoon butter in each; arrange in a shallow pan and heat in the oven while chicken broils (see preceding recipe)—about 5 to 10 minutes. To serve, spoon hot peas and onions into the artichokes and arrange 2 on each plate. Makes 4 servings.

VEGETABLE-FRUIT SALAD

Arrange slices of avocado, papaya or orange, and cucumber on lettuce on individual salad plates. Garnish with cherry tomatoes and pour over a blue cheese dressing.

PUMPKIN CAKE

  ½ cup butter, margarine, or shortening
1¼ cups sugar
    2 eggs
    2 cups unsifted all-purpose flour
    3 teaspoons baking powder
  ½ teaspoon each salt and soda
   1 teaspoon cinnamon
  ½ teaspoon each ground ginger and allspice
    1 cup canned pumpkin
 ¾ cup milk
  ½ cup chopped pecans or walnuts
    Orange Icing (recipe follows)

Cream together the butter or shortening and sugar until light. Add eggs, one at a time, and beat well after each addition. Sift flour with baking powder, salt, soda, and spices. Combine pumpkin and milk. Add flour mixture alternately with pumpkin to the creamed mixture, stirring just until blended. Stir in nuts. Spoon into a greased and flour-dusted baking pan (about 9 by 13 inches). Bake in a 350° oven for about 30 minutes, or until cake tests done. Cool in pan, then frost top. Cut in squares to serve. Serves 12.

Icing. Blend together ¼ cup soft butter, 2 cups sifted powdered sugar, 1 teaspoon grated orange peel, and 1 to 1½ tablespoons orange juice.

A Dinner Featuring Duck

ORANGE AND TUNA COCKTAIL

GLAZED DUCK

ASPARAGUS POLONAISE   RED CABBAGE

QUICK BLUEBERRY PIE

A particularly effective balance of rich and refreshing flavors gives this dinner that "special" quality you want your company meals to have. A cocktail of orange sections and tuna is the colorful start to the meal. The main course features duck, split lengthwise and roasted a glistening rich brown. Chilled asparagus and hot, tart red cabbage complement the duck. To finish, what could be better than warm, sugary-crusted blueberry pie?

There are no last-minute preparations. The first-course cocktail and the asparagus are prepared early in the day. The cabbage simmers slowly on top of the range, while duck and pie bake in the same oven.

ORANGE AND TUNA COCKTAIL

1 can (7 oz.) tuna, packed in broth
2 cups drained fresh orange sections
3 tablespoons thinly sliced green onion (including some of the green tops)
2 tablespoons orange juice
  Salt and pepper
  Lettuce cups (optional)
  Mayonnaise or sour cream

Drain tuna and break into chunks with a fork. Add orange sections, green onion, and orange juice. Toss lightly to mix. Season to taste with salt and pepper. Cover and chill. Serve in lettuce cups or seafood cocktail glasses, and top each serving with a dollop of mayonnaise or sour cream. Makes 4 to 6 servings.

GLAZED DUCK

Have your meatman split the duck lengthwise through breast and backbone.

4 to 5-pound duck, split lengthwise
⅓ cup soy sauce
1 clove garlic, crushed
3 tablespoons brown sugar
½ teaspoon monosodium glutamate (optional)
⅓ cup pineapple juice

Place duck in a shallow pan, cut side down. Mix the soy sauce, garlic, brown sugar, monosodium glutamate, and pineapple juice; pour over duck. Bake in a 350° oven for 2 hours, basting two or three times with pan juices. Makes 4 servings.

RED CABBAGE

1 tablespoon butter or margarine
1 medium-sized head red cabbage, shredded
1 tart apple, peeled, cored, and diced
1¼ cup dry red wine (more if needed)
1 teaspoon salt
3 tablespoons red wine vinegar
4 tablespoons brown sugar
2 whole cloves
Apple slices for garnish

Melt butter or margarine in a heavy pan. Add shredded cabbage, diced apple, ¼ cup of the wine, and the salt. Cover and cook, stirring occasionally, until cabbage is just limp, about 5 minutes. Add 1 cup more wine, the vinegar, brown sugar, and cloves. Simmer, covered, for about 1½ hours; stir occasionally. Add more wine if needed. Discard cloves. Garnish with apple slices. Makes 4 to 6 servings.

ASPARAGUS POLONAISE

Cook asparagus spears just until tender in well seasoned meat stock or canned bouillon; chill. To serve, drain and arrange on a platter. Garnish with finely chopped hard-cooked egg and hot croutons toasted in butter or margarine.

QUICK BLUEBERRY PIE

Use pastry scraps to make a flower or other design on the top of the pie, if you wish.

2 cups unsweetened frozen blueberries
Unbaked 9-inch pastry shell
¼ cup (⅛ lb.) butter or margarine
1½ cups sugar
2 eggs
Grated peel and juice of 1 lemon
Sweetened whipped cream (optional)

Pour berries into pastry shell. Mix together thoroughly the butter and sugar; beat in eggs. Add lemon rind and juice to creamed mixture and blend well. Spread over berries. Bake in a 350° oven for 1½ hours or until top is browned. Cool at least 40 minutes. Make a border of whipped cream, if you wish.

Roast Chicken Dinner

ROMAINE AND CUCUMBER SALAD WITH
FRENCH DRESSING
POULET FARCI CASSINI
ASPARAGUS WITH SOUR CREAM TOPPING
CRESCENT ROLLS
LIME BUTTERMILK PIE

A roasting chicken is a flavorful and attractive entrée for a small dinner party. Stuffed with a meaty dressing of ham, chicken livers, and mushrooms, the chicken will serve four to six people. Present it on a platter garnished with kumquats and watercress, if you wish.

The pie, your favorite French dressing, the sour cream topping for the vegetable, and the chicken stuffing can all be prepared in the morning of the dinner. Be sure to refrigerate the stuffing until you are ready to place it in the chicken and cook it.

POULET FARCI CASSINI

½ cup (¼ lb.) butter or margarine
½ pound mushrooms, sliced
¼ pound chicken livers, chopped
6 slices bacon, diced and crisply fried
½ pound ground cooked ham
4 cups soft bread cubes
½ teaspoon each salt and sage
⅛ teaspoon each pepper and nutmeg
¼ cup chicken stock
5 to 6-pound roasting chicken
1 clove garlic, mashed
½ cup dry Sherry (optional)

Melt about 3 tablespoons of the butter in a frying pan; brown the mushrooms and chicken livers in it. Blend mushroom mixture with bacon, ham, bread cubes, and seasonings. Melt remaining butter and add about ¼ cup of it with stock to make a moderately moist dressing.

Prepare chicken for roasting, filling cavity with the dressing. Bake any extra dressing separately, covered, in a buttered casserole. Blend garlic with remaining butter and brush part of the mixture over the chicken. Roast in a 325° oven about 2 hours, basting occasionally with remaining garlic butter. About 1 hour before the chicken is done, pour on some of the Sherry, repeating at 15-minute intervals and basting with each addition. Makes 4 to 6 servings.

ASPARAGUS WITH SOUR CREAM TOPPING

    ½ cup soft bread crumbs
    2 tablespoons butter or margarine, melted
    1 cup (½ pt.) sour cream
    1 teaspoon prepared mustard
    2 teaspoons lemon juice
    ¼ teaspoon salt
    1½ pounds fresh asparagus or 2 packages (10 oz.
        each) frozen asparagus spears
        Boiling salted water

Brown the bread crumbs in the butter. Blend sour cream with mustard, lemon juice, and salt (this can be done ahead); heat sour cream mixture slowly until warm. Cook asparagus in a small amount of boiling salted water about 15 minutes or until just tender, or cook frozen asparagus according to package directions. Drain and place in heated serving dish; top with hot sour cream mixture, then bread crumbs. Serve immediately. Makes about 6 servings.

LIME BUTTERMILK PIE

This pie has a sponge-like texture on top and a custardy layer beneath.

    3 eggs, separated
    ¾ cup sugar
    2 tablespoons flour
    ¼ teaspoon salt
    3 tablespoons butter or margarine, melted
    1 cup buttermilk
    1 teaspoon grated lime peel
    ¼ cup lime juice
        Green food coloring
        Unbaked 9-inch pastry shell
        Sweetened whipped cream
        Lime slices

In a large bowl, beat egg yolks slightly. Blend ½ cup of the sugar with flour and salt; stir into the egg yolks. Add butter or margarine, buttermilk, grated lime peel, and lime juice; blend well. Stir in a few drops of green food coloring to tint pale green. Beat egg whites until frothy. Add remaining ¼ cup sugar gradually, beating until rounded peaks are formed. Fold meringue into buttermilk mixture; pour into pastry shell.

Bake in a 450° oven for 10 minutes; reduce heat to 350° and continue baking for 20 to 25 minutes longer, or until knife inserted near center comes out clean. Cool, and serve garnished with whipped cream and lime slices. Makes 6 servings.

Supper from the Freezer

LEMON CHICKEN WITH RICE
ITALIAN GREEN BEANS
PICKLED BEETS   MARINATED ONION SLICES
HOT FRENCH BREAD
ICE CREAM DESSERT CUPS

It's reassuring to know that you have the makings of a complete supper waiting in the freezer and the pantry for a day when there's just not time for preparation. In this menu for four, you can freeze the entrée and dessert for up to a month before serving.

The chicken goes directly from freezer to oven in a temperature-resistant pan. Let it heat for an hour, then thicken the sauce and add the lemon juice just before serving. Meanwhile slice 1 large red onion, pour your favorite French dressing over it, and marinate it in the refrigerator. Drain and chill canned picked beets. Just before serving time, cook the rice and frozen Italian green beans; heat the bread in the oven. If you wish, take the ice cream dessert from the freezer for about 15 minutes and place in the refrigerator to mellow.

LEMON CHICKEN WITH RICE

    4 whole chicken breasts, split and boned
    ¼ cup each flour and butter or margarine
    ¼ teaspoon salt
    ⅛ teaspoon pepper
    1 cup regular-strength chicken broth
    ½ cup whipping cream
    2 tablespoons water
    1 tablespoon lemon juice
      Chopped parsley for garnish
      Steamed rice

Pound each piece of boned meat between sheets of waxed paper to about ¼-inch thickness. Lightly coat the chicken pieces with 2 tablespoons of the flour. Shake off excess flour and brown chicken, about 2 pieces at a time, in 2 tablespoons

of the butter heated in a large frying pan. Overlap chicken pieces in a 9-inch square or round pan (metal, disposable foil, or temperature-resistant ceramic). Heat remaining butter in the frying pan, add salt and pepper, and blend in the chicken broth and cream; pour over chicken. Cover with foil and freeze, or refrigerate if you plan to bake it later in the day.

Place frozen chicken directly into a 350° oven; bake, covered, about 1 hour, or until heated through (if it has been refrigerated only, bake only about 40 minutes).

To serve, remove chicken to a warm serving plate. Combine the remaining 2 tablespoons flour with 2 tablespoons water; gradually stir this into the liquid in the pan and cook over moderate heat until gravy is smooth and slightly thickened, about 2 minutes. Stir in lemon juice and pour over chicken on platter. Garnish with chopped parsley, if you wish. Serve with steamed rice. Makes 4 servings.

ICE CREAM DESSERT CUPS

For each serving, form a rounded scoop of strawberry or peppermint ice cream and roll quickly in crushed macaroons, sugar cooky crumbs, or chopped nuts. Put in fluted paper cups and freeze about 1 hour. Then spoon a little chocolate sauce (canned or homemade) over each. Return to freezer until sauce is set. Wrap carefully in plastic film or foil and store in freezer.

Hearty Casserole Dinner

MEAT AND SPINACH CASSEROLE
RAW VEGETABLES   MARINATED ARTICHOKES
HOT CRUSTY ROLLS
APPLES BAKED IN CARAMEL CREAM

This meal is planned around a casserole which resembles the layered Italian dish, lasagne, but is greatly simplified without sacrificing flavor. Layers of a rich meat sauce, noodles, spinach, sour cream, and cheese make up the casserole. You can freeze the meat sauce well ahead, or make it a day ahead and refrigerate it. The casserole can be assembled ahead and refrigerated.

Celery, green peppers, carrots, turnips, and zucchini make good choices for the vegetable tray. They will be best if prepared early enough to chill and crisp. Buy the marinated artichokes.

Heat the rolls in the oven with the casserole. The apples also bake at the same temperature and continue to cook during the meal to be served hot at dessert time.

MEAT AND SPINACH CASSEROLE

1 package (10 or 12 oz.) bow tie or butterfly-
   shaped noodles, cooked and warm
   Meat Sauce (recipe follows)
2 packages (10 oz. each) frozen chopped spinach,
   thawed and very well drained
2 cups (1 pt.) sour cream
1 cup grated or shredded Parmesan or
   Romano cheese

Combine noodles with the meat sauce and let cool. Spread half of this mixture over the bottom of a shallow 2½ to 3-quart casserole. Scatter half the spinach over noodles and dot evenly with half the sour cream, then spread gently to make an even layer. Sprinkle with half the cheese. Repeat layers of meat and noodles, spinach, and sour cream; top evenly with remaining cheese. If assembled ahead, keep covered and chilled until ready to bake.

Bake uncovered in a 375° oven for 40 to 50 minutes or until heated through and lightly browned on top. Makes 6 to 8 servings.

Meat Sauce. Crumble ½ pound bulk pork sausage and 1 pound lean ground beef in a wide frying pan; cook until meat loses pink color. Add 1 large onion, chopped, and 1 clove garlic, minced; cook, stirring occasionally, until soft but not brown. Blend in 1 large can (15 oz.) tomato sauce, 1 can (6 oz.) tomato paste, 1½ cups water (or 1 cup dry red wine and ½ cup water), ¼ teaspoon *each* rosemary, basil, marjoram, oregano, savory, and black pepper, and about 1½ teaspoons salt (or to taste). Simmer slowly, uncovered, until reduced to about 6 cups, about 30 minutes.

APPLES BAKED IN CARAMEL CREAM

 6 or 8 medium-sized Winesap apples
¼ cup (⅛ lb.) butter or margarine
⅓ cup brown sugar, firmly packed
½ cup whipping cream
¼ teaspoon cinnamon
   Maraschino or candied cherries (optional)

Remove cores from apples and cut a strip of peel from around the middle of each apple. Bring to a boil the butter or margarine, brown sugar, cream, and cinnamon. Arrange apples side by side in baking pan and pour butter mixture over them.

Bake uncovered in a 375° oven for 45 to 55 minutes or until apples are tender when pierced. Baste several times as they cook. Serve with the sauce; decorate with maraschino or candied cherries, if you like. Makes 6 to 8 servings.

Special Occasions

& Themes

These menus suit a variety of special occasions. They can serve a few guests or many. They range from simple get-togethers such as a family birthday dinner or a spring tea for six ladies to more elaborate meals, many of which have foreign themes and will appeal to the cook who likes to experiment with new and unusual recipes.

Even a relatively simple menu can take on a special theme with the proper staging. Use inexpensive props—Japanese parasols and giant paper fish, fish nets and glass floats, paper flowers, balloons, streamers, straw mats, baskets—to create a mood. In addition to the theme ideas in this section, you'll find more possibilities in the following two sections on holiday parties and parties for large groups.

The menus that follow are not complicated. In many cases most of the preparation can be done ahead of time. Ingredients for the foreign menus are readily obtainable in our markets, or if they are not, a substitution is suggested. In the introductions to the menus, you will find ideas for serving the meal, as well as suggestions to simplify its preparation.

Wine-Tasting Picnic

CHEESE COURSE:
Potted Cheese, Green Onions, Roasted Almonds,
Pumpernickel; Cocktail or Pale Dry Sherry

FISH COURSE:
Crab in Mayonnaise, Wheat Crackers with Sesame Seeds;
Pinot Chardonnay, Pinot Blanc, or White Pinot

MEAT COURSE:
Sliced Beef Tongue, Celery Hearts with
Spiced Tomato Sauce; Chianti or Vino Rosso

DESSERT COURSE:
Pound Cake, Fruit; White or Pink
Champagne, Sparkling Burgundy, or Sparkling Muscat

This is a picnic to eat in courses, with a wine to complement each part of the meal. If you live within comfortable driving distance of a winery, you may want to begin your picnic by touring the establishment and sampling their product. Perhaps you'll want to purchase wines for the meal while you are there.

Two of the four wines on our picnic menu (those for the second and fourth courses) are best well chilled, so you'll need icing equipment. The wines for the first and third courses may be served at room temperature or faintly chilled. The salad, the meat, and the vegetable should also be kept cold. Most of the foods can be prepared the day before. The pound cake can be a frozen or bakery one. The menu is planned to serve six picnickers.

POTTED CHEESE

2 cups shredded sharp Cheddar cheese
1 cup crumbled Gorgonzola or blue cheese
½ cup (¼ lb.) soft butter
⅓ cup dry Sherry

Beat all ingredients together. Pack in a small container. Cover and chill at least 24 hours. Carry un-iced to picnic; serve at room temperature. Makes about 2 cups.

CRAB IN MAYONNAISE

1 jar (6 oz.) marinated artichokes
2 cups (about 1 lb.) crab meat, fresh,
    frozen, or canned
1 cup mayonnaise
2 teaspoons tarragon vinegar
½ teaspoon tarragon
¼ cup finely chopped parsley
¼ cup minced chives
    Lettuce

Drain and save oil from artichokes. Cut artichokes into small pieces and mix lightly with the crab meat. Blend the reserved oil with mayonnaise, tarragon vinegar, tarragon, parsley, and chives. Toss with the crab mixture and keep well chilled until time to serve. Spoon onto lettuce-lined plates or large scallop shells. Makes 6 servings.

SLICED BEEF TONGUE

1 beef tongue (about 3 pounds)
2 carrots, sliced
1 onion, sliced
1 bay leaf
8 peppercorns
2 teaspoons salt
  Water

Wash beef tongue well and place in a deep kettle. Add carrots, onion, bay leaf, peppercorns, and salt. Cover with water, bring to a boil; cover, and simmer for 3 to 3½ hours or until very tender. Let cool in stock. Remove skin and return tongue to stock (overnight, if desired) until you are ready to take it to the picnic. Then lift tongue from stock and wrap in foil; keep on ice until ready to slice and serve. (Save stock for soups.) Makes about 9 servings.

CELERY HEARTS WITH SPICED TOMATO SAUCE

6 whole celery hearts
  Water
2 bouillon cubes
1 teaspoon salt
  Tomato Sauce (recipe follows)

Trim celery hearts to the same length, cutting off all leaves. Tie a string around top of each heart. In a wide shallow pan, heat to boiling enough water to almost cover celery hearts. Add bouillon cubes and salt. Add celery and cook, covered, for 10 to 15 minutes or until just barely tender. Chill in stock (overnight if desired).

To transport to picnic, drain celery and wrap in foil; carry in ice chest. Sauce need not be chilled. Remove strings from celery, arrange on serving dish and drizzle with sauce. Offer extra sauce to ladle over each celery heart. Makes 6 servings.

Tomato Sauce. Rub a small bowl with a cut clove of garlic. Mix in the bowl ½ small clove minced garlic, 1 cup catsup, 2½ tablespoons salad oil, 1 tablespoon wine vinegar, 1½ teaspoons celery seed, and ¼ teaspoon salt.

Spring Tea for Six

SANDKAKA

PETIT-SUISSE MOLD

FRESH STRAWBERRIES

TEA OR COFFEE

A small informal tea is a friendly, warm way to celebrate a variety of occasions. It can be a means to introduce a new neighbor, to celebrate a friend's accomplishment, to end a meeting or card game, or just to get several friends together for a chat. This is a menu to serve four to six. It includes a golden cake, fresh strawberries, and a molded cream cheese. You can prepare it all in the morning (or bake the cake the night before) and have only the tea or coffee to make just before serving time.

SANDKAKA

Sandkaka, or Sand Cake, is a Swedish cake made with oat flour. It has a coarse, compact texture and a subtle lemon flavor.

1½ cups quick-cooking rolled oats
1 cup (½ lb.) soft butter
1¼ cups sugar
4 eggs
Grated peel of 1 lemon
2 tablespoons lemon juice
2 teaspoons vanilla
1¼ cups unsifted regular all-purpose flour
Fine dry bread crumbs

Whirl oats in a blender until ground to a flour; reserve. In the large bowl of your electric mixer, cream butter with sugar until fluffy. Beat in eggs, one at a time. Add lemon peel, lemon juice, and vanilla; stir to blend. Gradually stir in the oat and all-purpose flours until smooth. Butter and coat with crumbs a small tube-type mold (1-quart size) or a loaf pan (5¼ by 9¼ inches); spoon in batter and smooth out. Bake in a 325°

oven for about 1 hour 10 minutes, or until a cake tester, inserted, comes out clean. Makes 8 to 10 servings.

PETIT-SUISSE MOLD

Petit-Suisse is an unsalted, cream-type French cheese that is generally available only in Europe. It is excellent with fresh fruit for dessert. This recipe combines simple ingredients that will give a product resembling the authentic French cheese, with an added nut topping.

1 large package (8 oz.) cream cheese
2 tablespoons sour cream
¼ teaspoon grated lemon peel
2 teaspoons sugar
1 teaspoon finely chopped nuts

In a bowl, blend well the cream cheese, sour cream, lemon peel, and sugar. Pack mixture into 5 or 6 small, lightly greased paper cups or muffin cups. Chill 2 hours or longer. Turn out by running a blade around edge and inverting container. Arrange on serving dishes, and sprinkle finely chopped nuts over each. Makes 5 or 6 servings.

A Birthday Dinner

TROPICAL FRUIT CUPS
CORNED BEEF   MUSTARD SAUCE
OVEN FRENCH FRIES   BRUSSELS SPROUTS
BIRTHDAY CAKE   ICE CREAM IN CUPS

A corned beef dinner with cake and ice cream offers an expandable menu well suited to a family gathering for a birthday celebration or other special occasion.

TROPICAL FRUIT CUPS

1 small fresh pineapple, peeled, cored, and cut in chunks
1 papaya, peeled, seeded, and sliced
2 bananas, peeled and sliced
1 can (11 oz.) mandarin oranges, drained

Combine the fruits, and serve chilled in small dessert bowls or cocktail or wine glasses. Makes 8 to 10 servings.

CORNED BEEF

Place a 4 or 5-pound corned beef in a large pot with 1½ quarts water and 1 peeled onion, stuck with 3 whole cloves. Bring to a boil and simmer 2½ to 3 hours, or until tender when pierced with a fork. Drain off liquid. Place roast on a rack in a baking pan and bake uncovered in a 375° oven 20 minutes, or until browned. Serve hot, sliced, with Mustard Sauce (recipe follows).

MUSTARD SAUCE

2 tablespoons each dry mustard, sugar, water, and white wine vinegar
1 tablespoon butter
1 teaspoon cornstarch
1 egg, beaten
½ cup whipping cream

Mix together in a small saucepan the mustard, sugar, water, and vinegar. Add butter and cornstarch. Stirring constantly, cook until sauce comes to a full rolling boil and is thick and clear. Stir sauce into beaten egg, return to pan, and cook over low heat 2 or 3 minutes longer. Chill. Whip cream until stiff, and fold in just before serving. Makes 1½ cups sauce.

BIRTHDAY CAKE WITH ORANGE FROSTING

Make up your favorite birthday cake or bake a packaged orange cake mix in two 9-inch layer cake pans as directed; cool. Spread orange frosting (recipe follows) between layers and on top and sides of cake. Let stand at room temperature until set. Makes about 12 servings.

Orange Frosting. Cream ¼ cup (⅛ lb.) butter until light and blend in 1 package (1 lb.) powdered sugar alternately with 1 egg and 4 tablespoons frozen orange juice concentrate, undiluted and thawed. Beat in 1 teaspoon grated orange peel.

ICE CREAM IN CUPS

Scoop out several different flavors of ice cream, such as vanilla, strawberry, and chocolate or coffee, and place each ice cream ball in a fluted paper or foil baking cup. Cover and return to freezer. At serving time, insert a small candle in each ice cream, if desired, and light. Then pass ice creams on a tray, letting guests select their favorite flavor.

Two-Family Snow Picnic

SAUSAGES: SALAMI, THURINGER

SWISS CHEESE

GREEK KASSERI OR CHEDDAR CHEESE

MUSTARD-FLAVORED MAYONNAISE

DARK RYE BREAD

MARINATED ARTICHOKE HEARTS

MARINATED WHOLE MUSHROOMS

FRESH PINEAPPLE

FROZEN RASPBERRY-SWIRL COFFEE CAKE

ORANGE SNOW CONES   HARD CANDIES

APPLE JUICE   BARBERA (OR OTHER RED WINE)

An exhilarating morning on the slopes builds up appetites for lunch. And a lunch you bring yourself is quicker, more convenient, and usually better eating than lunch in a crowded cafeteria. Two or more families may enjoy pooling lunch resources and arranging a noon rendezvous for a cooperative meal such as this one. Since packing ski gear for a trip leaves little time for food preparation, the best fare is the no-cook, prepackaged variety, from a delicatessen or the refrigerated section of a supermarket.

Bring along a square of oilcloth to use as a tablecloth. You will also need a cutting board and knife for on-the-spot food preparation, and plastic straws, paper cups, and toothpicks for serving. Bring mayonnaise seasoned with mustard in a plastic container.

To make the snow cones, drizzle concentrated fruit juice—orange, grape, pineapple-grapefruit, or lemonade—over clean snow packed into paper cups. Sip with plastic straws, or use plastic spoons for eating.

At the picnic site, halve the pineapple, cut out the core, and cube the fruit. Have an ample supply of hard candies and miniature boxes of raisins to stuff into children's pockets for the afternoon runs.

Alternatives or additions to the above menu might include dried beef or prosciutto and mushroom-flavored cheese spread; smoked oysters, cream cheese, and crackers; canned cashews or macadamia nuts and fruit cake or packaged chocolate cookies. And take fresh fruit.

Tea Party for Mothers

WHOLE STRAWBERRIES WITH SUGAR CONES
CINNAMON CRISPS
CHOCOLATE SPRINKLE ROUNDS
CHOCOLATE RIBBON CAKES
SPICY ORANGE TEA   LEMON SLICES

"Please come to tea, Saturday at three," the invitations might read when young girls plan a real tea party for their mothers. Two girls could be hostesses to their own mothers and a few friends and their mothers; or a not-too-large Brownie or Bluebird group might use this flexible party idea. One mother can be on hand to help.

A packaged cake mix and refrigerated sugar cooky dough are baking short-cuts for the desserts. The girls will enjoy personalizing them by frosting and cutting the cake into diamond-shaped petits fours and decorating the cooky dough for two kinds of party cookies. It works best to complete these two baking jobs a day or two in advance. In fact, both items freeze well if the girls wish to make them even a week or two ahead—a practical plan for a Brownie or Bluebird group. The other items on the menu are quickly prepared just before the tea.

WHOLE STRAWBERRIES WITH SUGAR CONES

Wash 6 whole strawberries per serving, leaving stems on; let drain on paper towels. To make the powdered sugar cones, spoon powdered sugar into a 2 or 3-ounce conical glass or other container (such as a jigger or egg cup) and tap sugar down until well packed. Turn each sugar-filled glass upside-down on a serving plate, a little to one side, and carefully remove glass by lifting it straight up. Surround each with 6 berries.

CINNAMON CRISPS

- 1 package (1 lb. 2 oz.) refrigerated sugar cooky dough
- 1 tablespoon whipping cream
- 2 teaspoons cinnamon
- 4 tablespoons sugar
- ½ cup sliced almonds

Cut sugar cooky dough into ¼-inch-thick slices. Place on a lightly greased baking sheet, spacing them 2 inches apart. Brush lightly with the cream. Sprinkle with a mixture of the cinnamon and sugar, and lay on sliced almonds. Bake in a 350° oven for 10 to 12 minutes, or until lightly browned. Remove to racks and let cool. Makes about 3 dozen.

CHOCOLATE SPRINKLE ROUNDS

**1 package (1 lb. 2 oz.) refrigerated sugar
    cooky dough
⅓ cup chocolate sprinkles**

Cut cooky dough into ¼-inch-thick slices. Dip one side of each slice in chocolate sprinkles and place, coated side up, on a lightly greased baking sheet; space cookies 2 inches apart. Bake in a 350° oven for 10 to 12 minutes, or until lightly browned. Remove to racks and let cool. Makes about 3 dozen.

CHOCOLATE RIBBON CAKES

**1 package (1 lb. 3 oz.) yellow cake mix, plus
    water and eggs specified on package
2½ cups unsifted powdered sugar
2 tablespoons light corn syrup
¼ cup milk
½ teaspoon vanilla
2 ounces semisweet chocolate
1 tablespoon butter or margarine
2 teaspoons light corn syrup**

Prepare the cake mix as directed on the package and turn batter into a buttered and floured 10 by 15-inch cake pan (jelly roll pan); spread evenly. Bake in a 350° oven for 30 to 35 minutes, or until a pick inserted in the center of the cake comes out clean. Let cool in the pan on a rack.

For frosting, combine the powdered sugar, 2 tablespoons corn syrup, milk, and vanilla in a bowl; mix until smooth. Spread with a spatula over entire surface of cake.

To make chocolate ribbons, in top of double boiler combine the chocolate, butter or margarine, and 2 teaspoons corn syrup. Place over hot water and stir until melted. Fashion a paper cone with a double thickness of waxed paper, making an opening ⅛ inch wide at the tip; secure cone with tape or a staple. Spoon in chocolate. Carefully squeeze out chocolate in lengthwise stripes, spaced 1 inch apart on the cake. With a small spatula or knife, draw perpendicular stripes, 1 inch apart, through frosting and chocolate stripes, letting the chocolate run.

When the frosting has set, cut cake into diamonds by making lengthwise cuts, 1 inch apart, then cutting through diagonally 1 inch apart. Makes about 6 dozen pieces.

SPICY ORANGE TEA

Prepare spicy orange tea using tea bags. Offer a pitcher of milk for those who wish their tea additionally flavored.

Committee Meeting Lunch

OVEN-GLAZED CORNED BEEF

INDIVIDUAL EGG BRAID LOAVES

SWEET BUTTER   MUSTARD

PREPARED HORSERADISH

MIXED GREEN SALAD

BROILED PINEAPPLE AND BANANA WITH ICE CREAM

The hostess who planned this menu calls this "conversation cooking." It is her answer to the problem of how to serve lunch to a committee meeting at her home and still participate in the discussions. Her objective is to serve a fine meal without the food's becoming obtrusive. It must be ready at the convenience of the group and available as long as the group chooses to nibble.

This menu qualifies on all counts. Guests make their own hot corned beef sandwiches with individual loaves of homemade egg bread—the fragrance of bread baking is a delightful prelude to the meal, and after the meal each guest can wrap up what's left of his loaf to take home.

The secret of having fresh bread ready for lunch is to use a packaged roll mix. If you start it around 9 in the morning, it should be baked sometime shortly before noon, with a minimum of attention required once the dough has been mixed and kneaded. The corned beef is cooked ahead—earlier in the morning or the day before —and the glazing sauce is mixed ahead.

The glaze is poured over the corned beef and it goes into the oven about 30 minutes before serving time; but the meat waits well, being almost equally good hot, warm, or cold. Have salad greens washed, dried, and crisped in the refrigerator; at the last minute, mix with a simple oil-and-vinegar dressing. The dessert is so quick to make that you can prepare it while your guests watch.

OVEN-GLAZED CORNED BEEF

If you have a pressure cooker, the corned beef can be cooked in about 1 hour; if you simmer it, allow 3 or 4 hours for it to cook tender.

4 pounds corned beef brisket or eye of round
 Water
1 cup catsup
1 tablespoon brown sugar
½ teaspoon celery seed
1 tablespoon dry mustard
2 tablespoons each Worcestershire and water
 Dash cayenne pepper or liquid hot-pepper seasoning

Wash the corned beef well in cold water. To cook it under pressure, follow the directions that came with your pressure cooker—this size piece will take about 50 minutes to cook tender at 15 pounds pressure. If you don't have a pressure cooker, put the meat into a large pan; cover with water and simmer (do not boil) for 3 to 4 hours, or until tender.

For the glazing sauce, combine the catsup, brown sugar, celery seed, dry mustard, Worcestershire, 2 tablespoons water, and cayenne; mix until well blended and set aside until you're ready to use it.

Shortly before serving, put the meat in a shallow baking pan with the fat side up. Pour the glazing sauce over the top. Put into a 350° oven about 30 minutes, or until heated through and glazed. Remove to serving board and cut in thin slices for sandwiches. Makes 6 to 8 servings.

INDIVIDUAL EGG BRAID LOAVES

Bake these little loaves of braided egg bread in individual-loaf-sized pans if you have them. The loaves can also be braided and baked side by side on a cooky sheet or shallow baking pan.

2 packages (14 oz. size) hot roll mix
1 cup warm (not hot) water
4 large whole eggs
1 egg, separated
1 teaspoon salt

Sprinkle the yeast from both packages of hot roll mix over the water in a large mixing bowl; stir until dissolved. Mix in the 4 eggs plus the egg yolk and salt. Add the dry mix from both packages and stir until blended. Turn out on a floured board and knead until smooth and satiny, about 8 to 10 minutes. Put into a greased bowl, cover, and set in a warm place (85° to 90°) to rise until almost double in size, about 45 minutes. (If you don't have a warm spot in your kitchen, set the dough in an unheated oven with a pan of hot water on a shelf underneath.)

Punch down the dough and divide into 6 equal portions. Working with 1 portion at a time on a lightly floured board, divide into 3 equal pieces; roll each with your hands to form a 5-inch strip (this will be easier if you let the dough pieces rest 5 to 10 minutes). Loosely braid the 3 strips together, sealing the ends and turning them under to fit a small bread pan (3 by 7 inches).

Grease well 6 small bread pans or a shallow baking pan about 12 by 15 inches. Set the loaves in the small pans or arrange them on the baking pan. Brush tops lightly with the slightly beaten egg white. Cover loosely with a cloth and allow to rise again in a warm place until almost double in size. Bake in a 375° oven until deep golden brown, about 25 minutes.

BROILED PINEAPPLE AND BANANA WITH ICE CREAM

Serve the caramel-glazed fruit piping hot with scoops of vanilla ice cream melting over the top.

4 to 6 slices fresh or canned pineapple
2 to 3 firm, ripe bananas
⅓ cup brown sugar
¼ cup (⅛ lb.) butter
1 tablespoon lemon juice
1 pint vanilla ice cream

Allow 1 slice of pineapple and ½ banana for each serving. Cut each banana in half lengthwise and then crosswise to make 4 pieces—2 per serving. Arrange the banana pieces and pineapple slices in a single layer in a baking dish. Sprinkle brown sugar over the top, dot with butter, and sprinkle with lemon juice. Set the fruit about 8 inches below broiler heat source and broil for 5 to 7 minutes, basting several times, until the fruit is glazed. Serve hot in individual dessert dishes, topping each serving with a scoop of vanilla ice cream and spooning some of the hot butter sauce over top of ice cream.

Indonesian Dinner for Four

GRILLED CHICKEN ON SKEWERS (SATE AJAM)

SALAD (GADO GADO)

PEANUT SAUCE (BUMBU RATJANG)

PUFFED SHRIMP CHIPS (KERUPUK)

RICE (NAZI)

CHICKEN AND VEGETABLE SOUP (SOTO AJAM)

COCONUT DESSERT (LAPIS)

TEA OR COFFEE

This Indonesian dinner for four will interest the cook who prefers trying unfamiliar foreign dishes on a small group. It is unusual enough to provoke conversation, but in general the flavors are not really unfamiliar to the American palate. Many of the recipes can be prepared wholly or partially in advance, and only last-minute grilling, heating, and adding of sauces and dressings need be done after your guests arrive.

On the morning of the dinner, you can prepare the vegetables for the salad and store them in separate covered containers in the refrigerator, make the soup to reheat just before serving, fry the shrimp puffs, and make the dessert. Prepare the skewered chicken and the Peanut Sauce a couple of hours before grilling. Have rice measured for 6 servings and ready to start cooking as you do the last-minute tasks.

GRILLED CHICKEN ON SKEWERS
(Saté Ajam)

Skewered chicken pieces, marinated in a lemon-soy mixture, are grilled and then served with a peanut sauce.

  3 whole chicken breasts (6 split breasts)
¼ cup soy sauce
  1 tablespoon lemon juice
¼ medium-sized onion, finely chopped
    Salad oil
  1 cup Peanut Sauce (recipe follows)
  2 tablespoons soy sauce
  1 tablespoon lemon juice

Skin and bone the chicken breasts. Cut in strips (about 1 by 3 inches), roll strips, and string on bamboo or metal skewers—if you use the bamboo ones, use 2 placed side by side for each saté. (Reserve small scraps of chicken for the soup—you'll need 1 cup or more.) Combine the soy sauce and the lemon juice in a shallow pan; marinate the skewered chicken for about 2 hours, turning occasionally to coat all sides. Broil chicken in oven broiler about 8 inches from heat for 6 to 7 minutes on each side, turning once; or cook over charcoal about 6 inches from medium-hot coals for about 10 minutes per side.

Meanwhile, fry onion in 1 to 2 tablespoons salad oil in frying pan until well browned; drain. Combine half the onion with 1 cup Peanut Sauce (recipe follows), soy sauce, and lemon juice; heat sauce until just warm, stirring to prevent burning on the bottom. When the chicken is done, arrange skewers on a warm serving platter. Sprinkle with remaining onion and either top with the sauce or pass sauce separately. Makes 4 servings.

SALAD
(Gado Gado)

The salad most popular in Indonesia is called Gado Gado. It is made of layers of cooked and raw vegetables topped with some of the Peanut Sauce.

2 quarts water
1½ teaspoons salt
1 cup fresh bean sprouts
½ medium-sized head of cabbage, leaves cut in 2-inch squares
1½ cups fresh green beans, cut in 1½-inch pieces (or 1 package, 9-oz., frozen cut green beans)
1 large potato, cooked, peeled, and diced
1 cucumber, peeled, cut in half lengthwise, then thinly sliced crosswise
¾ cup Peanut Sauce (recipe follows)
2 hard-cooked eggs, sliced

In a large kettle, bring the salted water to a boil; add bean sprouts and cook just until tender crisp, about 3 minutes; remove with a strainer or slotted spoon and drain. Chill in refrigerator.

In the same water, cook cabbage until tender (about 4 minutes), remove from water, drain, and refrigerate. Cook green beans in same water just until tender (8 to 10 minutes); remove, drain. Reserve vegetable stock for the soup. Allow vegetables to cool.

Layer vegetables on the platter in this order: cabbage, diced potatoes, cucumbers, green beans, and bean sprouts. Pour over Peanut Sauce. Arrange hard-cooked egg slices over top. Refrigerate a few minutes before serving. Makes 4 to 6 servings.

FRIED SHRIMP CHIPS
(Kerupuk)

In Indonesia, Kerupuk is always served when you serve Gado Gado. You can fry these white chips in a matter of minutes. Buy the uncooked chips in a Chinese market or specialty food store, or you can use ready-to-eat fried shrimp chips available in most supermarkets.

If you buy uncooked Kerupuk, fry as follows: Bring 3 to 4 inches of salad oil to a temperature of 325° in a deep-fat fryer or deep saucepan. Measure out about half of an 8-ounce package of chips, and drop about 12 chips at a time into the hot fat. They will puff and rise to the top in about 20 seconds. Remove and drain immediately. (If you want to keep leftover chips to serve later, store in an airtight container. If they become moist, dry them on a baking sheet in a 175° oven.)

PEANUT SAUCE
(Bumbu Ratjang)

This sauce is an ingredient for the sauce used on the grilled chicken and for the dressing used on the salad. You can prepare it while the chicken marinates.

½ medium-sized onion, finely minced
Salad oil
1 clove garlic
1 jar (12 oz.) chunk-style peanut butter
1 cup coconut milk (commercially frozen or made as directed below)
2 tablespoons dark brown sugar
1 teaspoon salt
3 dried hot red chiles (seeds removed), mashed into a paste with a little water

Fry onion in ½ inch of hot salad oil in a frying pan until very brown and crisp. Pour off excess oil and remove onions to a mortar (or round-bottomed bowl); mash onions with garlic to make a smooth paste. Return onions to frying pan along with peanut butter, coconut milk, brown sugar, salt, and chiles. Stir over low heat until smooth, adding water to make it a gravy-like consistency. Makes about 3 cups sauce.

Coconut Milk. Pour 2 cups boiling water or scalded milk over 4 cups finely grated fresh coconut; let stand 20 minutes. Strain through a double thickness of cheesecloth. Squeeze tightly to remove all liquid. Makes 2 cups.

(continued)

CHICKEN AND VEGETABLE SOUP
(Soto Ajam)

The soup is made of the stock used for cooking the salad vegetables, small pieces of chicken saved from the skewered chicken, and additional vegetables and seasonings. It is served over rice on the dinner plate.

> Stock from salad vegetables, or 5
>   cups water
> 1 cup (or more) small pieces of chicken
> 1 teaspoon grated fresh ginger root
> 1 small clove garlic, minced or mashed
> 1 can (1 lb.) black-eyed peas, drained
> 1 medium-sized onion, thinly sliced
>   Salad oil
> 1 tablespoon lemon juice
> 1 cup thinly sliced celery
> 2 hard-cooked eggs, cut in thick slices

Add to kettle of vegetable stock, the chicken pieces, ginger root, and garlic. Cover, bring to a boil, and simmer 15 to 20 minutes. Meanwhile fry black-eyed peas and onion in ½ inch of oil in a large frying pan for about 7 minutes, or until onions are golden; discard oil. Just before serving, add fried peas and onions, lemon juice, celery, and egg slices to the stock; heat through. Serve in a large bowl. Makes 4 to 6 servings.

COCONUT DESSERT
(Lapis)

Coconut is the predominant flavor in this red and white layered dessert. This is a very firm pudding that is served in small squares and eaten with the fingers.

> 6 tablespoons cornstarch
> ½ cup sugar
> 2 cups thawed, frozen coconut milk, or fresh
>   coconut milk made as directed in Peanut
>   Sauce recipe, or 1 cup coconut milk and
>   1 cup half-and-half (light cream)
> 1 teaspoon vanilla
> ⅛ teaspoon red food coloring

Mix together the cornstarch and sugar in the top of a double boiler. Slowly stir in the thawed coconut milk and vanilla and cook over boiling water, continuing to stir to prevent sticking, for about 10 minutes or until thickened. Remove from heat and quickly spread half of the mixture into a lightly greased 8-inch cake pan. Immediately stir the food coloring into the remaining mixture; then carefully spread over the first layer. Cool completely in a cool place or in the refrigerator. Cut into 1½-inch squares or small wedges. Makes approximately 1½ dozen pieces.

Informal Viennese Dinner

**BEEF SOUP WITH LIVER DUMPLINGS
(RINDSUPPE MIT LEBERKNÖDELN)**

VIENNESE VEAL CUTLET (WIENER SCHNITZEL)

BUTTER-BROWNED NEW POTATOES

TOMATO SALAD (PARADEISSALAT)

CUCUMBER SALAD (GURKENSALAT)

STUFFED EGG HALVES

DINNER ROLLS

VIENNESE NUT CAKE (NUSSTORTE)

DEMITASSE OF STRONG COFFEE

This informal dinner party menu for six is Viennese and planned specifically to enhance the enjoyment of *Wiener schnitzel*.

Because Wiener schnitzel must be hot and freshly fried to be at its best, plan on cooking it in the last 5 minutes or so just before dinner. But you can prepare the rest of the meal ahead.

Make the two salads 2 to 3 hours before dinner and allow them to stand in the refrigerator for best flavor. Bake the cake for dessert the day before, assemble the next morning, then let the completely decorated dessert wait in your refrigerator.

Of the hot foods, cook the potatoes ahead (or use canned new potatoes) and do the browning in the oven just before dinner. You can make the liver dumplings ahead, then drop them into the hot soup to cook about 10 minutes before serving.

BEEF SOUP WITH LIVER DUMPLINGS
(Rindsuppe mit Leberknödeln)

½ **pound beef or calf liver**
3 **slices white bread, crusts removed**
2 **tablespoons finely chopped onion**
2 **tablespoons bacon drippings or butter**
1 **teaspoon finely chopped parsley**
1 **egg**
  Dash each salt, pepper, and marjoram
¼ **to ½ cup fine dry bread crumbs**
1½ **quarts clear beef soup or 2 or 3 cans
    (10½ oz. each) condensed beef consommé
    Finely chopped parsley (optional)**

First prepare the dumplings: Cut liver in pieces and whirl in the blender or put through a meat chopper with a fine blade. Soak the bread in a little water, then squeeze as dry as possible. Put bread into blender with liver and whirl, or put the liver and bread again through the meat chopper. In a small frying pan, sauté the onion in the bacon drippings or butter until golden; add parsley and leave a minute or two over low heat, then remove. Combine the liver and bread with the onion mixture. Add egg, salt, pepper, marjoram, and ¼ cup of the bread crumbs, adding more

(continued)

bread crumbs until mixture is a consistency you can form into soft walnut-sized balls with two teaspoons. You can cover the bowl at this point and refrigerate the dumpling mixture until you are ready to heat the soup.

To serve, heat your own beef soup or the canned consommé, diluted with an equal amount of water, until it is boiling. Spoon dumpling mixture quickly into the boiling broth, a walnut-sized portion at a time, cover, reduce heat, and simmer for 6 minutes. Sprinkle a little finely chopped parsley on each serving of soup. Makes 6 servings.

VIENNESE VEAL CUTLET
(Wiener Schnitzel)

>   **2 to 3 pounds boneless veal cutlet, cut**
>   **⅓ inch thick**
>   **Salt and pepper**
>   **2 eggs**
>   **About ¾ cup flour**
> **1½ cups fine dry bread crumbs**
>   **Butter, margarine, or shortening**
>   **2 or 3 lemons**
>   **Parsley**

Carefully trim away any skin or fat from the outside of each cutlet. Depending on the size of the cutlet, leave it whole or divide it into 2 or 3 pieces, following the natural divisions of the meat. If the veal wasn't pounded at the market, put one piece at a time between two pieces of waxed paper and pound with a smooth-surfaced mallet to flatten it evenly to about ¼-inch thickness or a little less—don't pound so hard that the meat tears. With kitchen scissors, make very small cuts along the edges of the cutlets to keep them from curling while frying. Lightly sprinkle salt and pepper on each side.

Beat eggs with a fork until very well blended. Working with one piece of meat at a time, dust cutlets with flour, dip in egg, then in bread crumbs. Lay cutlet on board and pat crumbs in well with your hands so they won't fall off in the frying. You can do this much ahead and refrigerate the cutlets, covered, in a single layer or between sheets of waxed paper, until you are ready to fry them.

If you use two fairly large frying pans, you can fry enough schnitzel for six in about 4 or 5 minutes. With only one pan, allow about 10 minutes; have a shallow pan coated with paper towels inside a warm oven and transfer each cutlet to it as soon as it is browned. Over medium-high heat, melt just enough butter, margarine, or shortening in the frying pans to cover the pan bottoms completely; have more of the fat close at hand. Heat until the fat shows ripples when you tip the pan. Add the breaded cutlets; they should turn golden brown in about 1 minute. Turn and cook to golden brown on the other side, adding more fat as needed to keep pan bottoms well covered. If you are using only one pan for frying, it's a good idea to use half butter and half shortening; the fat will be less likely to burn when you re-use it.

Top each hot schnitzel with a lemon slice. Garnish platter with lemon wedges and parsley sprigs and serve immediately. Makes 6 to 8 servings.

BUTTER-BROWNED NEW POTATOES

Peel or scrub well about 2 pounds small new potatoes; cook in boiling salted water until just tender, about 20 minutes. Drain and set aside until you are ready to brown them in the oven. Or use 2 cans (1 lb. *each*) small new potatoes, drained. About 45 minutes before serving time, heat ¼ cup (⅛ lb.) butter or margarine in a shallow baking pan in a 400° oven. Put in the drained potatoes, turning in the melted butter until coated all over. Bake, turning the potatoes or shaking the pan several times, until the potatoes are nicely browned all over, about 40 minutes. (If browned before dinner is ready, cover with foil and leave in a warm oven.)

TOMATO SALAD
(Paradeissalat)

>   **2 pounds small, firm tomatoes, peeled and**
>   **thinly sliced**
>   **2 onions (about same size as tomatoes),**
>   **thinly sliced**
> **½ teaspoon salt**
>   **Dash cayenne pepper**
> **¼ teaspoon Worcestershire**
> **¼ teaspoon powdered sugar**
> **½ cup red wine vinegar**
> **¼ cup salad oil or olive oil**

Alternate tomatoes and onions in layers in a bowl. Mix together salt, cayenne pepper, Worcestershire, powdered sugar, vinegar, and salad oil or olive oil. Cover; chill about 2 hours. Drain off marinade. Makes 6 servings.

CUCUMBER SALAD
(Gurkensalat)

4 medium-sized cucumbers, thinly sliced
    (peel if waxed)
2 teaspoons salt
⅓ cup white wine vinegar
¼ teaspoon garlic salt
⅓ cup olive oil or salad oil
    Freshly ground pepper and paprika
    Stuffed egg halves for garnish (optional,
      recipe follows)

In a bowl mix together the cucumbers and salt. Let stand, covered, for about 30 minutes. Drain cucumbers well. Pour over them a mixture of the vinegar, garlic salt, and olive oil or salad oil. Sprinkle with freshly ground pepper and paprika. Cover; chill 2 to 3 hours. To serve, drain off liquid; if you like, garnish with stuffed egg halves (recipe follows). Makes 6 servings.

STUFFED EGG HALVES

Make these several hours before dinner and chill, covered.

3 hard-cooked eggs
3 tablespoons mayonnaise
1 teaspoon Dijon-style mustard
1 teaspoon chopped capers
    Whole capers for garnish

Carefully cut eggs in half lengthwise. Remove yolks and mash with a fork in a small bowl. Add mayonnaise, mustard, and chopped capers; blend together well. Spoon mixture into the egg halves and top each stuffed egg half with a whole caper. Serves 6.

VIENNESE NUT CAKE
(Nusstorte)

6 eggs, separated
1 whole egg
¾ cup powdered sugar (unsifted)
1½ cups finely ground walnuts (whirl in
    blender or grind with nut grinder)
⅓ cup graham cracker crumbs
    Whipped Cream Filling (recipe follows)
½ cup currant jelly
    Icing (recipe follows)
12 whole walnut halves

Beat the 6 egg whites until frothy, then spoon out 1 tablespoon and set aside for icing. Beat remaining whites until they hold firm but moist peaks; set aside. In the large bowl of your electric mixer, beat the 6 egg yolks and the whole egg with powdered sugar until light and fluffy. Fold in walnuts and cracker crumbs. Then gently fold in beaten egg whites. Pour into two 8-inch layer cake pans (greased, bottoms lined with paper, and greased again). Bake in a 300° oven for 35 to 40 minutes, or until tops spring back when gently touched. Let stand 10 minutes; remove from pans, peel off paper, and cool on wire racks.

When cake is cool, cut each layer in half, horizontally, to make 4 layers. Place one cake layer on serving plate; spread with half the Whipped Cream Filling (recipe follows). Arrange second layer and spread with half the jelly. Add third layer and spread with remaining cream, then position the top layer and spread remaining jelly evenly over top.

Position 4 strips of waxed paper under the cake edges. Carefully spoon icing over jelly on top of cake to cover evenly; let icing drizzle down sides. Arrange walnut halves on top of cake. Chill in refrigerator until ready to serve. Gently remove waxed paper strips. Makes 12 servings.

Whipped Cream Filling. Whip 1 cup heavy cream until stiff. Stir in ¼ cup powdered sugar and 1 teaspoon vanilla.

Icing. Mix together the reserved 1 tablespoon egg white from the cake recipe and 1¾ cups sifted powdered sugar. Dissolve 2 teaspoons instant coffee powder in about 1½ tablespoons boiling water. Add sufficient liquid to the sugar mixture to make a glaze that is thick enough to drizzle slowly down the sides of the cake.

Indian Buffet

LAMB CURRY

GINGER COCONUT RICE

INDIAN MIXED VEGETABLES

YOGURT RELISH   CHUTNEY

CARDAMOM BREAD

PINEAPPLE SHERBET   ALMOND COOKIES

COFFEE   DARJEELING TEA

This buffet dinner is based on authentic Indian foods, but the recipes are adapted to ingredients available here. The curry is a typical Indian one with flavors derived from a special blend of seasonings; an electric blender makes the preparation easy. To further recommend this curry, the flavor improves when the dish is made ahead and reheated before serving, and it doesn't suffer when kept warm on the buffet table for an extended period. The rice stays hot and fluffy in an Oriental basket set over steaming water that is kept simmering gently over the burner unit of a chafing dish; it will hold this way for an hour, or even two hours, with no perceptible loss of flavor or texture.

Plan to start the lamb curry several days before your party; reheat to serve. Start the rice about an hour before dinner. Have the vegetables all washed and cut; cook them during the last 20 minutes. Prepare the bread and wrap it in foil ready to heat for the last 20 minutes. Make the yogurt relish the day before and keep it covered in your refrigerator. Have a good chutney ready to serve; you can buy one or make it yourself. Buy pineapple sherbet or another tropical or citrus fruit sherbet for dessert and serve it with simple almond cookies, homemade or purchased from the bakery. Serve Darjeeling tea from India, but offer coffee, too, for those who prefer it.

This dinner is designed to serve 12, but the recipes can be doubled to serve twice that number.

LAMB CURRY

This dish has a smooth, exotic flavor, and as an extra bonus, your kitchen will be filled with a delicious aroma all the time it cooks. The yogurt base loses its identity but contributes an interesting tart flavor to the sauce.

    2 medium-sized onions
    2 cloves garlic
    2 tablespoons ground coriander (or whole
        coriander seed ground with a mortar and
        pestle)
    2 teaspoons each salt and cumin seed
    1½ teaspoons each black pepper, ground
        cloves, and ground cardamom
    1 teaspoon each ground ginger, ground
        cinnamon, and poppy seed
    ⅓ cup lemon juice
    2 cups yogurt
    5 pounds boneless lamb, cut in 1½-inch
        cubes
    ¼ cup (⅛ lb.) butter
        Curry powder (optional)

Cut 1 of the onions and 1 clove of the garlic directly into an electric blender. (If you don't have a blender, grate the onion and mash the garlic and combine in a bowl.) Add coriander, salt, cumin, pepper, cloves, cardamom, ginger, cinnamon, poppy seed, and lemon juice; whirl or beat until smooth and thoroughly blended. Blend in yogurt. Pour this sauce over the meat in a large container, stirring until all the meat pieces are coated. Cover and let stand 1 to 2 hours at room temperature, or overnight in the refrigerator.

Melt butter in a large frying pan or other heavy pan; thinly slice the remaining onion and 1 clove of garlic, and sauté in the butter until golden. Add the meat, including the marinating sauce. Cover and simmer slowly until the lamb is tender, about 2 hours. This makes quite a mild curry, so taste and add prepared curry powder (2 or 3 teaspoons) if you want to increase the curry spiciness. Makes about 12 servings.

GINGER COCONUT RICE

Use any untreated natural straw basket for serving the rice. To hold the basket above the steaming water, set it on a 7-ounce tuna can with top and bottom removed.

    ½ cup (¼ lb.) butter
    2 medium-sized onions, thinly sliced
    2-inch piece fresh ginger, grated, or
        1 teaspoon ground ginger
    3 cups uncooked regular long grain rice
    4½ cups regular-strength chicken broth
    ¾ cup fresh or packaged grated coconut

Melt the butter in a large, heavy pan. Add the onion and ginger; sauté until the onion is limp, but not browned. Add the rice and continue cooking slowly until the rice turns opaque. Stir in the chicken broth; cover, reduce heat, and simmer slowly for 10 minutes. Stir in the coconut, then continue cooking about 15 minutes, or until rice is tender and liquid has been absorbed. Transfer to basket and set in a large container over about 1 inch of gently boiling water; keep covered except to serve. Makes 12 servings.

(continued)

INDIAN MIXED VEGETABLES

The spice, turmeric, gives a golden color to this dish. The vegetables can be cut ahead, but cook them just before serving.

¼ cup (⅛ lb.) butter
1 medium-sized onion, sliced
¼ teaspoon turmeric
½ teaspoon summer savory
1 large potato, peeled and cubed
1½ cups water
1 small head cabbage, shredded
1 small cauliflower, cut in small pieces
1 cup fresh or frozen peas
2 fresh tomatoes, peeled and cut into wedges
1 bunch spinach, washed and stems removed
About 2 teaspoons salt

In a large pan (about 5-quart size), melt the butter; add onion, turmeric, and savory. Sauté until the onion is limp, about 5 minutes. Add the potato and water; cover and cook about 5 minutes. Add the cabbage and cauliflower and simmer about 5 minutes. Add the peas, tomatoes, and spinach; cook about 3 to 5 minutes. Add salt to taste and stir gently. Transfer to serving bowl immediately and keep warm over candle warmer or on electric hot tray on buffet table. Makes 12 servings.

CARDAMOM BREAD

Mexican flour tortillas, spread with cardamom-flavored butter and heated in foil in the oven, resemble the Indian bread called *nan*.

¾ cup (⅜ lb.) soft butter
¾ teaspoon ground cardamom
2 packages (2 dozen) flour tortillas

Blend the butter with the cardamom. Spread lightly on each tortilla, and stack, making 2 stacks. Wrap each separately in foil, so the second package will keep hot while you serve the first one. Heat in a 300° oven about 20 minutes. Serve in the stack and each guest can roll or fold the tortilla on his plate, or roll each one with the buttered side in.

YOGURT RELISH

There is good reason why a yogurt condiment is served with nearly every meal in India—the temperature and flavor contrast perfectly with curry. The simplest version, used often in India, is just yogurt seasoned with cayenne pepper, according to one's tolerance for hotness. This yogurt relish is seasoned with cumin, an especially interesting flavor note with this menu.

3 cups yogurt
¼ cup finely chopped green onion
1 teaspoon each salt and sugar
1 tablespoon ground cumin (or whole
    cumin seed ground with mortar and
    pestle)
4 small zucchini or 2 cucumbers

Combine yogurt, onion, salt, sugar, and cumin. Scrub the zucchini well, or trim or peel the cucumber; shred and stir in. This keeps well for several days in the refrigerator. Serve cold; you might nest the bowl in ice. Makes 12 servings.

Tahitian Buffet

COCONUT CHICKEN WITH FRESH FRUIT

RAISIN PILAF   CRESCENT ROLLS

CURRY-DRESSED GREEN SALAD

FRUIT SHERBET

TOASTED POUND CAKE FINGERS

The Tahitians have combined French, Chinese, and Polynesian cuisines with lavish use of tropical fruits. Some of these flavors are incorporated in this colorful, simplified Tahitian dinner.

Early in the day you can wash, dry, and refrigerate the salad greens and prepare the dressing. Also you might make scoops of sherbet using one or several flavors. Freeze them on a shallow pan, then pile the sherbet balls in an attractive bowl, cover, and store in the freezer.

Just before dinner, cook the chicken and the pilaf, heat frozen or brown-and-serve rolls, and mix the salad.

COCONUT CHICKEN WITH FRESH FRUIT

2 tablespoons butter or salad oil
8 large split chicken breasts (4 whole
   breasts)
1 tablespoon finely chopped fresh ginger,
   or ¾ teaspoon ground ginger
⅓ cup toasted coconut (toast flaked coconut in
   a 300° oven for about 10 minutes,
   until lightly browned)
½ teaspoon salt
1 cup (½ pint) whipping cream
3 large, firm, ripe bananas
1 large, ripe papaya
   Lime wedges

In a large frying pan (12-inch) with a lid, heat butter or oil, and brown chicken breasts on all sides. Sprinkle chicken with the ginger, 3 tablespoons of the coconut, and the salt. Pour cream over all, cover, and cook over medium heat about

10 minutes or until meat is white throughout (cut gash in thick portion to test).

Peel and quarter the bananas. Peel, halve, seed, and slice the papaya. Remove chicken from pan and arrange on a large platter with the fruit. Spoon sauce from pan over chicken and sprinkle the remaining toasted coconut over all. Garnish with lime to be squeezed over chicken and fruit. Serves 6.

RAISIN PILAF

Add ¼ cup raisins to 1 package chicken-flavored rice mix; cover and cook as package directs.

CURRY-DRESSED GREEN SALAD

¼ cup salad oil
2 tablespoons lemon juice or lime juice
½ teaspoon sugar
¼ teaspoon curry powder
   Dash salt
8 cups torn salad greens

In a small jar combine salad oil, lemon juice, sugar, curry powder, and salt. To serve, shake dressing and mix with salad greens. Serves 6.

TOASTED POUND CAKE FINGERS

Purchase 1 frozen pound cake. Cut 5 slices, each ¾ inch thick; then cut each slice in 4 lengthwise strips. Toast the pound cake pieces, turning to lightly brown all sides. Serve hot or cooled. Makes 6 servings.

Turkish Buffet

RICE-STUFFED VEGETABLES (DOLMAS)
LEMON WEDGES
BARBECUED LAMB CHOPS
MIXED GREENS SALAD
ARMENIAN CRACKER BREAD OR SOUR FRENCH BREAD
FRESH FRUIT

Rice-stuffed vegetables, called *dolmas,* dominate this menu, an ideal choice for a patio buffet. These dolmas are served at room temperature and should not be confused with the meat-stuffed dolmas often served hot as a main dish in Turkey. In Turkey the cool dolmas are served as the first or appetizer course, often with the pepper, tomato, and eggplant dolmas arranged together. The cabbage and grape leaf dolmas are usually served alone. You could simplify this menu by serving a smaller assortment of the vegetables.

The filling for the dolmas, as well as the stuffed and cooked vegetables themselves, may be made a day ahead, leaving very little to do to complete preparations on the day of your party. If you make the dolmas in advance, keep them in the refrigerator, but take them out about an hour before serving. They should be served at room temperature.

Even though the same filling is used, each stuffed vegetable is cooked separately. The filling takes on a distinct taste in each vegetable, so don't mix the flavors by cooking several kinds together. Also, the vegetables have different cooking times and shouldn't be overcooked or they will lose their shape. Olive oil is essential to the flavor, so don't substitute another salad oil, or butter or margarine, which will solidify when cold.

Dress the salad greens with olive oil and vinegar, then salt and pepper to taste. Greek bakeries and delicatessens often carry the Armenian cracker bread (also called Lavash), but if it isn't available in your area, serve French bread. Have plenty of lemon wedges available for your guests to squeeze on the cabbage and grape leaf dolmas.

DOLMA FILLING

This recipe for dolma filling makes about 10 cups, an ample amount to stuff 12 to 15 *each* of the small tomatoes, small peppers, Oriental eggplant, cabbage leaves, and about 2½ dozen grape leaves—enough for 8 to 12 guests. Omit the mint and dill from the filling used for the cabbage leaves. Short grain rice (such as California Pearl) is best for the filling, but if your market doesn't carry it, use regular long grain rice.

   6 cups boiling water
   2 cups uncooked short grain rice
   1 cup olive oil
   8 large onions, chopped
   ¼ cup pine nuts or slivered almonds
   4 teaspoons salt
   2 large tomatoes, chopped, or 2 cups
      tomato pulp
   2 cups boiling water
   ¼ cup currants or chopped raisins
   1½ teaspoons each pepper and allspice
   2 teaspoons sugar
   1 tablespoon crushed dried mint leaves
      (omit for cabbage dolmas)
   2 teaspoons dill weed (omit for cabbage
      dolmas)

Pour the 6 cups boiling water over rice; cover, and let stand until the water cools to room temperature. Turn rice into a wire strainer and run cold water through it for a few minutes; let the rice drain thoroughly.

(continued)

In a large frying pan, heat olive oil. Add the onions, pine nuts, and salt; stir over medium heat until the onions are golden brown. Add the drained rice and continue to stir until it browns lightly, about 10 more minutes. Reduce heat to low and add tomatoes, the 2 cups boiling water, currants, pepper, allspice, sugar, and the mint and dill, if used. Heat and stir about 5 more minutes, until the rice has absorbed the liquid. Remove from heat and turn onto a platter so the rice will cool quickly. Makes about 10 cups.

STUFFED GREEN PEPPERS
(Biber Dolmasi)

    **12 to 15 small green peppers or halved
       medium-sized peppers**
    Dolma Filling
1½ teaspoons salt
  2 tablespoons olive oil
  ½ cup boiling water

Cut tops off the small green peppers, remove stems, but keep tops with matching peppers; remove seeds. Or cut the medium-sized peppers in half lengthwise through the stem (don't cut out stem end, it helps hold pepper in shape); remove seeds. Fill each pepper about ⅞ full with Dolma Filling. Don't pack stuffing, for the rice expands

while cooking. Put tops back on small peppers or cover top of each pepper half with small piece of foil. Arrange peppers close together in a heavy pan. Sprinkle the salt and olive oil over top. Pour the boiling water down the inside of the pan. Cover and simmer 25 to 30 minutes (add a little more water, if needed; it should be almost cooked away when the vegetables are tender). Cool in the pan.

STUFFED TOMATOES
(Domates Dolmasi)

  **About 15 medium-small tomatoes (ripe,
    but very firm)**
  Dolma Filling
1½ teaspoons salt
  2 tablespoons olive oil
  ½ cup boiling water

Cut off tops of tomatoes, keeping tops with matching tomatoes; remove tomato pulp with a small spoon (this pulp can be used in the stuffing recipe). Stuff tomatoes about ⅞ full without packing. Put tops back on. (It is best to use a rack in the bottom of the cooking pan for these—tomatoes hold their shape better if not resting in the water.) Arrange the tomatoes close together on the rack in the cooking pan. Sprinkle salt and olive oil over the top. Pour boiling water down inside of pan. Cover and simmer until tomatoes are tender, 15 to 20 minutes, adding a little more water if needed. Cool in the pan.

STUFFED EGGPLANT
(Patlican Dolmasi)

Small finger-shaped eggplants are available in markets that sell Italian or Oriental foods. If you can't find them, you can use regular eggplants.

  **About 12 small finger-shaped eggplants or
    2 regular eggplants**
  Dolma Filling
  3 tablespoons olive oil
1½ teaspoons salt
  ½ cup water

Remove stems from the small eggplants, cut in half, and use an apple corer to hollow out centers; if you use the regular large eggplants, cut each in 6 wedges; carefully slit each wedge with a sharp knife from point to within about ½ inch of peel. Spoon Dolma Filling into hollows or openings in eggplants to about ⅞ full; cover ends of the small ones with a small piece of foil, or cover cut edges of the wedges with foil. Arrange close together in a heavy cooking pan. Sprinkle with the olive oil and salt. Pour boiling water down the inside of the pan. Cover pan and simmer until tender, 15 or 20 minutes, adding water if needed. Cool in the pan.

STUFFED CABBAGE
(Lahana Dolmasi)

4 to 5-pound head of cabbage
2 quarts boiling water
3 tablespoons salt
Dolma Filling (without mint or dill added)
2 tablespoons olive oil
½ cup boiling water

Core the cabbage and separate the leaves, being careful not to tear them. You'll need about 2 dozen large leaves, about 5 to 6 inches wide. (If the leaves don't separate easily, put the whole head into the 2 quarts boiling water with salt and separate them after they are cooked.) Cook the leaves in the salted water just until they become pliable. Remove and spread leaves on wire racks to drain.

Working with one leaf at a time, cut out hard portions of leaf and overlap cut sections. Spoon on about 1 tablespoon of the Dolma Filling, fold sides over, then roll up. Pour olive oil into bottom of heavy cooking pan, arrange rolled leaves close together. Place a heatproof plate on top of the rolls. Pour the ½ cup water over plate. Cover pan and simmer for 20 minutes—the water should almost cook away. Cool before removing the plate.

STUFFED GRAPE LEAVES
(Yaprak Dolmasi)

2½ to 3 dozen fresh Thompson Seedless grape
  leaves or 1 jar grape leaves preserved
  in brine
  Boiling salted water (optional)
  Dolma Filling
2 tablespoons olive oil
  Juice of ½ lemon
½ cup water

If you use fresh grape leaves, wash them well in warm water, or you can blanch them quickly in boiling salted water to make them more pliable. The preserved leaves will need to be separated carefully and rinsed in warm water. Lay the leaves on wire racks to drain thoroughly.

To roll, lay each leaf with the stem end toward you and with the veined side (or underside) up. Spoon ½ to 1 tablespoon Dolma Filling in center, near stem. Fold sides over loosely. Start at stem end to roll up. Pour olive oil into the bottom of a heavy cooking pan and arrange the rolls close together in the pan; place a heatproof plate on top to keep them from unrolling. Pour the lemon juice and ½ cup water over the plate. Cover the pan and simmer until the leaves are tender, about 30 minutes—the water should be almost absorbed. Cool in the pan before removing the plate.

BARBECUED LAMB CHOPS

Prepare the lamp chops as the Turks do: Rub the meat on both sides with a cut clove of garlic, brush with olive oil, then sprinkle with crushed marjoram leaves and salt and pepper to taste. Barbecue or broil them in your usual way.

Latin American Fiesta Tray

FIESTA TRAY

CRUSTY BREAD

AVOCADO CREAM

SWEET BRAZILIAN COFFEE

A giant platter of cold meats and vegetable salad, beautifully arranged, is served as a fiesta dish on many occasions throughout Latin America. You'll find this one-dish meal—if you can call the largest platter or tray you own a "dish"—perfect as a party meal in hot weather, when it's too warm to cook. The little cooking that's required is done ahead—you can do it in the cool of the evenings, several days before. Only the arranging is a last-minute job, and you can even do that well before guests arrive if your refrigerator is large enough to hold the tray. It takes just a few minutes to make the Avocado Cream in a blender.

Use your imagination in arranging the foods on the tray, placing them symmetrically with an eye to color contrast. Garnish with pimiento strips, and have the capers and cheese ready to sprinkle over the salads just before serving.

FIESTA TRAY

Make the dressing several days before the party; marinate vegetables in it for two to three days.

- **1 large head cauliflower**
- **3 cups diced carrots**
- **3 cups fresh or thawed frozen peas**
- **3 cups diced green beans**
- **3 cups diced potatoes**
  Salad Dressing (recipe follows)
- **4 or more eggs**
- **2 heads Boston lettuce**
- **4 pounds meat—choose at least 5 of these:**
  sliced cooked chicken or turkey, salami, bologna, mortadella, corned beef, tongue, roast pork, roast beef, ham, or any summer sausage
  About 1 pint each pitted ripe olives and gherkins
- **1 can (4 oz.) pimientos, cut in strips**
- **¼ cup capers**
- **½ pound queso fresco or any mild cheese (even cream cheese or ricotta), shredded or chopped**

Cook each vegetable separately. Break cauliflower into small pieces and cook in salted water until barely tender; drain. Cook carrots, peas, beans, and potatoes separately in salted water; do not overcook. Drain and cool vegetables; combine. Pour dressing over and marinate two to three days, carefully turning two or three times so the flavors will mingle.

The day before serving, hard cook the eggs, wash and crisp lettuce, and slice the cold meats. When you are ready to arrange tray, make nests of the lettuce; pack vegetable mixture into custard cups and unmold on lettuce. Then arrange the rest of the ingredients on the tray. Garnish with pimiento strips; sprinkle capers and cheese over the salads just before serving. Serves 12 or more.

Salad Dressing. Combine 1 cup olive oil, 1 cup vinegar, 2 teaspoons salt, 1 teaspoon freshly ground black pepper, ¼ cup minced parsley, 1 teaspoon dry mustard, and ½ cup canned consommé. Mix well.

AVOCADO CREAM

This simple dessert requires very ripe avocados, and it should be made only an hour or so before it is to be served.

2 large ripe avocados, peeled, seeded, and diced
5 tablespoons powdered sugar
2 to 3 tablespoons lemon or lime juice

Whirl diced avocado in a blender along with the powdered sugar and lemon or lime juice to taste. If you prefer, press the avocado through a wire strainer and blend in the sugar and citrus juice.

Spoon the avocado cream into individual serving dishes and chill about 1 hour. Makes 6 servings.

SWEET BRAZILIAN COFFEE

The Brazilians are fond of after-dinner coffee, usually served in the living room for sipping in a leisurely fashion. To make it the way they do, add a little strong, hot coffee to a demitasse cup nearly half full of sugar, then fill with warm milk.

German Rouladen Buffet

CUCUMBER AND LETTUCE SALAD

BUTTERED PUMPERNICKEL

BEEF ROULADEN WITH MUSHROOM SAUCE

POTATO PARMESAN SOUFFLE

FUDGE TORTE A LA MODE   RASPBERRY SAUCE

Stuffed beef rolls with mushroom sauce, potato soufflé, sliced cucumber salad, and pumpernickel make handsome buffet fare. The beef rolls take time to prepare, but they are not difficult. The other dishes go together readily.

Bake and freeze the brownie-style torte whenever you like. It keeps well from 1 to 2 months. Make the raspberry sauce ahead, too; it keeps 2 to 3 days when refrigerated. Plan to assemble the meat rolls, ready for baking, a day ahead. (You can freeze them, and you can freeze the sauce prepared without the mushrooms; add the mushrooms to the sauce when you reheat it.) The soufflé goes together fast; you can have everything ready and simply fold in the egg whites at the last minute. The rouladen and soufflé bake at the same oven temperature.

Dress a sliced cucumber and lettuce salad with an oil and vinegar dressing, sweetened with a touch of sugar. Offer hot slices of buttered pumpernickel.

BEEF ROULADEN

A small sirloin tip roast, sliced ¼ inch thick, provides excellent tender steaks for these compact stuffed meat rolls. Ask your meatman to slice a roast for you.

   3-pound sirloin tip roast, sliced ¼-inch thick
   2 large onions, finely chopped
  10 tablespoons butter or margarine
1½ pounds mushrooms
   ¾ pound cooked ham, sliced ⅜ inch thick
   ¾ cup grated Parmesan cheese
   1 cup dry red wine
   1 cup regular-strength beef broth
   1 teaspoon salt
     Freshly ground pepper
   2 tablespoons each cornstarch and cold water
   2 tablespoons finely chopped parsley

Cut away fat from each meat slice. Place 1 slice at a time between pieces of waxed paper and pound lightly with the smooth side of a wooden mallet until meat is about 1/16 inch thick. Then cut each pounded piece into rectangles about 4 by 6 inches.

In a large frying pan, sauté onions in 2 tablespoons of the butter until limp; transfer onions to a bowl. Finely chop half the mushrooms (save the smallest ones for the sauce) and sauté the chopped mushrooms in 2 tablespoons of butter; add to the onions. Cut ham into julienne strips about ½ inch long and ⅛ inch wide and add to stuffing mixture with cheese; mix lightly.

Place 1 heaping tablespoon filling on each meat rectangle; fold the long sides of the meat over the filling about ½ inch on each side and roll up the meat; secure with a toothpick. Repeat until all the meat rolls are filled. Using 2 large frying pans, melt 2 tabespoons butter in each pan and brown meat rolls, turning to brown all sides. Pour in wine and broth and season with salt and pepper. Cover and simmer gently for 10 to 15 minutes, or until beef is fork tender. Remove toothpicks from meat rolls and transfer to an ovenproof serving dish.

Combine wine juices in a single frying pan and bring to a boil. Stir in cornstarch blended with the water, and cook, stirring, until thickened. In the other frying pan over medium heat, sauté the remaining whole mushrooms (if larger than bite size, slice them) in 2 tablespoons butter for about 5 minutes or until tender, and add to the meat sauce. Pour the mushroom sauce over the meat rolls. If made in advance, let cool, then cover and refrigerate.

Heat, covered, in 375° oven for 20 minutes (45 to 50 minutes, or until heated through, if refrigerated). Sprinkle with parsley before serving. Makes about 3 dozen meat rolls. Makes about 10 servings.

POTATO PARMESAN SOUFFLE

Instant mashed potatoes speed the making of this soufflé, which is impressive to serve and particularly good with the meat rolls. If you need to hold the soufflé a few minutes before serving, leave it in the oven with the heat turned off.

8 servings instant mashed potatoes,
    prepared as package directs
6 eggs, separated
¾ cup shredded Parmesan cheese
½ teaspoon each salt and cream of tartar

Prepare instant mashed potatoes according to package directions for 8 servings. While still hot, beat in egg yolks, one at a time, and mix in cheese. (At this point, you can cover and let stand at room temperature a few hours.) About 1 hour before serving time, beat egg whites until foamy, add salt and cream of tartar, and beat until soft peaks form. Fold beaten whites into potato mixture. Spoon into two buttered 2-quart soufflé dishes or a 4-quart soufflé dish (or use baking dishes with straight sides).

Bake in a 375° oven allowing 45 minutes for small soufflés or 1 hour for a large soufflé. Makes 8 to 10 servings.

FUDGE TORTE A LA MODE

This delectably rich brownie recipe makes a double batch, as it is just as easy to make two pies as one. They freeze well if you want to serve them on separate occasions. Or you can cut one pie into squares for cooky bars.

4 ounces unsweetened chocolate
1 cup (½ lb.) butter or margarine
4 eggs
2 cups sugar
2 teaspoons vanilla
1 cup unsifted regular all-purpose flour
⅛ teaspoon salt
1 cup chopped macadamia nuts or walnuts
1 package (10 oz.) frozen raspberries
    Vanilla ice cream
    Unsweetened chocolate curls

Melt chocolate and butter in the top of a double boiler placed over simmering water. Set aside and let cool. Beat eggs until thick and lemon-colored and gradually beat in sugar, 1 tablespoon at a time, beating until very thick. Beat in vanilla. Mix in the melted chocolate and butter mixture and the flour and salt, mixing just until blended. Fold in chopped nuts. Turn into two buttered 9-inch pie pans. Bake in a 325° oven for 30 to 35 minutes, or until the top springs back when lightly touched. Let cool. Package and freeze, if desired. Before serving, let thaw completely at room temperature. Purée thawed raspberries and syrup in a blender, then pour through a wire strainer to remove seeds. Pour into a pitcher.

To serve each torte, top with balls of ice cream, allowing about 1 quart of ice cream for each pie. Then sprinkle with chocolate curls, made by peeling ½ bar of unsweetened chocolate with a vegetable peeler. At the table, pour the raspberry sauce over the torte, and cut into wedges to serve. Each pie makes 8 servings.

Holiday Entertaining

The mention of holiday menus immediately brings to mind the Thanksgiving feast and the busy end-of-the-year holiday season. These are important, of course, and often call for special party menus. But the year is filled with many holidays, and any one of them offers a good theme for entertaining or for treating the family to a special meal.

Many of the holiday menus included here can be cooperative affairs, with the work load shared with friends or relatives. Many are so simple that there really is no work load for anyone.

The traditional holidays frequently feature a traditional menu, but with unusual and interesting variations. A number of the meals are presented buffet style to make service easy on the hostess. There are picnics and barbecues for the summer holidays, including some that can be converted to relaxed meals at home if the weather should be uncertain.

Valentine's Day Luncheon

SWISS CHEESE SOUFFLE
INDIVIDUAL FRUIT SALADS   **PARKER HOUSE ROLLS**
MARASCHINO CHERRY ICE CREAM
FROSTED SUGAR COOKY VALENTINES
HOT CHOCOLATE   COFFEE

You may want to make this a special Valentine luncheon for children, but the foods are favorites of adults, too.

Make the ice cream a day ahead, too. Whip up the soufflé and arrange and chill the salads just before the luncheon. For the salad, combine canned mandarin oranges, thawed frozen pineapple chunks, sliced bananas, sliced Winesap apples, and seedless grapes; arrange on lettuce.

SWISS CHEESE SOUFFLE

This relatively foolproof soufflé utilizes instant-type flour for a quick, smooth cream sauce base.

**3 tablespoons each butter and instant-type
     all-purpose flour
1 cup milk
½ teaspoon salt
¼ teaspoon dry mustard
4 egg yolks
1 cup shredded Swiss cheese
6 egg whites
⅛ teaspoon each salt and cream of tartar**

Combine in a small saucepan the butter, flour, milk, ½ teaspoon salt, and dry mustard. Stirring constantly, cook until thickened. Remove from heat and stir in egg yolks and cheese.

Beat egg whites until foamy; add the ⅛ teaspoon salt and the cream of tartar, and beat until whites hold soft peaks. Stir about a fourth of the beaten egg whites into the sauce, then fold in the remaining egg whites. Turn into a buttered 2-quart soufflé dish or other straight-sided baking dish. Bake in a 375° oven for 25 to 30 minutes. Serve immediately. Serves 6.

MARASCHINO CHERRY ICE CREAM

**½ cup maraschino cherries
2 tablespoons maraschino syrup
1 quart vanilla ice cream
2 tablespoons finely chopped walnuts**

Purée cherries and syrup in a blender. Let ice cream soften slightly, then stir in puréed cherries and walnuts. Return to the freezer and freeze until firm. Serves 6.

FROSTED SUGAR COOKY VALENTINES

Cut the large heart-shaped cookies from your favorite sugar cooky dough and bake a day ahead. Let older children decorate them with frosting from a pressurized can that comes with different tube tips. Cookies decorated with guests' names can be used as place cards.

Father's Day Dinner

MIXED LETTUCE GREENS
BLUE ROGUE DRESSING
MARINATED LONDON BROIL
LONG GRAIN AND WILD RICE
PETITE PEAS WITH BUTTER-SAUTEED ONIONS
WHIPPED CREAM CAKE WITH MACADAMIAS AND PINEAPPLE

A steak dinner has unfailing popularity with fathers. This menu features a flank steak that marinates overnight in a wine-herb mixture and a zestful blue cheese dressing that can be made ahead.

Cook a packaged long grain and wild rice mixture to go with the steak. Lightly brown tiny canned onions in butter and mix with cooked frozen petite peas. For dessert, decorate a whipped-cream-frosted cake (your own recipe or a bakery one) with macadamia nuts, and serve with fresh pineapple.

BLUE ROGUE DRESSING

1 cup salad oil
3 tablespoons red wine vinegar
1 teaspoon salt
¼ teaspoon each pepper and paprika
1 clove garlic, minced
½ teaspoon celery salt
1 tablespoon each lemon juice and
    Worcestershire
½ cup (4 oz.) crumbled blue cheese

Mix salad oil, vinegar, salt, pepper, paprika, garlic, celery salt, lemon juice, and Worcestershire. Gradually mix this into the blue cheese. Chill, covered, for at least 8 hours to mellow flavors. Makes 1¾ cups; allow 1 tablespoon for each cup of salad greens.

MARINATED LONDON BROIL

⅔ cup dry red wine
⅓ cup olive oil or salad oil
1 tablespoon soy sauce
⅛ teaspoon each crumbled oregano,
    crumbled marjoram, and pepper
1¼ to 1¾-pound flank steak

Mix the wine, oil, soy sauce, oregano, marjoram, and pepper. Place steak in a deep bowl and pour marinade over it. Cover and chill at least 12 to 18 hours, turning meat once or twice.

Drain meat and broil 4 inches from heat for about 5 minutes on each side. Make thin slices across the grain and diagonal to the top surface of the steak; save the juices. Serve the steak with cooked rice mixed lightly with the meat juices. Makes 4 to 6 servings.

WHIPPED CREAM CAKE WITH MACADAMIAS AND PINEAPPLE

On a whipped-cream-frosted layer cake (white or yellow cake or sponge cake), make a border around top with 4 to 6 tablespoons minced macadamias. Garnish with a few whole nuts.

Split a medium-sized pineapple vertically, leaves and all. Cut fruit from shell and thinly slice or chop. Return to one of the half shells with juices. Spoon fruit and juices over each piece of cake. Makes 8 to 10 servings.

Tea for Mother's Day

TANGY CHEESE WAFERS

CARROT TEA BREAD SANDWICHES   **PECAN BARS**

MELON BALLS WITH MINT SPRIGS

TEAS OF YOUR CHOICE   **COFFEE (OPTIONAL)**

Finger foods make this an easy-to-serve menu for a Mother's Day tea party. Two or three teen-age girls might want to share in presenting the tea to honor their mothers. The foods are simple to prepare and can be done ahead.

You may want to serve several kinds of tea—perhaps an oolong, an orange and spice blend, and a minted tea.

To prepare the baked foods ahead, chill dough for the cheese wafers; slice and bake shortly before serving. Bake the bread a day ahead (or it can be baked and frozen for up to two weeks); the next day slice it, prepare the sandwiches, and wrap them in plastic film. The cookies can be baked a day or two in advance, cut, and wrapped until serving.

Arrange the melon balls in a bowl, chill, and garnish with mint. Use colorful wooden picks to spear them.

TANGY CHEESE WAFERS

½ cup (¼ lb.) soft butter or margarine
1 jar (5 oz.) sharp process cheese spread
1 cup unsifted regular all-purpose flour
    Dash each cayenne and nutmeg
    Poppy seed, sesame seed, or paprika

Cream butter with cheese spread until fluffy. Blend in flour, cayenne, and nutmeg. Shape into two 8-inch rolls, 1¼ inches in diameter; wrap in waxed paper or plastic film and chill for several hours or overnight until firm.

Slice about ⅛ inch thick. Sprinkle with poppy seed, sesame seed, or paprika. Bake on un-greased baking sheets in a 400° oven for 6 to 8 minutes or until edges brown lightly. Cool on wire racks. Makes 8 to 10 dozen.

CARROT TEA BREAD SANDWICHES

2⅓ cups unsifted all-purpose flour
1½ cups sugar
¾ teaspoon salt
1½ teaspoons baking powder
1 teaspoon cinnamon
¾ cup finely chopped pecans or walnuts
¼ cup milk
1 cup salad oil
1 teaspoon vanilla
3 eggs, slightly beaten
1½ cups finely shredded carrots (about 4
medium-sized carrots)
Whipped cream cheese

Sift flour, sugar, salt, baking powder, and cinnamon into a bowl (if using instant-type flour, mix ingredients well); stir in nuts. Mix together milk, oil, vanilla, eggs, and carrots. Add to flour mixture and stir just until combined. Spread in a greased 5¼ by 9¼-inch loaf pan. Bake in a 325° oven about 1 hour and 20 minutes or until bread is well browned and tests done in center. Cool and let stand overnight. Slice thinly; spread with whipped cream cheese, and cut into small sandwiches.

PECAN BARS

You'll need two 9-inch round cakepans with removable bottoms to make these cookies.

2 cups cake flour, sifted before measuring
1 tablespoon sugar
1 teaspoon salt
½ cup (¼ lb.) firm butter
About 6 tablespoons cold water
Pecan Filling (recipe follows)

Sift cake flour with sugar and salt into a bowl. Cut in butter until mixture resembles fine crumbs. Stir in water, one tablespoon at a time, until mixture clings together.

Divide into two equal parts. Roll each out to a circle a little larger than a 9-inch pan bottom. Place in bottom of pan, turning about ½ inch of dough up around edge; prick bottom with fork. Bake in a 450° oven for 10 to 12 minutes or until lightly browned. Remove pans to rack and cool slightly.

Spread pastry rounds with cooled Pecan Filling, leaving a 1-inch margin around edge. Bake in a 350° oven about 15 minutes or until mixture is bubbly and lightly browned. Let cool in pans for about 5 minutes, then remove. When filling is almost firm (about 15 minutes), cut to serve; if it becomes too hard to cut, return to oven for several minutes to soften. Trim off curved edges and cut square center into small bars, or cut outer two inches in bars and center in wedges. Makes about 4 dozen small cookies.

Pecan Filling. Heat ½ cup (¼ lb.) butter, 1½ cups unsifted powdered sugar, and ¼ cup honey until mixture boils. Remove from heat and let cool 15 minutes. Stir in 1½ cups chopped pecans.

Easter Brunch Buffet

ORANGE BASKETS WITH FRUIT
COLORED EGGS IN THE SHELL
SLICED WHITE BREAD   BUTTER
ROLLED HAM, SWISS CHEESE, AND THURINGER SAUSAGE
MARBLE POUND CAKE
COFFEE   HOT CHOCOLATE

After the traditional Easter morning egg hunt, a buffet-style brunch is a pleasant way to serve family and guests. The meal suits a range of ages and a flexible number of diners, and since only the beverages are hot it can be set up well ahead of time.

Table decorations are built right into the menu —dyed Easter eggs in a basket, pound cake baked in a fancy mold, and colorful orange-shell fruit baskets. Bake the cake a day in advance; or bake it and freeze it a week or more ahead. You can also make the orange baskets a day ahead, then mix in the other fruits just before serving.

Easter morning, arrange sliced boiled ham, cheese, and sausage on a large board. Set out the bread and cake and fill the orange baskets. Arrange all on a buffet, and time the beverages to be hot when everyone is ready to eat.

ORANGE BASKETS WITH FRUIT

Cut 4 medium-sized oranges in half, zigzag fashion; remove fruit with a grapefruit knife and cut into sections, discarding white membrane. Mix orange segments, 1 cup hulled strawberries, and 2 sliced bananas; pile into the orange shells. Cover and chill. Serves 8.

MARBLE POUND CAKE

A fancy bundt (fluted tube) pan will make an especially festive-looking cake, but you can use an ordinary 10-inch tube pan. Dust the cake with powdered sugar, if you wish.

    2 ounces unsweetened chocolate
    ⅓ cup hot water
    ¼ teaspoon soda
    6 eggs, separated
    1 cup (½ lb.) butter or margarine
    2 cups sugar
    2 teaspoons grated orange peel
 3¾ cups regular all-purpose flour
    3 teaspoons baking powder
    ¼ teaspoon salt
    1 cup milk

Melt chocolate in the top of a double boiler over simmering water; stir in the water and soda, then cool. Beat egg whites until they hold firm but moist peaks; set aside. Cream the butter and sugar together thoroughly. Beat in egg yolks and orange peel.

Sift flour, measure, then sift with baking powder and salt. Alternately add flour and milk to creamed mixture, mixing until blended after each addition. Fold in egg whites. Stir 2 cups of the batter into chocolate mixture. In a greased and flour-dusted tube pan, alternate the dark and light batters.

Bake in a 325° oven for about 1 hour 10 minutes, or until a toothpick inserted in cake comes out clean. Cool 15 minutes, remove from pan, and cool thoroughly. Makes 12 to 16 servings.

Easter Dinner

HAM IN A CRUST

FRESH PEAS WITH THYME

YAMS WITH ORANGE SAUCE

PINEAPPLE-ONION SALAD

BUTTER ROLLS   CURRANT JELLY

CINNAMON-CHOCOLATE TORTE

Ham baked in a seasoned crust headlines this Easter dinner menu designed for six. Much of the dinner can be prepared in advance, so it is surprisingly easy to serve.

You start the meal the day before Easter with the preparation of the gelatin salad and the Cinnamon-Chocolate Torte. On Easter morning, wash, cook, and peel the yams early in the day; reserve, covered, until about 30 minutes before dinner; then slice, add seasonings, and reheat in the oven with the ham. About 1½ hours before dinner, prepare the seasoned crust, enclose the ham in it, and bake. Shortly before serving, cook and season the peas, unmold and garnish the salads, and heat the ready-made rolls in the oven.

HAM IN A CRUST

  2 cups biscuit mix
  1 teaspoon dry mustard
½ teaspoon dry basil
    About ⅔ cup milk
  5-pound canned boneless ham (with
    excess gelatin removed)

Combine biscuit mix with mustard and basil. Add ⅔ cup milk, and mix as directed on the package for biscuits. Roll out dough on a lightly floured board into a rectangle about 14 by 22 inches. Place ham in the center of the dough; fold up the long ends over the ham, overlapping them. Carefully turn the ham over; tuck in dough ends as though wrapping a package, smoothing out surface with your hands. If you wish, cut a design in the top. Brush entire crust with milk; place on a buttered cooky sheet.

Bake in a 325° oven for 50 or 60 minutes or until crust is golden brown. Allow crust to cool slightly before slicing. (Use a knife with serrated blade for best results.) Makes 12 servings.

FRESH PEAS WITH THYME

  3 pounds fresh peas, shelled, or 2 packages
    (10 oz. each) frozen peas
  Salted water
  3 tablespoons melted butter
½ teaspoon dried thyme
  Butter

Cook peas in the salted water until tender; drain. Season with the 3 tablespoons butter and thyme. Spoon into a serving bowl and top with a slice of butter. Makes 6 servings.

YAMS WITH ORANGE SAUCE

  3 pounds yams, cooked and peeled, or
    2 cans (1 lb. 13 oz. each) yams, drained
  2 tablespoons brown sugar
½ teaspoon grated orange peel
  3 tablespoons melted butter

Slice yams in diagonal slices about 1 inch thick. Put in a shallow casserole in a single layer. Sprinkle with a mixture of the brown sugar and grated orange peel; pour melted butter evenly over the top. Cover with a lid or foil and place in a 325° oven for about 20 minutes or until heated through. (Allow 10 minutes longer if made ahead and refrigerated.) Remove cover and serve. Makes 6 servings.

PINEAPPLE-ONION SALAD

1 envelope unflavored gelatin
½ cup pineapple juice (or syrup from canned pineapple tidbits)
1½ cups boiling water
1 tablespoon lemon juice
½ cup sugar
1 can (about 14 oz.) pineapple tidbits, drained
½ can (3¼ oz.) capers, drained
1 can (3½ oz.) tiny pickled onions, drained
3 tablespoons chopped pimiento
Lettuce
Mayonnaise

Dissolve gelatin in pineapple juice; add boiling water, lemon juice, and sugar. Allow to set until thickened, but still runny, Stir in pineapple tidbits, capers, pickled onions, and pimiento. Pour mixture into either 6 individual molds or a 1-quart mold. Just before serving, unmold on crisp lettuce and garnish with mayonnaise. Makes 6 servings.

CINNAMON-CHOCOLATE TORTE

This make-ahead party torte has an intriguing cinnamon spiciness throughout its many layers.

Cinnamon Meringue (recipe follows)
1 package (6 oz.) semisweet chocolate pieces
2 egg yolks
¼ cup water
1 cup (½ pint) whipping cream
¼ cup sugar
¼ teaspoon cinnamon
½ cup whipping cream (optional)
8 walnut halves (optional)

Prepare meringue shell first (see below). For the filling, melt chocolate pieces in a pan over hot water. While hot, spread 2 tablespoons chocolate over bottom of meringue shell. Into remaining warm chocolate beat egg yolks and water. Chill.

Combine the 1 cup cream with sugar and cinnamon and whip until stiff. Spread half the cream over the chocolate-covered meringue. Fold remaining cream into chocolate mixture and spread on top. Chill several hours or overnight. If you wish, garnish with remaining ½ cup cream, whipped, and walnuts. Makes 8 servings.

Cinnamon Meringue. Beat 3 egg whites with ¼ teaspoon salt and ½ teaspoon white vinegar until soft peaks form. Mix ¼ teaspoon cinnamon into ½ cup sugar and gradually add to egg whites, beating until stiff. Place buttered waxed paper on a baking sheet. Spread meringue on paper, forming a shell 18 inches across with sides 1¾ inches high and bottom ½ inch thick. Bake in a 300° oven 1 hour; turn off heat and keep in oven with door closed 1 hour longer. Peel off paper. Cool.

Greek Easter Barbecue

ATHENIAN GREEN SALAD

BARBECUED BUTTERFLIED LAMB   **RICE PILAF**

GREENS PIE (SPANAKOPITA)   **BREAD RING (KOULOURA)**

RED HARD-COOKED EGGS

GREEK PASTRIES   **ORANGES**

RETSINA OR DRY RED WINE   **TURKISH COFFEE**

Greek families often celebrate Easter out-of-doors, where they can stage such traditional activities as dancing, cracking red-dyed eggs, and partaking of the grand feast. Adapt their foods and customs as you wish for your own dinner. The dishes on this barbecue menu are uniquely Greek yet delicately seasoned to appeal to all tastes and ages.

Much of the menu can be prepared ahead. You'll have to visit a delicatessen or Greek market to buy several ingredients that make the picnic authentic: a goat cheese called *feta*, thin *fila* pastry, Greek-style olives, and a doughnut-shaped bread called *kouloura* (or substitute a sweet French bread).

You can bake and freeze the specially-shaped pastries in advance and prepare the vegetables a day ahead. Marinate the lamb overnight. Just for fun, dye hard-cooked eggs a brilliant red, allowing at least one per person. Children will enjoy the game of tapping eggs together, trying to crack friends' eggs without cracking their own.

Cook the pilaf just before you leave and pack it in an insulated bag. Mix the salad and brew the coffee at the picnic site. Bring a jar or can of instant Turkish-style coffee and a Turkish coffee pot or other small pot. Follow package directions for amounts, and cook over the barbecue fire. Offer a resinated red wine, if you like; otherwise a light dry red wine is appropriate.

ATHENIAN GREEN SALAD

Tear the greens and mix the dressing at home, then complete this handsome salad when you reach the picnic site.

> 1 head each iceberg lettuce, butter lettuce,
>   and romaine
>   Salad Dressing (recipe follows)
> 1 avocado, peeled and sliced
> 2 tomatoes, cut into wedges
> ¼ pound feta cheese
> 2 dozen Greek-style olives or pitted
>   ripe olives
> 1 can (2 oz.) anchovy fillets, drained

Wash and dry the greens and tear into bite-sized pieces. Place in a plastic bag and chill. To serve, pile into a large salad bowl and pour dressing over; mix thoroughly. Arrange avocado slices and tomato wedges on top. Crumble the cheese and scatter the olives and anchovy fillets over top. Makes 12 servings.

Salad Dressing. Pour into a jar ¾ cup olive oil, ¼ cup red wine vinegar, ½ teaspoon *each* salt and garlic salt, and freshly ground pepper. Cover and shake well. Chill. Makes 1 cup.

(continued)

BARBECUED BUTTERFLIED LAMB

Have your meatman bone and butterfly the legs of lamb. Squeeze lemons over the meat at serving time for extra zest.

**2 legs of lamb (each 5 to 6 lbs.), boned
    and butterflied
6 cloves garlic, slivered
½ cup each lemon juice and olive oil
2 teaspoons salt
½ teaspoon pepper
1 tablespoon dried oregano
3 lemons
    Oregano**

Lay meat out flat and insert garlic into both sides. Place each piece of meat in a large shallow pan. Mix the lemon juice, olive oil, salt, pepper, and 1 tablespoon oregano; pour evenly over the meat. Turn meat to coat both sides, cover and refrigerate overnight.

Barbecue over medium low coals, allowing about 20 minutes to brown one side; turn to brown other side, cooking about 20 minutes more for medium rare meat. Place on a large carving board and reshape into two roasts. Cut lemons in half, zigzag fashion, sprinkle with oregano, and place around roasts. Slice to serve. Makes 12 to 14 servings, with some left over.

RICE PILAF

**7½ cups water
1 tablespoon each salt and salad oil
3 cups uncooked long grain rice
1 cup golden raisins
1 cup butter**

Bring water to a boil in a large pan. Add salt, salad oil, and rice; cover and simmer 25 minutes, or until rice is barely tender; remove from heat. Mix in raisins with a fork. Heat butter until it bubbles and starts to brown, then pour over rice and stir with a fork. Cover 10 minutes. Carry to picnic in insulated container. Serves 12 to 14.

GREENS PIE
(Spanakopita)

These pastry squares are excellent warm or chilled. You need tissue-thin sheets of dough, called fila, available in 1-pound packages from Greek markets and many delicatessens.

**1 bunch each Swiss chard, spinach, chicory
    (curly endive), and parsley
  About 6 green onions
¼ cup olive oil
1 teaspoon salt
½ teaspoon pepper
4 eggs, beaten
¾ pound feta cheese, crumbled
10 sheets fila (about 12 by 16 inches each)
½ cup butter, melted
    Ground cinnamon**

Wash and finely chop all the greens; pat dry with paper towels. Mix in the olive oil, salt, pepper, eggs, and cheese.

Lay out fila and cover with plastic film to keep from drying out. With a pastry brush, lightly butter 5 sheets fila, one at a time, and layer one on top of another in a buttered 9 by 13-inch baking pan. Place the greens mixture over the dough and smooth the top. Sprinkle lightly with cinnamon. Fold any overhanging fila back over the greens. Arrange 5 more buttered sheets of fila, cut to fit top of pan, one at a time on top.

Cut squares through the top layers only, making three lengthwise and five crosswise cuts. Bake in a 400° oven for 1 hour; cover with foil if crust browns ahead of time. Finishing cutting into squares and remove to a wire rack so bottom layers of fila stay crisp. Serve at room temperature. Makes 24 squares.

EASTER SHORTBREAD
(Koulourakia)

This traditional Greek Easter cooky with toasted sesame seed topping resembles shortbread.

**½ cup each butter and sugar
3 egg yolks
¼ cup half-and-half (light cream)
2¼ cups regular all-purpose flour
1 teaspoon baking powder
¼ teaspoon salt
    Sesame seed**

Cream butter and sugar until light and fluffy. Beat in two of the egg yolks, one at a time. Mix in 3 tablespoons of the half-and-half. Sift flour, measure, then sift again with baking powder and salt. Add to the creamed mixture and stir until well blended. Chill thoroughly.

Pinch off ¾-inch balls of dough and roll each with lightly floured hands into an 8-inch-long strand. Form each into a pretzel shape and place on a greased baking sheet.

Beat remaining egg yolk with remaining 1 tablespoon half-and-half and brush on tops of the cookies. Sprinkle lightly with sesame seed. Bake in a 350° oven 20 to 25 minutes, or until nicely browned. Makes about 30.

SUGAR-COATED BUTTER CAKES
(Kourabiedes)

To prepare nuts for these sugary cookies, grind almonds finely in blender; toast in a 350° oven about 7 minutes, or until light brown.

  1 pound sweet (unsalted) butter
¼ cup powdered sugar
  2 egg yolks
  2 tablespoons Cognac or Brandy, or
     1 teaspoon vanilla
  1 cup toasted ground almonds
4¼ cups regular all-purpose flour
  1 teaspoon baking powder
    Whole cloves for garnish (optional)
    About 1 pound (1 package) powdered
     sugar

Cream butter until light and fluffy. Mix in the ¼ cup sugar and egg yolks, blending well. Add Cognac or vanilla. Mix in almonds. Sift flour, measure, and sift again with baking powder. Gradually add to creamed mixture until smooth.

Pinch off pieces of dough the size of a walnut and shape into crescents or flatten into rounds. Place on an ungreased baking sheet. If you wish, insert a whole clove in center of each round. Bake in a 325° oven 30 minutes, or until very lightly browned.

Let cool in pan on rack for 5 minutes. Sift a ⅛-inch-thick layer of powdered sugar over waxed paper and transfer cookies to it. Sift more sugar over the top to cover. Let stand until cool, then store in a lightly covered can. Makes about 5 dozen.

ALMOND CAKE
(Amigthalopeta)

Hot lemon syrup soaks into this tender, light nut sponge cake, lacing it with tangy flavor.

  6 eggs, separated
  1 cup sugar
½ cup regular all-purpose flour
  1 teaspoon baking powder
¼ teaspoon almond extract
  2 cups very finely ground blanched almonds
⅛ teaspoon each salt and cream of tartar
  1 teaspoon grated lemon peel
    Lemon Syrup (recipe follows)

Beat the egg yolks until light; gradually beat in ½ cup of the sugar, beating until thick and lemon-colored. Sift flour, measure, then sift again with baking powder. Stir into yolk mixture. Add almond extract and half of the almonds, and mix just until well distributed.

Beat egg whites until foamy, add salt and cream of tartar, and beat until whites hold soft peaks. Beat in remaining ½ cup sugar, a tablespoon at a time. Fold in lemon peel and remaining almonds. Add a fourth of the white mixture to yolk mixture and mix until blended. Gently fold yolk mixture into remaining white mixture. Turn into a buttered 9 by 13-inch baking pan. Bake in a 350° oven for 30 minutes, or until top springs back when touched lightly.

Cool on a rack 10 minutes. Cut into diamond-shaped pieces (make five lengthwise cuts, then cut diagonally 1¼ inches apart). Pour hot Lemon Syrup over, and let cool. Cover and hold at room temperature until serving time. Makes about 30 pieces.

Lemon Syrup. Combine in a small pan ¾ cup sugar, 3 tablespoons lemon juice, and ¼ cup water. Bring to a boil and cook just until sugar is dissolved.

Memorial Day Picnic

SKIRT STEAKS TERIYAKI

SNOW PEA SALAD WITH SESAME DRESSING

HOT BUTTERED FRENCH BREAD

CRUNCH-TOP OATMEAL CAKE   FRESH FRUIT

This barbecue picnic can take place either at home or away without a change in the menu. If you plan to barbecue the pinwheel-shaped steaks away from home, carry them in their soy marinade in a covered container.

Keep the salad cool, and add the dressing just before you serve it. Heat the bread, wrapped in heavy foil, on the grill while the steaks cook.

SKIRT STEAKS TERIYAKI

1 teaspoon unseasoned meat tenderizer
6 to 8 skirt steak pinwheels
¼ cup each Sherry and soy sauce
¼ teaspoon each ground ginger and garlic
    powder
Dash pepper

Rub tenderizer into both sides of each steak; place in a shallow container that can be tightly covered. Combine Sherry, soy sauce, ginger, garlic powder, and pepper; pour over meat. Cover and chill for several hours or overnight; turn once or more, if possible. Barbecue for 6 to 8 minutes on each side, or until steaks are well browned. Makes 6 to 8 servings.

SNOW PEA SALAD WITH SESAME DRESSING

1 package (7 oz.) frozen Chinese (edible
    pod) peas
Boiling salted water
½ head cauliflower, separated into bite-sized
    clusters (about 2 cups)
1 can (5 oz.) water chestnuts, drained and
    sliced
1 tablespoon chopped pimiento
Sesame Seed Dressing (recipe follows)

Cook peas in a small amount of boiling salted water until barely tender, about 1 minute after water boils again; drain. Cook cauliflower clusters in boiling salted water until tender but still crisp, about 3 minutes after water boils again; drain. Combine peas and cauliflower with water chestnuts and pimiento; cover and chill. Just before serving, mix with about 3 tablespoons dressing. Makes 4 to 6 servings.

Sesame Seed Dressing. Place 2 tablespoons sesame seed in a shallow pan in a 350° oven for 5 to 8 minutes or until golden brown; cool. In a jar combine ⅓ cup salad oil, 1 tablespoon *each* lemon juice, vinegar, and sugar, a half clove garlic, minced or mashed, ½ teaspoon salt, and the toasted sesame seed. Cover and chill. Shake well before using.

CRUNCH-TOP OATMEAL CAKE

1¼ cups boiling water
  1 cup quick-cooking rolled oats
½ cup (¼ lb.) soft butter or margarine
  1 teaspoon vanilla
  1 cup each firmly packed brown sugar and
     granulated sugar
  2 eggs
1⅓ cups unsifted all-purpose flour
  1 teaspoon each soda, cinnamon, and
     nutmeg
½ teaspoon salt
  Coconut Topping (recipe follows)

Pour water over rolled oats; mix well, and let cool slightly. Cream butter with vanilla and sugars until fluffy. Beat in eggs, one at a time, until mixture is light-colored. Stir in rolled oat mixture. Sift together the flour, soda, cinnamon, nutmeg, and salt (if using instant-type flour, mix together well); stir into butter mixture until well blended.

Spread in a greased 9 by 13-inch pan. Bake in a 350° oven for about 30 minutes or until top is golden brown and cake tests done when a thin wooden skewer is inserted; cool slightly in pan. Spread with Coconut Topping; place pan about 6 inches from broiler unit and broil until bubbly and golden, 3 to 5 minutes.

Coconut Topping. Cream 6 tablespoons soft butter or margarine with ½ cup granulated sugar and ¼ cup firmly packed brown sugar. Beat in ¼ teaspoon vanilla and ¼ cup half-and-half (light cream) until fluffy. Stir in 1 cup *each* flaked coconut and finely chopped walnuts or pecans.

Fourth of July Picnic

SPREAD EAGLE CHICKEN

RED AND WHITE POTATO CASSEROLE OR SALAD

RAW VEGETABLE RELISH

CORN ON THE COB OR CORN SOUP

SLICED TOMATOES   BUTTERED ROLLS

BANNER SHORTCAKE

Versatility is the special feature of this picnic. You can serve it in the patio at home or make a few adjustments and pack it in a hamper to eat, perhaps at the picnic grounds after the big parade or before the fireworks display.

Corn on the cob is no problem to serve at home, but away from home you'll find fresh hot corn soup from a vacuum bottle easier to manage. Serve the soup as a separate course before the chicken.

The hot potato casserole, too, is simple to serve at home, but you may want to make the potato salad version for a picnic away from home. The chicken is good either hot or cold.

If you're staying at home, you can assemble the shortcake several hours ahead. But to transport, it's best to keep the whipped cream and berries chilled separately and then put the cake together when you serve it.

SPREAD EAGLE CHICKEN

Allow a 2½-pound broiler-fryer chicken for each 2 or 3 servings. Have your meatman cut through the length of the back of each chicken. Open each out flat, breaking the breast bone so chicken stays flat. Sprinkle with salt and pepper. Broil or grill over medium-hot coals about 6 inches from heat source about 45 minutes or until thigh is tender when pierced with tip of sharp knife; turn occasionally and baste frequently with melted butter. Serve hot or cold, cut in halves or pieces.

RED AND WHITE POTATO CASSEROLE

You can make this casserole several hours ahead, chill, and bake when ready to serve, allowing about 35 to 40 minutes to heat.

    6 to 8 medium-sized boiling potatoes
    6 cups water
1½ teaspoons salt
    2 cans (4 oz. each) sliced pimientos
    ½ cup chopped green onions
    3 tablespoons butter
    3 tablespoons flour
    2 cups milk or light cream
    ¾ cup shredded Swiss, jack, or medium-
        sharp Cheddar cheese

Peel potatoes and cut in very thin slices, dropping slices into a bowl of cold water as you cut them. Bring the 6 cups water to a boil with the salt. Drain potatoes and add to hot water; cook just until tender, 6 to 8 minutes. Drain and mix with pimientos and onions.

Melt butter; blend in flour, and gradually add milk or cream. Cook until thickened, stirring. Gently mix with the cooked potato mixture. Pour into a 2-quart casserole and sprinkle with cheese. Bake in a 350° oven for about 20 minutes or until bubbling. Serves 6 to 8.

Red and White Potato Salad. Follow directions for the casserole, cooking the potatoes and mixing with pimientos and onions. Then, instead of making sauce, just blend 1 cup prepared Italian-style oil and vinegar dressing with potatoes. Chill. Serves 6 to 8.

CORN ON THE COB

Allow at least 1 or 2 ears for each serving. Remove husks and silk and drop corn into boiling unsalted water to cover. Let simmer 5 minutes; drain. Serve with butter, salt, and pepper.

CORN SOUP

2 tablespoons butter
  Kernels from 5 ears of corn
    (about 2½ cups)
2 tablespoons flour
4 cups milk or light cream
1 cup regular-strength chicken broth
  About 1 teaspoon salt
  Pepper
1 cup sour cream
  Dill weed

Melt the butter in a wide pan and add corn; cook, stirring, for 2 or 3 minutes. Blend in flour and gradually add milk or cream and broth. Cook, stirring, until boiling. Reduce heat and simmer about 5 minutes, stirring occasionally. Season to taste with salt and pepper. Remove from heat.

Blend some of the hot mixture with the sour cream, then stir into soup. Serve hot (from a vacuum bottle) in mugs or bowls. Sprinkle dill weed on top of each serving. Serves 6.

BANNER SHORTCAKE

This shortcake has qualities of both a biscuit and a cake. It soaks up fruit juices without becoming mushy.

2½ cups cake flour, sifted before measuring
  2 cups powdered sugar, sifted before
    measuring
  1 teaspoon baking powder
¼ teaspoon salt
½ cup (¼ lb.) soft butter
  2 eggs, slightly beaten
  2 cups whipping cream
   Granulated or powdered sugar
 2 cups sliced strawberries
  1 cup blueberries

Sift flour and powdered sugar together with baking powder and salt into a bowl. Add butter and eggs and mix until well blended. Spread batter evenly over bottom of buttered and waxed-paper-lined 8 or 9-inch square pan. Bake in a 300° oven for 45 minutes. Cool 5 minutes, then turn onto a wire rack and peel off paper. When cake is cool, carefully split to make two layers.

Whip cream until stiff and sweeten with sugar. Spread half on one layer of the cake and cover with half the strawberries and all the blueberries. Top with remaining section of cake, cover with remaining cream, and arrange remaining strawberries in strips on the cream. (You can save a few blueberries for decorating, too, but they should be added at the last moment because they discolor the cream.) Chill, lightly covered, until ready to serve (as long as 2 or 3 hours). Serves 8 or 9.

Fourth of July Neighborhood Barbecue

APPLE AND AVOCADO GREEN SALAD

SKILLET POTATOES ANNA

GRILLED EGGPLANT SLICES

BARBECUED SIRLOIN WITH ROSEMARY

TOASTED FRENCH BREAD

HOMEMADE MACADAMIA NUT ICE CREAM

Several families could join for this barbecue, each family being made responsible for one or two of the dishes. One chef should preside at the barbecue, cooking the steak, grilling the eggplant, and toasting the bread. The potatoes cook in the hostess' oven, and the salad is mixed at the last minute.

Homemade ice cream is a traditional favorite that's particularly appropriate for this holiday. Turn the crank—or the switch, if your freezer is electric—anytime from 1 to 3 hours before you plan to serve the ice cream.

APPLE AND AVOCADO GREEN SALAD

3 heads butter lettuce
1 small bunch watercress
1 red-skinned apple, peeled and cored
1 ripe avocado, peeled
6 tablespoons olive oil
2 tablespoons white wine vinegar
¼ teaspoon each salt and crumbled dried
     tarragon
3 tablespoons finely chopped walnuts

Tear lettuce into bite-sized pieces and add the leaves of the watercress. Dice half of the apple and slice the remainder. Dice half the avocado and slice the rest. Add diced fruit to greens. Mix the olive oil, vinegar, salt, and tarragon. Pour over the greens and diced apple and avocado; mix lightly. Arrange the apple and avocado slices in a pinwheel design on top. Sprinkle with chopped walnuts. Serves 10.

SKILLET POTATOES ANNA

Peel and slice 6 to 8 large baking potatoes. Melt ½ cup butter. Brush a 10-inch heavy ovenproof frying pan or shallow baking dish with part of the melted butter and overlap the potato slices in the pan, sprinkling each layer with salt and pepper to taste. Pour over the remaining melted butter. Bake uncovered in a 450° oven for 45 minutes, or until the top is crusty and the potatoes are tender. Serves 10.

GRILLED EGGPLANT SLICES

Slice 2 large eggplants ¾ inch thick. Brush cut sides with olive oil and sprinkle with salt, pepper, and paprika. Grill over medium barbecue coals about 7 minutes on each side, or until tender. Serves 10 to 12.

BARBECUED SIRLOIN WITH ROSEMARY

If your barbecue doesn't have a hood, make one with heavy aluminum foil.

1 boneless top sirloin about 2 inches thick (about 4½ lbs.)
2 tablespoons fresh rosemary (or 2 teaspoons dried rosemary)
Salt and pepper

Press rosemary into the meat, coating both sides. Place over medium barbecue coals and cover with barbecue hood. Barbecue about 15 minutes on each side for rare meat, or until the meat thermometer registers 135°. (You can insert a meat thermometer into the meat after barbecuing one side.)

Place on a carving board; season with salt and pepper. Slice on the diagonal. Serves 10 to 12.

MACADAMIA NUT ICE CREAM

This creamy nut ice cream must be made in an ice cream freezer—either electric or crank style.

4 egg yolks
1 cup sugar
1 tablespoon vanilla
   Dash salt
1 pint half-and-half (light cream)
4 cups (2 pints) whipping cream
1 cup chopped salted macadamia nuts (or blanched almonds)
2 tablespoons butter

Place egg yolks, sugar, vanilla, salt, and half-and-half in an electric blender and blend until smooth (or beat with a rotary beater until smooth). Pour into the chilled freezer can and add the whipping cream; adjust dasher and cover.

Pack freezer with 5 parts crushed ice to 1 part rock salt. Freeze until ice cream is whipped thick but still soft. Meanwhile, sauté the nuts in butter until lightly browned; cool. Add to the ice cream and continue freezing until firm. Drain off water from ice, remove dasher and pack ice cream down into container. Replace lid and repack freezer with 8 parts crushed ice to 2 parts rock salt. Cover with towels and let mellow at least 1 hour. Makes about 2 quarts.

Fourth of July Patio Potluck

ASSORTED RAW VEGETABLES   BLUE CHEESE DIP

PINEAPPLE BARBECUED SPARERIBS

HUSK-ROASTED CORN ON THE COB

BACON POTATO SALAD   SLICED TOMATOES

HARD ROLLS   BUTTER

HOMEMADE TOASTED ALMOND ICE CREAM

FRESH PEACH SLICES

A patio supper is a good way to celebrate the Fourth of July away from holiday crowds. Family and friends can make it a cooperative effort —all the foods are made or assembled ahead and can be transported easily—or you can prepare the whole menu yourself without difficulty.

For the first course, offer several of these: celery hearts, carrot sticks, raw asparagus, turnip sticks, green onions, radishes, green pepper strips, and cauliflower buds. Buy or make blue cheese dip.

Both the corn and spareribs are served from the grill, but you should soak the corn at least an hour ahead and can parboil the spareribs and prepare the baste several hours ahead.

Combine and refrigerate the ice cream mixture, ready to freeze after picnickers are assembled. The ice cream can be turned anytime from 1 to 3 hours before it's time for dessert; you pack it in ice. Sprinkle fresh peach slices with lemon juice to prevent discoloring.

PINEAPPLE BARBECUED SPARERIBS

10 pounds spareribs
  Water
12 whole black peppers
 6 whole cloves
 2 bay leaves
 2 cloves garlic
  Pineapple Barbecue Sauce (recipe follows)

Place spareribs in water that almost covers; season with peppers, cloves, bay leaves, and garlic.

(If you don't have a pan large enough, cook half at a time with half the seasonings.) Bring to a boil, cover, and simmer for 30 minutes, or until almost tender. Drain, then cover and refrigerate.

At the picnic, arrange spareribs on the barbecue grill over hot coals; cook about 30 minutes, turning occasionally. During the last 15 minutes, baste with Pineapple Barbecue Sauce; cook until ribs are glazed and tender. Remove onto warm platter. Serves 10 to 12.

Pineapple Barbecue Sauce. Combine 2 tablespoons brown sugar, 2 medium-sized onions, finely minced, ⅔ cup soy sauce, ¼ cup catsup, 1 can (1 lb.) crushed pineapple (including syrup), ⅔ cup dry white wine, ½ teaspoon black pepper, and 1 teaspoon salt. Makes about 4 cups.

HUSK-ROASTED CORN ON THE COB

Soak corn in the husks in cold salted water to cover for about an hour. Fold back the husks and remove silk. Rub corn with soft butter. Bring husks back up to cover kernels as well as possible. Roast on the grill for about 20 minutes, turning 3 or 4 times so all surfaces are exposed to the heat. Serve with husks on, to keep corn steaming hot.

(continued)

BACON POTATO SALAD

Serve this salad cool but not cold to bring out its flavors. Because the dressing is not yet mixed in, you can take the salad out of the refrigerator about two hours before serving.

10 potatoes
½ cup finely minced green onions
½ pound bacon, cooked until crisp,
    then drained and crumbled
1 cup white wine vinegar
6 tablespoons bacon drippings
1½ teaspoons salt
1 cup mayonnaise
6 hard-cooked eggs, sliced
    Green pepper slices

Boil potatoes in their jackets until tender but still firm; cool just enough to handle. Peel carefully and slice into a bowl, sprinkling with onions and bacon. Heat vinegar, bacon drippings, and salt to simmering; pour over the potatoes. Let stand 30 minutes; stir occasionally so the vinegar permeates the potatoes evenly. Drain off any excess vinegar; turn potatoes into serving bowl and refrigerate.

To serve, spread top with the mayonnaise and garnish with egg slices and a few green pepper slices. Serve cool but not chilled. Serves 10 to 12.

TOASTED ALMOND ICE CREAM

You'll need a 2-quart ice cream freezer, electric or hand-turned, to make this dessert.

2 cups milk
1 tablespoon cornstarch
¼ teaspoon salt
1 cup sugar
4 egg yolks
1 cup chopped almonds
¼ teaspoon almond extract
1 teaspoon vanilla
2 cups whipping cream

Scald the milk. Combine cornstarch, salt, sugar, and egg yolks. Beat in a little of the scalded milk, then combine the two mixtures and cook over low heat (or in a double boiler), stirring constantly, until thick and smooth.

Spread almonds on a cooky sheet and toast in a 350° oven until browned, about 5 to 10 minutes; add to the custard. Add almond extract and vanilla. Chill.

When it is time to make the ice cream, stir whipping cream into the custard and pour into freezer can; adjust dasher in can and cover. Pack freezer with 1 part ice cream salt (rock salt) to 8 parts ice. Crank until very hard to turn, 15 to 30 minutes. Drain off excess water from freezer; remove dasher from can, pack ice cream down, and replace cover. Pack freezer with more salt and ice, this time 2 parts salt to 8 parts ice. Cover with newspapers or towels and let the ice cream mellow for at least an hour. Makes about 1½ quarts.

Labor Day Barbecue

CHEESE AND CRACKER TRAY
ORANGE BAKED CHICKEN
GRILLED VEGETABLES   BREAD STICKS
STEAMED RICE OR BAKED POTATOES
CHOCOLATE CHIP DATE CAKE

This Labor Day meal is one you can serve indoors or outdoors. You can prepare the food at home and carry it with you in insulated bags or take it to the picnic site and barbecue it there. At home, this is a good menu for adapting to changeable weather; barbecue the chicken and vegetables on an outdoor grill or do them in your kitchen oven.

Prepare the vegetables early in the day and let them marinate until you are ready to cook them. You can bake the cake ahead. The chicken can be prepared, wrapped in foil, and refrigerated until you are ready to pack or bake it.

ORANGE BAKED CHICKEN

2½ to 3½-pound cut-up broiler-fryer chicken
  Salt and pepper
4 tablespoons thawed frozen orange juice
    concentrate
4 tablespoons butter

Sprinkle each serving of chicken with salt and pepper and place it on a piece of heavy duty foil. Pour 1 tablespoon orange juice concentrate over each; dot each with 1 tablespoon butter. Wrap foil around each serving, sealing edges tightly. Bake in hot coals or in a 350° oven about 1 hour, or until thigh meat is tender when pierced with tip of sharp knife. Makes 4 servings.

GRILLED VEGETABLES

Serve about 1 cup vegetables per person; a good selection includes frozen artichoke hearts (thawed), cucumber slices, eggplant cubes, small whole mushrooms, green pepper squares, and cherry tomatoes. Marinate for several hours in your favorite French dressing or a mixture of 1 cup salad oil, ⅓ cup lemon juice, ¼ teaspoon salt, and a dash *each* pepper and sugar.

Just before cooking, remove vegetables from marinade and string on skewers. Place over coals or under a broiler; cook until slightly browned, 3 to 5 minutes, turning once. Baste with some of the marinade while vegetables are cooking.

CHOCOLATE CHIP DATE CAKE

½ pound pitted dates, cut fairly fine
1 teaspoon soda
1 cup hot water
½ cup (¼ lb.) butter
1 cup sugar
2 eggs
1¾ cups regular all-purpose flour, sifted before
    measuring
1 tablespoon cocoa
⅛ teaspoon salt
1 teaspoon vanilla
1 package (6-oz. size) semisweet
    chocolate pieces
½ cup chopped walnuts

Mix dates with soda and water; set aside to cool. Cream butter with sugar; add eggs, beating well. Sift flour with cocoa and salt. Add dry mixture to creamed mixture alternately with dates and water. Fold in vanilla, half the chocolate chips, and walnuts.

Pour batter into greased 9-inch square pan; sprinkle with remaining chocolate chips. Bake in a 350° oven for 40 to 45 minutes. Let cool.

German-American Thanksgiving

OPEN-FACED SANDWICHES   RHINE WINE PUNCH

BUTTER LETTUCE SALAD

ROAST TURKEY

APPLE-HERB STUFFING   TURKEY GRAVY

SPATZLE   SWEET-SOUR RED CABBAGE

FRESH CRANBERRY RELISH   CRISP VEGETABLE TRAY

APPLE KUCHEN

The traditional American Thanksgiving meal can be interpreted in rich variety. A German-American family based this Thanksgiving menu on the food of a German harvest feast, substituting turkey for goose. The generous amount of meat in the stuffing is typically European.

Prepare sandwich ingredients ahead; assemble an hour or so before serving, or let guests make their own. Use pumpernickel, buffet rye, or French bread. Top with sliced hard-cooked egg, pickled herring, and pimiento; dilled egg salad; or anchovy butter, tomato slices, and onion.

For the punch, pour two bottles (⅘ qt. each) chilled Rhine wine and a quart of ginger ale over an ice ring in a punch bowl. Mix lettuce and cucumber salad with an oil and vinegar dressing. Prepare Swiss *spätzle* (free-form noodles) as the package directs and season with butter and parsley (you'll find packaged spätzle mix in a store with an imported food section).

Present the turkey on a platter lined with butter lettuce and decorated with spiced crabapples on pear halves.

GERMAN APPLE-HERB STUFFING

Shredded apples give this German stuffing an elusively sweet flavor.

  1 loaf (15 oz.) firm white bread, cubed
¼ cup each milk and lukewarm water
  1 pound ground beef chuck, crumbled
    Turkey liver and heart, finely chopped
  2 tablespoons butter or margarine
  2 cups finely chopped celery
  1 large onion, chopped
½ cup chopped parsley
  1 large apple, peeled, cored, and shredded
  2 eggs, slightly beaten
  1 teaspoon each salt and poultry seasoning
⅛ teaspoon pepper

Put the bread in a large bowl and add milk and water; set aside. Brown ground beef and turkey liver and heart in butter; stir in celery, onion, parsley, and apple. Cook over low heat, stirring occasionally, until celery is soft; cool slightly. Blend lightly with soaked bread, eggs, salt, poultry seasoning, and pepper. Makes about 10 cups.

If you have more stuffing than the turkey will hold, bake it in a covered, greased casserole for the last 30 to 45 minutes the turkey roasts.

SWEET-SOUR RED CABBAGE

2 medium-sized heads red cabbage
2 tart apples
5 whole cloves
1½ teaspoons salt
½ cup white wine vinegar
4 cups boiling water
¼ cup butter
2 tablespoons sugar

Shred cabbage and apples into a large, deep pan. Add cloves, salt, vinegar, and boiling water. Bring to a gentle boil and simmer, uncovered, for 1½ hours; stir occasionally. Add butter and sugar; cook 30 minutes longer. Serves 10 to 12.

FRESH CRANBERRY RELISH

Using medium blade, grind together in food chopper 1 package (1 lb.) cranberries, 2 peeled, cored tart apples, and 1 unpeeled, coarsely chopped, seedless orange. Blend in 1½ cups sugar. Makes 4 cups.

APPLE KUCHEN

Serve this nut-garnished dessert warm or cold, with sweetened whipped cream, if you like.

1¾ cups unsifted regular all-purpose flour
¼ cup sugar
½ cup butter
1 egg, well beaten
½ teaspoon vanilla
1 teaspoon grated lemon peel
4 large apples, peeled and sliced about
    ¼ inch thick
1 teaspoon cinnamon
½ cup sugar
⅓ cup chopped filberts

Sift the flour with the ¼ cup sugar. Cut in butter. Stir in egg, vanilla, and lemon peel; mix with your hands and shape into a ball. Press into bottom and up 1¼ inches of the sides of an ungreased 9-inch cheesecake pan (with removable bottom or spring-released sides).

Arrange apple slices in crust in circular pattern. Sprinkle with mixture of cinnamon, ½ cup sugar, and filberts. Bake in a 350° oven for 1 hour or until apples are tender.

French-American Thanksgiving

CREAMED CRAB IN PATTY SHELLS

TRUFFLED ROAST TURKEY

CHESTNUT STUFFING   TURKEY GRAVY

FRENCH ROLLS   BUTTER-BROWNED NEW POTATOES

SPINACH AND MUSHROOMS AU GRATIN

GREEN SALAD WITH MUSTARD DRESSING

FRENCH CHEESE TRAY   CRACKERS

MELON WEDGES

GENOISE CAKE

Many courses are considered essential for an important dinner in France. In adapting French foods to this American holiday meal, the classic French style of menu has been followed, but you could serve the crab dish for an early lunch or the cheese and fruit for late supper if you want to spread out the riches a bit.

The crab-filled pastries are made from prepared patty shells, frozen or from a bakery. To fill 12 shells you'll need 1½ to 2 pounds crab meat; bind it with 2 cups rich cream sauce flavored with Sherry.

The truffles for the turkey are optional. If you use them, buy a small can; thinly slice the truffles and slip them under the skin of the turkey the day before you roast it. Work from the back opening of bird and gently separate skin from flesh with your fingers. Add any bits of truffles and the liquid to stuffing. Roast turkey as usual, basting occasionally with butter.

For Spinach and Mushrooms au Gratin, layer creamed spinach and butter-sautéed mushrooms in a casserole. Sprinkle with shredded Gruyère cheese and buttered crumbs; heat through.

Possible selections for the cheese tray include Camembert, Brie, Pont l'Eyeque. Buy a cake from the bakery.

FRENCH CHESTNUT STUFFING

Dried chestnuts, available in markets that handle imported Italian or French groceries, are a convenience in making this stuffing. You'll need ½ pound dried chestnuts or about 2½ pounds chestnuts in shells.

1 loaf (15 oz.) firm white bread, crusts
    removed
3 cups coarsely chopped cooked chestnuts
    (directions follow)
½ pound bulk pork sausage
    Turkey liver and heart, finely chopped
6 tablespoons butter or margarine
1 large onion, chopped
2 cups thinly sliced celery
1 teaspoon thyme
3 tablespoons chopped parsley
2 eggs, slightly beaten
¼ cup brandy or chicken or turkey broth

Cut bread in cubes and combine with chestnuts in a large bowl. In a frying pan, stir the sausage over medium heat until it releases some fat. Add the chopped liver and heart; cook until the meats lose their pink color. Add to bread mixture, discarding the drippings. In same pan, melt the butter; sauté the onion until golden brown, then add butter and onion to dressing. Add the celery, thyme, parsley, eggs, and brandy or broth. Mix lightly until blended. Makes about 10 cups.

To bake dressing left over after turkey is stuffed, put it in a greased casserole, cover, and place in oven for last 30 to 45 minutes the turkey is roasting.

To cook dry chestnuts. Cover ½ pound dry chestnuts with cold water, bring slowly to boil, cover, and boil 2 minutes. Remove from heat; let stand for 1 hour. Drain and pick out any skin remaining in crevices of each nut. Cover again with water; add 1 teaspoon salt and 2 bay leaves; bring to a boil, cover, and cook until tender, about 30 minutes. Drain and coarsely chop.

To cook chestnuts in shells. Slit an X in the skin of each of 2½ pounds chestnuts. Drop into boiling water to cover; simmer, uncovered, 15 minutes; drain. Pull off the skins with a knife. Put nuts in a pan, cover with water, and add 1 teaspoon salt and 2 bay leaves; simmer, covered, for 20 minutes or until tender. Drain and chop.

BUTTER-BROWNED NEW POTATOES

Peel 3 pounds uniformly small new potatoes; wash and dry. Melt ¾ cup butter in a Dutch oven over medium heat; add potatoes (they should just cover pan bottom) and cook, uncovered, for 15 minutes, stirring carefully. Reduce heat to low, cover, and cook 10 to 15 minutes, until tender. Uncover, increase heat to moderately hot, and turn potatoes until crisped and browned. Lift out with slotted spoon. Sprinkle with salt, pepper, and chopped parsley. Serves 12.

MUSTARD DRESSING

Combine 1 tablespoon *each* Dijon-style mustard and chopped shallots, ½ teaspoon salt, ⅛ teaspoon pepper, ¼ cup tarragon wine vinegar, ¾ cup olive oil. Mix well. Makes enough for 3 quarts greens (include some Belgian endive or chicory in greens for a bitter accent).

Scandinavian-American Thanksgiving

APPETIZER SMORGASBORD TRAY

ROAST TURKEY WITH SAUSAGE STUFFING

POACHED APPLES   LINGONBERRIES

BROWN-SUGAR-GLAZED POTATOES

CAULIFLOWER WITH CHEESE SAUCE

BUTTERED CARROTS

MIXED VEGETABLE SALAD

HOT ROLLS   WHIPPED BUTTER

CRANBERRY FRUIT SOUP   COOKIES AND PASTRIES

This menu incorporates Scandinavian cuisine into Thanksgiving dinner. The first and last courses of the meal retain their Scandinavian identity; all the elements can be purchased. Choose several of these appetizers: herring, anchovies, sliced smoked salmon, caviar; sliced ham, veal loaf (sylta), hot meatballs in sauce, Danish salami, and other sausages; pickled beets, red cabbage, fresh cherry tomatoes; Danish blue, Brie, kuminost, and Havarti cheeses; hard-cooked eggs; assorted breads and crackers; whipped butter. At the bakery you can buy an assortment of cookies and pastries for dessert, as well as dinner rolls.

Start your preparations early in the day by making the cranberry dessert and arranging the appetizer and dessert trays. To the salad greens, you might add chilled cooked peas, sliced celery, and diced apple. To garnish turkey, poach apple halves until tender; serve warm or cooled, filled with currant jelly.

BROWN-SUGAR-GLAZED POTATOES

2 dozen small potatoes
  Boiling salted water
¾ cup brown sugar
¼ cup (⅛ lb.) butter
3 tablespoons milk

Cook potatoes in boiling salted water until tender; drain and peel. Heat brown sugar, butter, and milk in large frying pan, stirring to blend. Add potatoes; cook 4 to 5 minutes over medium heat, turning to glaze. Serves 12.

SCANDINAVIAN SAUSAGE STUFFING

You can prepare the seasoned sausage mixture ahead. Refrigerate it, then combine with the eggs, milk, and bread just before filling the bird.

    1 pound bulk pork sausage
    ½ pound ground lean beef
    1 medium-sized onion, finely chopped
      Turkey liver, heart, and gizzard, cooked
        (optional—directions follow)
    1 tablespoon chopped parsley
    ½ teaspoon each rubbed sage and whole thyme
    1½ teaspoons salt
    ¼ teaspoon each pepper and allspice
    2 eggs, slightly beaten
    ½ cup milk
    4 cups toasted firm white bread cubes

Crumble sausage and beef into a frying pan; add onion and cook just until meat loses its pink color. Drain off drippings. Finely chop the cooked turkey giblets; add to meat. Stir in parsley and seasonings. Beat eggs with milk; mix gently with meat and bread. Makes 8 cups.

Any extra stuffing can be baked in a greased casserole, covered, for 30 to 45 minutes with the turkey.

To cook giblets. Simmer gizzard in water to cover with ½ onion and a sprig of parsley for 30 minutes. Add heart and liver; cook 15 minutes more, or until tender.

CRANBERRY FRUIT SOUP

    3 cups each cranberry juice cocktail and water
    ¾ cup sugar
    6 tablespoons cornstarch
    1 stick cinnamon
    2 whole cloves
      Sweetened whipped cream
      Sliced almonds

Combine cranberry juice, water, sugar, cornstarch, cinnamon, and cloves in a pan. Bring to a boil; simmer, stirring, until juice is clear and slightly thickened. Chill. Serve in individual glasses, topped with whipped cream and sliced almonds. Makes 12 servings.

Thanksgiving Dinner Buffet

APPETIZER TRAY:

Deviled Eggs with Salted Almonds;
Salmon-Cream Cheese Rolls;
Cheese-Stuffed Celery Sticks; Cherry Tomatoes
with Smoked Oysters; Pickle and Salami Cornucopias

GREEN SALAD FRESH FRUIT PLATTER

TWO ROAST TURKEYS

SHERRIED WILD RICE AND SAVORY GIBLET STUFFINGS

RICH GRAVY MOLDED WHOLE CRANBERRY SAUCE

CAULIFLOWER WITH CHIVE HOLLANDAISE

BUTTERED YAMS GLAZED ONIONS WITH ALMONDS

MUSHROOM CAPS WITH PEAS

DINNER ROLLS RED CURRANT JELLY

PUMPKIN SOUFFLE PUDDING GINGER WHIPPED CREAM

ICE CREAM BALLS MINCEMEAT SAUCE, FLAMBE

This is a meal that gives credence to the picture of a table sagging beneath the weight of Thanksgiving culinary bounty. Preparing the two turkeys and impressive array of accompaniments doesn't have to end in exhaustion for anyone if the work load is shared by several families.

Serve appetizers in the living room. Have salads waiting at each place in the dining room. Then diners proceed to the buffet. Serve the desserts buffet-style, several hours after dinner.

Carve one of two roasted hen turkeys (about 12 pounds each) in the kitchen and arrange on a platter. Time the second to come out of the oven just before dinner; it will stay hot for second helpings and add to the festive appearance of the table. To garnish the tray, dip small bunches of green grapes in slightly beaten egg white, then in granulated sugar to frost tips; arrange on grape leaves.

Your plans for sharing the work will depend on the group with whom you celebrate. One family could bring the appetizers, preparing the tray and covering it with plastic film for the drive to the host's home or bringing makings and assembling them there. A second family could bring salad ingredients; fruit to cut for the fresh fruit platter; the cranberry sauce, ready to unmold; and the rolls.

Have a third family stuff and roast one turkey and transport it in a covered roasting pan wrapped in several layers of newspaper. The host family can provide the vegetable dishes and the second turkey and stuffing. Perhaps another guest can be responsible for dessert; the soufflé ingredients can be ready to assemble and put into the oven about an hour before it is to be served. If dessert will immediately follow dinner, put the soufflé in the oven after the turkey comes out.

(continued)

DEVILED EGGS WITH SALTED ALMONDS

> 9 hard-cooked eggs
> 3 tablespoons each mayonnaise and
>   sour cream
> 1 teaspoon salt
> 2 teaspoons Swedish or Russian-style
>   mustard
> ¼ cup chopped salted almonds

Halve the eggs and scoop out yolks; mash yolks with mayonnaise, sour cream, salt, and mustard. Press through a pastry tube with a star-shaped tip or use a spoon to fill the whites. Sprinkle almonds over the centers. Makes 18.

SALMON-CREAM CHEESE ROLLS

> 2 small packages (3 oz. each) cream cheese
> 2 tablespoons half-and-half (light cream)
> ¼ teaspoon onion salt
> ½ teaspoon dill weed
> ¾ pound thinly sliced, lightly smoked
>   salmon (lox), cut into pieces about
>   2 inches square
> Tiny sprigs of parsley for garnish

Blend the cream cheese, half-and-half, onion salt, and dill weed. Spread this mixture thinly over each piece of salmon. Roll each into a log shape. Arrange on the tray with cut sides down and garnish with sprigs of parsley tucked into the ends. Makes 18.

PICKLE AND SALAMI CORNUCOPIAS

For each appetizer, place a sliced bread-and-butter pickle on a thin slice of salami. Fold salami over the pickle into a cornucopia shape, and secure with a toothpick.

CHERRY TOMATOES WITH SMOKED OYSTERS

Cut down through each tiny tomato to within about ¼ inch of the base; spread apart and slip a canned smoked oyster inside each one. (A 3-oz. can contains about 40 tiny smoked oysters.)

FRESH FRUIT PLATTER

> 1 large melon (Casaba, Crenshaw, or
>   Persian), chilled
> 3 large papaya, chilled
> 1 large (or 2 medium-sized) pineapple
>   (or 2 cans sliced pineapple, 1 lb.
>   14 oz. each), chilled
> Lime slices and fresh mint for garnish

Cut melon into balls or cubes. Peel papaya, remove seeds, and cut into wedges. Peel, core, and slice pineapple. Arrange on a large serving tray and garnish the papaya with lime slices and the pineapple with mint.

GREEN SALAD WITH AVOCADO AND SHRIMP

> ¾ cup salad oil
> ⅓ cup vinegar
> 1 teaspoon each salt and dry mustard
>   Dash pepper
>   Cut garlic clove (optional)
> 6 quarts torn crisp greens (such as 1 large
>   head each romaine, red leaf lettuce,
>   and iceberg lettuce)
> 2 large ripe avocados
> ½ pound cooked and chilled shrimp
> ⅓ pound Roquefort cheese

For the dressing, shake together in a jar the salad oil, vinegar, salt, mustard, and pepper. Rub a large salad bowl with the cut clove of garlic, if you like; add torn greens to the bowl. Peel and slice the avocados and add to the greens with the shrimp; crumble in the cheese. Add the dressing and mix gently. Makes 18 servings.

SHERRIED WILD RICE STUFFING

1½ cups uncooked wild rice
  3 cups hot turkey or chicken broth
    (regular strength)
  1 tablespoon olive oil or butter
  6 strips bacon, diced
  3 cups chopped celery
  1 cup chopped onion
 ½ cup dry Sherry
 ½ cup filberts, coarsely chopped or halved

Wash rice well and soak for 2 hours in water to cover; drain. Combine rice, hot turkey broth, and olive oil or butter in a pan; cover and simmer 25 minutes, or until rice is almost tender and the liquid has been absorbed.

Meanwhile, fry bacon until crisp and remove from pan; discard all but ¼ cup drippings. Add celery and onion to the pan and cook until limp. Lightly mix the sautéed vegetables and bacon into the cooked rice; add Sherry and mix lightly. Stir in nuts. Use to stuff a 12-pound turkey.

SAVORY GIBLET STUFFING

 ½ pound ground beef chuck
  Turkey giblets, chopped, or ½ pound
    chicken livers, chopped
 ½ cup (¼ lb.) butter or margarine
  3 medium-sized onions, chopped
 ½ cup golden raisins, chopped
  4 large carrots, peeled and shredded
  2 large stalks celery, chopped
 ½ cup walnuts, chopped
  2 teaspoons salt
  1 cup turkey or chicken broth (regular strength)
1½ teaspoons each poultry seasoning and
    cinnamon
  2 teaspoons nutmeg
 ½ teaspoon ground cloves
  1 package (6 oz.) zwieback, finely crushed
  6 eggs

Brown the meat and chopped giblets in butter. Add the onions and sauté until golden. Turn into a large pan; add raisins, carrots, celery, nuts, salt, and broth. Cover and simmer for 2 hours or until very soft. Add poultry seasoning, cinnamon, nutmeg, and cloves and simmer 30 minutes longer. Mash well with a potato masher. Mix in zwieback. Cool slightly. Beat eggs until light and mix in. Use to stuff a 12-pound turkey.

CAULIFLOWER WITH CHIVE HOLLANDAISE

  2 large whole heads cauliflower
    Boiling salted water
  1 can (6 oz.) Hollandaise sauce
 ¼ cup sour cream
  1 tablespoon lemon juice
  1 tablespoon minced chives

Cook cauliflower in boiling salted water just until tender, about 20 minutes; drain. Arrange on a serving plate and spoon over quick Hollandaise made by stirring canned Hollandaise sauce, sour cream, and lemon juice over medium heat until heated through. Sprinkle cauliflower with chives. Makes 18 servings.

BUTTERED WHOLE YAMS OR SWEET POTATOES

Peel and cook about 5 pounds small yams or sweet potatoes in a small amount of boiling salted water until tender; drain and season to taste with butter, salt, and pepper. Or use 4 cans (1 lb. 10 oz. *each*) whole yams or sweet potatoes in syrup; heat as directed on the can. Makes 18 small servings.

GLAZED ONIONS WITH ALMONDS

  4 cans (1 lb. each) small whole onions
 ¼ cup slivered blanched almonds
  6 tablespoons butter
  3 tablespoons flour
1½ teaspoons Worcestershire
1½ tablespoons brown sugar
  1 teaspoon salt
 ½ teaspoon paprika
 ⅛ teaspoon pepper

Drain onions and save the liquid. Arrange onions in a greased 2-quart casserole. In a saucepan, brown almonds in butter; add flour and stir until bubbly. Remove from heat and stir in 1½ cups of liquid from onions and the Worcestershire, brown sugar, salt, paprika, and pepper. Cook, stirring, until slightly thickened; then pour over onions in casserole. Cover and bake in a 375° oven for 25 minutes or in a 325° oven for about 1 hour. Makes 18 small servings.

(continued)

MUSHROOM CAPS WITH PEAS

18 large mushrooms (2 to 2½ inches in
    diameter)
¼ cup (⅛ lb.) butter
    Salt and garlic salt to taste
 2 packages (10 oz. each) small frozen peas
    Butter, salt, and pepper

Wash mushrooms and carefully remove stems. Sauté the caps in butter until lightly browned and tender. Sprinkle with salt and garlic salt to taste and arrange on serving plate with cauliflower (see preceding page).

Meanwhile cook peas as directed on the package; drain. Season to taste with butter, salt, and pepper; spoon inside mushroom caps. Makes 18.

ICE CREAM BALLS

The day before Thanksgiving, scoop vanilla ice cream (about 2 quarts) into 18 to 24 balls; pile these into a serving bowl and keep them in the freezer. If you wish, hollow out a pumpkin in advance and set the bowl of ice cream balls inside it at serving time. Serve with Mincemeat Sauce.

Mincemeat Sauce, Flambé. Heat 1 large jar (12 oz.) prepared mincemeat just before serving, or have ready and hot in a chafing dish. Warm ¼ cup brandy, ignite, and pour flaming over mincemeat. Serve over ice cream balls.

PUMPKIN SOUFFLE PUDDING

This pudding has a soufflé topping and a custard-like base. Bake it in two soufflé dishes or casseroles.

 6 eggs, separated
 ⅛ teaspoon cream of tartar
1⅓ cups brown sugar, firmly packed
  2 tablespoons flour
  1 teaspoon salt
  2 teaspoons ground ginger
  4 teaspoons cinnamon
 ½ teaspoon ground cloves
  3 cups milk
  1 can (1 lb.) pumpkin (2 cups)
  2 tablespoons melted butter

Beat egg whites until foamy; add cream of tartar and beat until soft peaks form. Gradually beat in ⅔ cup of the brown sugar; beat until stiff but not dry. Set aside. Mix together remaining ⅔ cup brown sugar, flour, salt, ginger, cinnamon, and cloves. Beat egg yolks until thick, and beat in the sugar-spice mixture. Stir in milk and pumpkin.

Fold half the beaten egg whites into the yolk mixture, blending until smooth. Carefully fold in remaining whites and melted butter. Turn into two buttered soufflé dishes or straight-sided casseroles (1½ or 2-quart size; use foil collar to extend a 1½-quart dish). Set in a pan of hot water and bake in a 375° oven for 45 to 50 minutes, or until a knife inserted in center comes out clean. Serve with Ginger Whipped Cream. Makes 16 to 18 small servings.

Ginger Whipped Cream. Just before serving, whip 1 pint cream and flavor to taste with powdered sugar, vanilla, and ground ginger. Turn into a serving bowl for guests to spoon on top of warm Pumpkin Soufflé Pudding.

Christmas Open House

FROTHY EGGNOG PUNCH   HOT CIDER PUNCH
CARAMEL NUT TARTLETS   FRUITCAKE
MINIATURE FRUITCAKES

When you invite friends to an afternoon or evening open house, try this simple menu which requires little last-minute attention.

The fruitcake can be made weeks in advance and aged. You can bake the tartlets a day before the party or several days in advance and freeze.

HOT CIDER PUNCH

3 quarts cider or apple juice
2 to 3 quarts Sauterne (or substitute more cider)
12 cloves
4 cinnamon sticks
Unpeeled orange slices for garnish

Mix the cider, Sauterne, cloves, and cinnamon sticks in a large kettle; let stand at least 30 minutes. Immediately before serving, heat until hot, but not to simmering. Garnish with orange slices. Makes 18 servings.

FROTHY EGGNOG PUNCH

14 eggs, separated
1¼ cups sugar
1 quart milk
1 cup (½ pint) whipping cream
1 cup (½ pint) each light rum and brandy

Beat egg yolks until blended. Combine with ¾ cup *each* of the sugar and milk in a large saucepan; place over medium-low heat; cook, stirring, until mixture thickens to a soft custard (about 12 minutes); cool. Beat egg whites until frothy; add remaining ½ cup sugar and beat until they form soft peaks; spoon into cooled custard. Whip the cream in the same bowl. Add whipped cream and remaining 3¼ cups milk to beaten whites and custard; gently mix together. Refrigerate, covered, for several hours or overnight. Just before pouring into punch bowl, stir in the rum and brandy. Makes 15 to 20 servings.

CARAMEL NUT TARTLETS

½ cup (¼ lb.) butter or margarine
1 package (3 oz.) cream cheese
1¼ cups unsifted regular all-purpose flour
1 egg
¾ cup dark brown sugar, firmly packed
¼ teaspoon salt
1 tablespoon melted butter
½ teaspoon vanilla
1 cup chopped walnuts or pecans

In the small bowl of your electric mixer, cream together the butter and cream cheese until light and fluffy. Gradually mix in the flour until blended.

Place 1 rounded teaspoonful of the pastry in each cup of a pan for miniature muffins (cups about 1½ inches in diameter). Shape into shells using fingertips to press dough to cups.

To make filling, beat the egg well and then beat in the sugar and salt. Add butter, vanilla, and chopped walnuts; mix until smooth. Spoon filling into the shells. Bake in a 350° oven for about 25 minutes or until the pastry is delicately browned. Cool in pan. Makes 24 tartlets.

MINIATURE FRUITCAKES

Make your favorite fruitcake; use part of the batter to bake in fluted paper bonbon cups. Fill each cup about ¾ full of batter and bake 15 to 20 minutes. If you wish, ice the cakes and decorate them with nuts or candied cherries.

Christmas Roast Beef Dinner

PAPAYA WITH SMOKED SALMON
ROLLED BEEF ROAST   **BLENDER BEARNAISE**
BAKED CHEESE TOMATOES
DUCHESS POTATO MOUNDS
CROISSANTS
CREAM PUFF STAR

This Christmas dinner is a festive meal. The rolled rib eye roast is surrounded with browned potato puffs and Swiss cheese baked tomatoes, and enhanced by a simplified whole-egg Béarnaise sauce. The cream puff dessert is a star-shaped variation of the French pastry *croquenbouche;* you bake and freeze the cream puff shell ahead, then fill it the day of the dinner.

For the first course, serve each person a quartered, peeled papaya topped with a strip of smoked salmon and a wedge of lime. Roast the beef until done to the stage you prefer. (Choices of roast include a rolled rib, sirloin tip, cross rib, or shoulder clod.) You can make the Béarnaise sauce ahead and reheat it. The tomatoes and potatoes bake together after the roast comes out of the oven.

BLENDER BEARNAISE

3 tablespoons white wine vinegar
1 teaspoon each tarragon (crumbled) and
    chopped chives or green onions
2 eggs
2 tablespoons lemon juice
1 cup hot melted butter

Simmer vinegar with tarragon and chives or green onions until reduced to about 2 teaspoons. Place in a blender container with eggs and lemon juice. Blend a few seconds; then, with blender turned on, slowly pour in the hot melted butter. Turn into a sauce bowl. (If made ahead, reheat over a pan of hot tap water.) Makes 1½ cups.

BAKED CHEESE TOMATOES

Cut a thin slice off the tops of medium-sized tomatoes, season with salt, pepper, and basil, and sprinkle lightly with shredded Swiss cheese. Bake at 375° for 10 to 15 minutes. Allow 1 per person.

DUCHESS POTATO MOUNDS

Prepare instant mashed potatoes as directed on package for 8 servings. Beat in 2 egg yolks and 3 tablespoons soft butter. Pile potatoes into mounds on a buttered baking sheet. Bake at 375° for 15 minutes. Makes 8 servings.

CREAM PUFF STAR

  1 cup regular all-purpose flour
  1 cup water
  ⅛ teaspoon salt
  ½ cup (¼ lb.) butter or margarine
  4 eggs
    Rum Cream Filling (recipe follows)
  ⅓ cup sugar
  3 tablespoons sliced almonds

Sift and measure flour. In a saucepan combine water, salt, and butter; heat until butter is melted. Bring to a full rolling boil, add flour all at once, remove from heat, and stir until paste leaves sides of pan.

Add eggs, one at time, beating until smooth after each addition. Spoon paste into pastry bag with star tip and press out onto a greased baking sheet into a 5 or 6-pointed star about 13 inches across. Bake in a 400° oven 20 minutes; reduce heat to 375° and bake 30 minutes longer. Let cool on rack. Freeze if desired; thaw to fill.

To serve, split shell in half and fill with Rum Cream Filling. Heat sugar until it melts and turns a light amber color, then quickly dribble over puff and sprinkle with almonds. Chill, lightly covered, until time to serve. Makes 12 servings.

Rum Cream Filling. Mix 1 package (3 oz.) egg custard mix and 1¼ cups milk in a saucepan. Bring to a boil, stirring, and remove from heat. Cool and stir in 2 tablespoons rum *or* ½ teaspoon rum flavoring. Beat 2 egg whites until soft peaks form, then beat in ¼ cup sugar, 1 tablespoon at a time. Fold into cool custard. Whip 1 cup heavy cream until stiff; fold into custard.

Christmas Dinner Spanish Style

DRY SPANISH SHERRY

GARLIC SHRIMP APPETIZER

PARSLEY AND PAPRIKA CHEESE APPETIZERS

ROMAINE-AVOCADO SALAD

SEVILLE CHICKEN (POLLO DE SEVILLA)

BROWN BUTTER RICE

HARD FRENCH ROLLS

RUM FLAN (FLAN DE RON)

This dinner for a small group features flamed roast chickens. The host flames the chickens with heated brandy just before carving them. The menu is based on recipes collected in Spain and is a fine choice for Christmas dinner. It is planned to serve 8.

Several hours before the meal, make the flan and chill it. You can also prepare the salad greens, assemble the appetizers, and dice the vegetables (except mushrooms) used in the chicken recipe. About an hour before your guests arrive, start roasting the chicken. When you're ready to heat the appetizers, you can place them in the oven with the chicken. Serve them in the living room with the Sherry. Cook your favorite rice and spoon browned butter over it before serving. Dress the salad at the table.

GARLIC SHRIMP APPETIZER

  1 pound small, shelled, and deveined raw shrimp
½ cup olive oil
  1 whole clove garlic
¼ teaspoon salt
  1 tablespoon minced parsley

Combine the shrimp with the oil, garlic, and salt in a shallow casserole; sprinkle parsley over the top and allow to marinate for 2 to 4 hours. Place the casserole uncovered in a 375° oven for 10 minutes; serve immediately, with toothpicks. Serves 8 to 10.

PARSLEY AND PAPRIKA CHEESE APPETIZERS

Slice 3 long sourdough French rolls into ¼-inch slices. Top each slice with a piece of mild Cheddar cheese about ⅛ inch thick and cut slightly smaller than the bread slice. Sprinkle each with a dash of Parmesan cheese; then sprinkle half of them with a dash of crumbled dried parsley and half with a dash of paprika. Place on a baking sheet in a 375° oven for 3 to 5 minutes or until cheese starts to melt. Serve hot. Makes about 36.

ORANGE-AVOCADO SALAD

  2 medium-sized heads romaine lettuce, washed and chilled
  2 large oranges, peeled and sliced
  1 ripe avocado, peeled and cut in slices
  4 green onions, sliced
⅓ cup olive oil or salad oil
¼ cup wine vinegar
  1 teaspoon sugar
½ teaspoon salt
½ teaspoon salad herb blend (or ¼ teaspoon each whole thyme and basil)
¼ teaspoon chile powder

Break salad greens into a bowl, arrange a layer of orange slices over greens, then avocado slices; sprinkle onion on top. Combine ingredients for the dressing in a jar or bottle. Shake to blend just before pouring over the salad. Mix and serve immediately. Makes 8 servings.

SEVILLE CHICKEN
(Pollo de Sevilla)

 2 roasting chickens (about 4½ pounds each)
   Salt
 4 tablespoons olive oil
 3 small carrots, peeled and sliced
 2 leeks, thinly sliced
 2 stalks celery, sliced
 1 medium-sized onion, chopped
10 whole black peppers
 2 cloves garlic
 2 bay leaves
 1 sprig fresh thyme (or ¼ teaspoon
       dried whole thyme)
 1 cup dry red wine
 3 to 4 tablespoons butter or margarine
¾ pound medium-sized mushrooms,
       sliced
 1 cup (4½-oz. bottle) Spanish-style,
       pimiento-stuffed olives, sliced
 3 to 4 tablespoons flour
 1 can (10½ oz.) condensed chicken broth
       (or 1¼ cups broth made from chicken
       bouillon cubes)
⅓ cup brandy (optional)

Wash and season the chickens with salt; truss. Rub each chicken with 2 tablespoons olive oil and place breast side up in a large open baking or broiling pan without rack. Put in a 400° oven for 20 minutes to brown. Then add the carrots, leeks, celery, onion, and a spice bouquet made of peppercorns, garlic, bay leaves, and thyme tied loosely in cheesecloth. Add ½ cup of the wine. Reduce heat to 375° and cook about 1½ hours longer. Remove spice bouquet. Spoon vegetables and liquid into a blender and whirl to purée vegetables (or force through a sieve).

Meanwhile, melt butter in a large frying pan and add the mushrooms and sauté until tender. Add the olives; heat through. With a slotted spoon, remove olives and mushrooms to a large platter; arrange chickens on top; keep warm. Stir flour into the remaining liquid and butter in the frying pan. Slowly stir in the puréed vegetables, the chicken stock, and the remaining ½ cup wine; cook, stirring, until thickened. Serve in a bowl.

If you wish, flame the chickens at the table by carefully pouring heated, flaming brandy over them. Carve and serve with sauce. Serves 8 to 10.

RUM FLAN
(Flan de Ron)

 6 eggs
⅔ cup sugar
⅛ teaspoon salt
1¾ cups milk or half-and-half (light cream)
¼ cup rum (or rum flavoring to taste)
   Date slices and pecan halves for garnish

Beat eggs with sugar and salt until smooth. Scald milk and beat gradually into the egg mixture. Beat in rum until blended. Pour into a buttered 8-inch cake pan or 1½-pint shallow baking dish; place in a pan of hot water and bake in a 350° oven for about 30 minutes or until a knife blade can be inserted about 2 inches from the side and come out clean. Cool at room temperature until just warm.

Run a knife around the edge of the pan; turn flan out on a serving plate; cover and refrigerate until ready to serve. Garnish with round, thin slices of dates and pecan halves. Cut in wedges. Serves 8.

Christmas Supper Buffet

HOT GLOGG
COLD RARE BEEF ROAST SMOKED BEEF TONGUE
SWEDISH LIVER LOAF CRAB AND CELERY ROOT SALAD
EDAM CHEESE BALLS AND SVEA-OST CHEESE
RUSSIAN RYE BREAD WHITE EGG BREAD
RIPE OLIVES, PICKLES, PICKLED RED PEPPERS
CHERRY AND APPLE-MINCE TARTS WHIPPED CREAM
FRESH FRUIT BASKET

This cold buffet calls for a maximum of advance cookery, a minimum of preparation on the supper day. It is planned to serve 24. While the menu suggests three sliced meats, you could serve two instead. You could also eliminate the tarts and instead offer a basket of grapes and Winesap apples for dessert. Paper plates or metal trays with paper liners would simplify the clean-up.

Roast to the rare stage a 6-pound boneless beef roast (sirloin tip, cross rib, or rolled rib), then chill and slice thinly. Simmer until tender, then chill a 4-pound smoked beef tongue. Serve your choice of cheeses, perhaps a 4-pound Edam and a 4-pound Swedish Svea-ost or Kuminost. Have 2 loaves each of dark Russian rye bread and white egg bread, and 1 jar (about 12 oz.) each of jumbo ripe olives, sweet pickles, and sweet pickled red peppers. Include prepared mustard and horseradish on the meat platters.

HOT GLOGG

6 oranges
 About 6 dozen whole cloves
1 cup warm rum
1 gallon (4 quarts) hot apple cider
3 sticks cinnamon

Stud each orange with 10 to 12 whole cloves. Place on a baking pan and bake in a 300° oven for 2 hours, or until juices start to run. Transfer to a heatproof 2-gallon serving bowl (or copper pan). Pour over warm rum, ignite, and flame. Then pour in hot apple cider and add cinnamon sticks. Keep hot over a warmer during serving time, ladling into small heatproof punch cups. If you wish, stir in additional rum. Makes about 32 servings.

SWEDISH LIVER LOAF

 3 tablespoons finely chopped onion
 1 tablespoon butter
1½ pounds calves liver (cubed)
 ⅓ pound bulk pork sausage
 2 slices bread
 1 cup half-and-half (light cream)
 4 eggs
1½ teaspoons salt
 1 teaspoon Worcestershire
 ¼ teaspoon each cinnamon, allspice,
  nutmeg, and cloves
  Sliced olives, hard-cooked eggs, and
  watercress for garnish

Sauté onion in the butter until tender. In a blender, purée in several batches, the calves liver, pork sausage, bread, onion, half-and-half, eggs, salt, Worcestershire, cinnamon, allspice, nutmeg, and cloves. Spoon the mixture into a buttered 5 by 9-inch baking pan, and cover top of pan with foil. Place in a pan containing 1 inch of hot water and bake in a 350° oven for 1 hour; remove foil and continue baking ½ hour longer.

Cool, then chill. To serve, turn out on a platter and garnish with sliced olives, hard-cooked eggs, and watercress. Makes 24 slices about ⅜ inch thick.

CRAB AND CELERY ROOT SALAD

3 celery roots, peeled and cut horizontally
    into ½-inch-thick slices
  Boiling salted water
  Juice of ½ lemon
¼ cup each olive oil and lemon juice
½ teaspoon salt
¼ teaspoon pepper
2 pounds crab meat, fresh, frozen, or canned
8 hard-cooked eggs, diced
  Salad Dressing (recipe follows)
  Chicory (curly endive)
2 cups halved cherry tomatoes

Cook celery roots in boiling salted water with juice from the ½ lemon for 20 minutes or until tender. Drain, let cool, and dice in ½ -inch cubes. Mix together the olive oil, ¼ cup lemon juice, salt, and pepper; pour over diced celery root, cover, and chill.

Reserve for garnish 6 crab legs from fresh crab or 6 large pieces of meat from frozen or canned crab. Add remainder of crab meat to salad along with diced hard-cooked eggs. Pour dressing over salad and mix lightly. Pile into a salad bowl lined with chicory; mound halved cherry tomatoes in center. Garnish with reserved crab legs. Makes 24 servings.

Salad Dressing. Mix together ⅔ cup *each* mayonnaise and sour cream, ¼ cup lemon juice, ¼ cup capers, 1 teaspoon grated lemon peel, ½ teaspoon *each* salt and crumbled dried tarragon, and ¼ teaspoon pepper.

EDAM CHEESE BALLS

Slice 1½ inches off the top of an Edam cheese. Use a melon ball cutter to scoop out balls. Refill the cheese shell with balls; use cheese scraps for another purpose.

CHERRY AND APPLE-MINCE TARTS

Purchase 2 dozen individual tart shells. Fill half with Cherry Filling and the remainder with Apple-Mince Filling.

Cherry Filling. Heat 1 can (1 lb. 5 oz.) prepared cherry pie filling with 1 tablespoon lemon juice and 2 tablespoons kirsch (optional); simmer 2 to 3 minutes and spoon into shells.

Apple-Mince Filling. Drain 1 can (1 lb. 4 oz.) cooked sliced apples and slice thinner; sauté in 1 tablespoon butter and 2 tablespoons brown sugar for 5 minutes. Add 1 cup prepared mincemeat and heat, simmering until juices are thickened. Spoon into tart shells. Makes 24 servings.

All-Day New Year's Buffet

GRILLED SANDWICHES:

White, Wheat, and Rye Bread; Sliced Cheddar, Swiss, Provolone, and Jack Cheese; Sliced Ham, Corned Beef, Turkey, and Cooked Salami

SPREADS:

Butter, Mustard, and Mayonnaise

SALADS:

Cottage Cheese and Peeled Grapefruit Wedges
with Peeled Orange Slices

DESSERTS:

Winesap and Golden Delicious Apples, Anjou and
Comice Pears with Camembert, Edam, Grape Cheese
(Tomme au Marc de Raisin)

BEVERAGES:

Cold Milk, Hot Coffee, and Individual Cans
of Fruit and Vegetable Juices

For football fans, Tournament of Roses viewers, and people who just want to relax on New Year's Day, here is a serve-yourself buffet that can last practically all day. It's an easy menu of make-your-own (when you want to) grilled sandwiches, salads, fruit, cheeses, juices, milk, and coffee for you to enlarge and elaborate as desired.

Arrange all the foods on a table in a convenient spot. To cook the sandwiches, have an electric sandwich griddle on the table and switch it on when you want to use it.

To keep the breads fresh, put them in an airtight plastic container or a large plastic bag. Lay sliced cheeses and meats on a refrigerated serving tray and cover with a plastic dome, if the tray is equipped with one, or cover with waxed paper or clear plastic film. You can devise a substitute for the tray by filling a broiler pan about half full with water and freezing. Then put the broiler rack on the pan and top with cheese and meats; cover with waxed paper. Set pan on a heavy towel to absorb condensation; it keeps food cool for about 6 hours. Set cottage cheese and fruit salad on the same tray. Keep the butter, mayonnaise, and mustard in deep little jars or pots that can be covered when not in use.

Arrange the dessert of fruit and cheese on a board, and cover it, if you wish. Have coffee in an electric coffee maker or over a candle warmer, milk in a vacuum bottle or insulated pitcher, and the cans of juice in a deep bowl partially filled with crushed ice or ice cubes.

If you serve on paper plates and cups, cleanup is minimized.

The Big Party

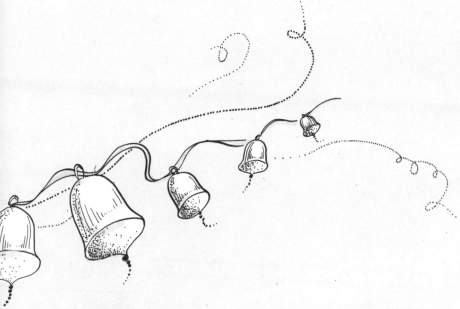

A party for a large group can be relaxed and fun for the host and hostess as well as for the guests. But this takes advance planning, and in many cases improvisation. The menus offered here are varied. They range from a picnic in the park to an elegant buffet dinner. All are carefully planned for easy, informal service. Most can be presented either indoors or out of doors, and the hours are flexible.

In addition to the menus presented here, many of those in the section on special occasions and special themes can also be adapted to serve a larger number of guests.

Equipment for serving a crowd is often a major consideration in planning a big party. You can often borrow extra furniture from friends and neighbors, and many party needs can be rented (check the yellow pages of the telephone directory). But improvising some of the necessities adds to the fun of the party and can emphasize its theme. For example, the lamb entrée in the barbecue menu on pages 182-183 was adapted from a classic Turkish dish, and the Turkish motif was carried out in the table decorations and seating arrangement. The low table was made from a damaged door purchased inexpensively at a building supply store and supported by a pair of wooden benches. The canopy that provided shade was made of inexpensive denim. Guests brought their own cushions.

A Barbecue Buffet

SHREDDED-VEGETABLE SALAD
LAMB KEBAB IN A BOWL
SWEET FRENCH ROLLS
GREEN PEPPER–YOGURT SAUCE
FRUIT   ALMOND COOKIES

The lamb entrée in this menu was adapted from a classic Turkish dish. The Turkish motif is carried out in the table decorations and seating arrangements. The menu, featuring barbecued meat served with salad and bread, makes simple, time-tested fare for a relaxed summer party, but it introduces some surprising flavor variations.

The meat and accompaniments are kept warm over the barbecue. The lamb is roasted in a covered barbecue, then suspended from a tripod above the coals. To make the tripod, lash together three sticks or dowels 2½ feet long. Drill small holes through lower ends of sticks and secure tripod to grill with wire.

SHREDDED-VEGETABLE SALAD

Finely shred 1 small head *each* red cabbage and white cabbage, and 1 bunch carrots. Make separate piles of the vegetables on a large serving plate or tray. Garnish with lettuce, olives, pickled hot peppers, and lemon wedges. Serve with olive oil and additional lemon wedges. Guests select vegetables, then drizzle them with olive oil and lemon juice. Makes 12 to 16 servings.

LAMB KEBAB IN A BOWL

For each 6 to 8 guests, you'll need about 1 quart of rich meat or chicken broth and about 1 dozen sweet French rolls. Split and toast the rolls and heat the broth ahead. For serving, you'll need large soup bowls or deep, rimmed plates.

Buy a large leg of lamb with bone in (about 6 lb.) for each 6 to 8 guests. Drill a small hole through end of shank bone. For each leg, crush 1 clove garlic, blend with 2 tablespoons olive oil and 1 teaspoon *each* crumbled oregano and whole thyme, and rub over surface. Roast lamb slowly in a barbecue that has a hood, allowing about 2½ hours. Use a meat thermometer and roast to about 150° for medium rare or 160° for medium well done. When done, remove the barbecue hood, take out all but a few ignited coals, attach tripod to grill, and suspend meat with wire.

To serve, place pan of rolls under meat, ladle a little hot broth over rolls, and carve meat thinly, letting it fall onto rolls. Each guest places bread in a bowl, piles meat slices on the bread, ladles broth over, then generously tops all with the yogurt sauce.

GREEN PEPPER–YOGURT SAUCE

6 green peppers, seeded and cut in
    ½-inch-wide strips
6 tablespoons olive oil
¾ teaspoon liquid hot-pepper seasoning
6 tablespoons flour
1 cup whipping cream
1 quart plain yogurt
1 tablespoon sugar

Put peppers in a bowl. Mix together the olive oil and liquid hot-pepper seasoning, and drizzle over peppers; refrigerate, covered, for 2 hours or overnight. In the top of a double boiler (or use an improvised pair of pans), blend flour with cream into a smooth paste; gradually stir in yogurt and sugar. Set over gently simmering water and heat slowly, stirring often, for 1 to 1½ hours.

Shortly before serving, turn green pepper strips and oil into a large frying pan; cook, stirring constantly, over high heat, until browned but still slightly crisp. Combine peppers and yogurt in a pan; keep warm on barbecue. Serves 6 to 8.

An Elegant Dinner Party

MUSCAT WINE PUNCH

SWISS TOAST   VIENNESE EGGS

SOLE MOUSSE WITH SHRIMP

GREEN PEA SALAD

MINIATURE HOT BUTTERED ROLLS

TOASTED ALMOND BLACKBERRY TORTE

Cold dishes deliciously flavored and beautifully decorated give this buffet its elegant tone. And they are made mostly the day before. That's the key to the easy serving of this dinner for 12 or—by simply doubling quantities in each recipe—24 guests. The only oven-tending duties are re-heating prepared appetizers and bread.

The appetizers and a wine punch form the first course. Guests then help themselves to mousse, salad, and hot rolls from the buffet. A fork, plate, and napkins are the only utensils each guest needs—there is no meat to cut or bread to butter.

About midday before your party, garnish the mousse and decorate the torte.

MUSCAT WINE PUNCH

3 bottles (4/5 qt. each) Riesling wine
1 bottle (4/5 qt.) Black Muscat wine
2 bottles (1 qt. each) sparkling water
2 cups washed and stemmed Muscat grapes
    (or a small cluster of the grapes)

Thoroughly chill the wine and sparkling water. To serve, blend wines and sparkling water in a punch bowl. Add grapes. Ladle the punch into wine glasses, adding a few grapes to each serving. From an ice bucket, add a piece of ice to keep each drink chilled. Makes 12 to 14 servings.

SWISS TOAST

The cheese mixture can be made several days ahead. You can spread it onto the bread and chill a day ahead, or assemble further ahead and freeze.

1 cup (¼ lb.) finely shredded Swiss cheese
1 egg yolk
⅓ cup half-and-half (light cream)
¼ teaspoon white pepper
½ teaspoon salt
½ teaspoon prepared horseradish
9 or 10 slices of heavy, coarse-textured
    pumpernickel bread, crusts removed

Mix cheese to a paste with egg yolk, half-and-half, pepper, salt, and horseradish. Spread bread slices evenly with cheese mixture and cut each slice in quarters. Arrange on baking sheet in single layer. Cover and chill, or freeze.

To serve, place uncovered in a 375° oven for 8 to 10 minutes, or until hot and the cheese is melted. Serve immediately. Makes 36 to 40 appetizers, enough for 12 guests.

(continued)

VIENNESE EGGS

You can cook and shell the eggs the day before and fill and decorate them early on the day of the dinner.

> 9 hard-cooked eggs, cooled and shelled
> ½ cup sour cream
> Salt to taste
> Lime slices for garnish
> About 1½ tablespoons black caviar

Cut eggs in half lengthwise and remove yolks, being careful not to tear whites. Mash yolks to a fine paste with a fork, blend in sour cream, and salt to taste. Spoon into whites, or force through a pastry bag fitted with a large rosette tip. Top each half egg with a quarter section of a thin slice of unpeeled lime and about ¼ teaspoon caviar. Cover the dish without touching the eggs and chill until ready to serve.

SOLE MOUSSE WITH SHRIMP

> 2 cups dry white wine
> 1 onion, thinly sliced
> 1 carrot, thinly sliced
> 2 sprigs parsley
> 1 teaspoon salt
> 8 to 10 whole peppercorns
> 2½ pounds sole fillets
> 2 envelopes unflavored gelatin
> 1 small onion, minced
> 3 tablespoons butter
> 2 tablespoons flour
> 1½ cups half-and-half (light cream)
> Salt
> Juice of 1 lemon
> 2 teaspoons Dijon-style mustard
> 2 cups heavy cream, whipped stiff
> 1 pound small cooked, deveined shrimp
> 1 cucumber, thinly sliced

In a wide, shallow pan, combine wine, sliced onion, carrot, parsley, salt, and peppercorns. Cover, bring to a boil, and simmer about 5 minutes. Poach the fish fillets in this stock a few at a time; cook 2 to 3 minutes, or until fish flakes. Lift fillets from stock with slotted spatula and place together in a pan. When all are cooked, drain into the stock any juice from pan containing the fish. Strain stock and save—you should have 2 cups (add water to make this amount if necessary). Grind fish through fine blade of a food chopper or whirl until smooth in a blender, using some of the stock to make a smooth paste.

Cool half of the stock, add gelatin, and set aside to soften. Meanwhile cook minced onion in butter until soft, but not browned. Stir in flour; blend in half-and-half. Cook, stirring, until thickened. Remove from heat, salt to taste, and stir in gelatin mixture until dissolved. Add fish, lemon juice, any remaining stock, and the mustard. Chill until partially set; fold in whipped cream. Pour into a straight-sided, flat-bottomed, round or square 3-quart mold. Cover and chill overnight.

To serve, unmold on a platter and decorate with shrimp and cucumber. Spoon extra shrimp over each serving. Makes 12 to 14 servings.

GREEN PEA SALAD

> 6 packages (10 oz. each) frozen peas
> ⅔ cup salad oil
> ⅓ cup red wine vinegar
> 1½ teaspoons salt
> 2 tablespoons crumbled dry or minced
>   fresh mint
> 1 cup finely diced celery
> ½ cup plain yogurt or sour cream
> Lettuce
> 4 tomatoes, cut in wedges

Early in the day, cook peas in a small amount of water until just heated through. Drain and reserve ½ cup cooking liquid; to this add the salad oil, vinegar, salt, and mint. Pour over peas; cover and chill.

Just before serving time mix in celery and yogurt or sour cream. Spoon onto a large lettuce-lined serving tray or bowl, and arrange tomato wedges around edge. Makes 12 to 14 servings.

MINIATURE HOT BUTTERED ROLLS

Prepare 2 packages (14 oz. *each*) hot roll mix according to package directions (or use your own recipe for yeast rolls). Shape as desired, but about a third the usual size. Let rise, then bake in a 375° oven for 10 to 15 minutes until browned. Cool on wire racks. Split and butter. Arrange in single layer close together on baking sheets, then seal in foil and freeze (or refrigerate overnight if you don't have a freezer). Before serving, heat, covered, in a 375° oven for about 10 minutes or until heated through.

TOASTED ALMOND BLACKBERRY TORTE

Bake the cake layers ahead and freeze them, if you wish. Assemble and decorate 4 or 5 hours before the dinner. To prepare almonds called for in this recipe, whirl nuts a few at a time in a blender, or grate on a nut grinder; to toast, arrange whole or chopped on cookie sheet and place in a 350° oven for 10 to 20 minutes, until golden, shaking occasionally.

10 eggs, separated
¾ cup sugar
1¾ cups ground blanched, toasted almonds
¼ teaspoon salt
 About ¾ cup white Port
 About ¾ cup seeded blackberry jam
1½ cups heavy cream, whipped stiff
 Sugar
 Mocha Butter Cream (recipe follows)

Beat yolks with ¾ cup sugar until thick and light colored. Stir in almonds and salt.

Whip egg whites until they hold short, distinct peaks; fold into yolk mixture. Pour into three buttered and floured 9-inch cake pans. Bake in a 350° oven for 20 minutes or until cake begins to pull away from sides of pan. Let stand 10 minutes, then turn out onto wire racks to cool (you can wrap in foil and freeze until time to assemble).

About 4 or 5 hours before guests are expected, sprinkle each layer with 3 or 4 tablespoons Port. Spread two layers generously with jam, reserving a few tablespoons. Stack layers, putting the plain one on top. Sweeten whipped cream to taste with sugar; spread smoothly on sides and top of cake, using a long spatula.

Decorate with Mocha Butter Cream forced through a pastry bag fitted with a ridged half moon tip. Pipe about five straight lines across top and down sides of cake; then pipe five more lines at right angles to the first (to make squares on top and straight lines down the sides). Pipe a border around the base and top edge. Fill alternate squares on top with jam. Chill.

Mocha Butter Cream. Mix ½ cup (¼ lb.) soft butter with 1 pound sifted powdered sugar. Add 2 teaspoons instant coffee powder and 3 tablespoons ground chocolate dissolved in 4 tablespoons hot water. Whip until smooth. Cover and let stand in a cool place (do not refrigerate) until ready to use.

Four Suggested Menus for a Relaxed Big Party

How do you give a big dinner party when by all the rules you haven't enough space, equipment, or time? Obviously, you begin by breaking those very rules that dictate niceties such as formal seating and matching dinner service, and by shaking up the order of the meal and the way it is served.

The four menus suggested here lend themselves nicely to the large-scale, easy-to-manage, open-end sort of party that provides enough nourishment to be called dinner, yet is relaxed for both guests and hosts. You can mix and match any of the parts, or make substitutions wherever you wish. Food quantities can be adjusted easily to serve any number of guests.

The physical set-up makes these menus work smoothly. All courses are presented at strategically separated locations indoors or outdoors, close enough to invite circulation, yet separated enough to avoid crowding. The food is brought out just before guests arrive and kept at ideal serving temperatures; it's ready to serve without plates and forks and requires no attention once guests have arrived. Guests serve themselves as frequently as they wish.

Be generous in your estimate of the amounts of food and drink—appetites can be surprising when guests have plenty of time and free rein. For one serving, allow 1 cup of soup, about ½ pound of meat for 3 or 4 sandwiches, a half bottle of wine, a big salad-size serving of vegetables, and fruit equal to the size of an apple.

When reasonable, keep foods whole or in large pieces; they look nicer and stay fresher. Avoid any food that requires much individual or last-minute attention. Use your imagination in the selection of serving containers—choose containers that will add to the fun. Have plenty of paper napkins and a waste receptacle at each station.

HOW TO PRESENT THE MEAL

It's best to place the aperitif station quite near the entry. Guests serve themselves. Choose an aperitif wine, champagne, a prepared punch, fruit juice, or any drink that needs no mixing. Allow one glass for each guest to use throughout the meal. If guests tend to be forgetful, give each guest a name tag to attach to his glass. You can use wine glasses (rented or borrowed) or plastic throwaway cups.

Then comes the soup. It should be hot and sippable. Have plastic throw-away cups to hold it, and hot pads to protect hands if ladle or soup container are apt to get too hot to handle. Make your own favorite soup ahead, or choose any good canned or dehydrated one.

For a meat course, a large cut like a roast is visually attractive and holds its flavor best. Let guests slice their own and make sandwiches; if you want a special bread, bake and freeze it, or order from a bakery.

Offer just one kind of wine for the whole meal; you might have the same varietal made by several vintners for comparison. Keep wine at a separate serving post.

Instead of serving salad dressing on or mixed with the salad, serve greens or vegetables separately and let guests dip them into a dressing or sauce. Raw or cold cooked vegetables, kept mostly whole (thus easier to prepare) and attractively arranged, have a fresh look.

A dessert of fruit and cheese is the perfect finale to this type of menu. Fruit should be mostly whole and decoratively presented (pears or apples to cut, pineapple cut in chunks and served from its shell, strawberries with stems). Pair fruit with cheeses. Leave cheese in large handsome pieces and let guests serve themselves. As an alternate or an addition, offer a sweet that can be eaten out of hand, such as cookies or a rich, uniced cake.

Coffee is easiest served unpretentiously from a large percolator urn. Make no apology about a miscellaneous collection of coffee cups—just tuck them into a picnic basket with buffers of colorful tissue paper. Provide cream and sugar. Or, if you wish, serve the coffee with lemon twists, sugar, whipped cream, and whiskey, and let your guests make coffee royals or Irish whiskey.

Cold Turkey Dinner

ICED CHAMPAGNE
CLEAR MUSHROOM SOUP
COLD TURKEY   PROSCIUTTO
PARKER HOUSE ROLLS
ARTICHOKES   HOLLANDAISE SAUCE
ALMOND MACAROONS   PINEAPPLE IN SHELL
PROVOLONE CHEESE

Begin the meal with iced champagne, and perhaps continue it through the meal. Or switch to a white wine such as Sauvignon Blanc, Pinot Blanc, Johannisberg Riesling. One icing tub can hold all the wine.

Serve the soup from a silver pitcher over a flame, or from an insulated jug or ceramic carafe. Carve a few slices from the turkey and arrange around the carcass with thinly sliced prosciutto (Italian-style ham). Accompany with prebuttered Parker House rolls on an electric warming tray. Group cold cooked artichokes in a large bowl to eat leaf by leaf, dipping into room-temperature hollandaise sauce. Provide a few spoons and knives for trimming hearts as exposed. Serve the pineapple in its shell and present provolone cheese for guests to slice themselves. Serve the macaroons in a large jar.

Baked Ham Dinner

SHERRY OR OTHER APERITIF WINE

ROSE OR RED WINE

SPLIT PEA SOUP

HOT OR COLD BAKED HAM   TINY CORN MUFFINS

BUTTER   RELISHES

CHERRY TOMATOES   GUACAMOLE

TORTILLA CHIPS

FRUITS IN SEASON   POUND CAKE

Sherry or some other aperitif wine precedes hot split pea soup, served thick and hot from a bountiful tureen on a warming tray. Both the ham and corn muffins may be served either hot (on electric trays) or cold. Serve with a pot of butter and relishes such as chutney or watermelon pickles. Choose either a chilled rosé or a mellow red wine such as Chianti or Vino Rosso to accompany the meal. As a dip for cherry tomatoes, serve homemade guacamole or thawed, frozen avocado dip. (Serve the dip in avocado shells.) Provide tortilla chips for extra dipping and salt for plain tomatoes. For dessert, serve any fruits in season accompanied by pound cake.

Pastrami Sandwich Supper

BURGUNDY OR ALE

ONION SOUP OR CLEAR BORSCHT

PASTRAMI   SWISS CHEESE   RYE BREAD

MUSTARD   BUTTER   PICKLES

CRISP RAW VEGETABLES   HOMEMADE MAYONNAISE

STRAWBERRIES   SUGAR   RICH, UN-ICED CAKE

For this sturdy fare, one beverage such as a full-bodied Burgundy or some ale would do nicely throughout the meal.

The onion soup (strained) or clear borscht might be served from a punch bowl. Keep the soup warm over low heat. Serve the pastrami cold on a board with a wedge of Swiss cheese, to be sliced and served on buffet-sized rye bread. Offer pots of mustard, butter, and pickles. Prepare bite-sized pieces of raw zucchini, Belgian endive, green beans, cabbage, and turnips; serve with homemade mayonnaise for dipping.

For dessert, offer strawberries to be dipped in powdered or granulated sugar; accompany with slices of rich, un-iced cake.

Roast Beef Supper

SHERRY, DRY VERMOUTH, BYRRH   RED WINE

HOT BROTH

RARE ROAST BEEF   SMALL ROUND ROLLS

SWEET BUTTER   LUMPFISH CAVIAR

DIJON-STYLE MUSTARD   PREPARED HORSERADISH

WATERCRESS OR CURLY ENDIVE

ROMAINE   RAW MUSHROOMS   RAW ASPARAGUS

GREEN GODDESS DRESSING

APPLES   CHEESE   COOKIES

Greet guests with a choice of aperitifs such as Sherry, dry Vermouth, or Byrrh, with ice and lemon twists. Barbera or any robust red wine is a good accompaniment to the meal.

Ladle the hot broth into cups from a tureen in front of the fire (you might keep the soup warm right in the fireplace, or use an electric warming tray or candle warmer). The beef, roasted rare (140°, or higher if you like) will stay moist and tasty for about 6 hours on an electric warming tray; an electric knife is handy for slicing. New York strip and cross-rib roasts are both suitable boneless cuts, as they can be trimmed of excess fat. Embellishments for the beef sandwiches include sweet butter, lumpfish caviar, Dijon-style mustard, prepared horseradish, and a bouquet of watercress or curly endive.

Serve the Green Goddess Dressing as a dip for tender inner leaves of romaine, raw mushrooms, and raw asparagus. To make the dressing, combine in a blender 3 egg yolks, 3 tablespoons vinegar, ⅔ cup lightly packed chopped parsley, 1 can (2 oz.) anchovy fillets and oil, 6 green onions, chopped (including most of the tops), and 1½ teaspoons crumbled tarragon. Cover and whirl to liquid consistency, then remove cover and, with motor running, gradually add 1¼ cups salad oil. Increase flow of oil as mixture thickens; turn off and on to blend. Cover and chill up to a week. Makes 1½ cups or 12 to 18 servings.

For dessert, serve a combination of Golden Delicious apples, a large chunk of Fontinella cheese and several small Danish Camemberts, and rich homemade or purchased cookies.

Patio Wine-Tasting Party

FISH COURSE:
Smoked Salmon, Cucumber, Sweet Butter, Dark Bread; Semillon

MEAT COURSE:
Beef Chunks Braised in Wine,
Sliced French Bread; Cabernet Sauvignon

CHEESE COURSE:
Fontina, Gorgonzola, Provolone,
Reblochon; Water Crackers; Barbera

DESSERT COURSE:
Fresh Strawberries, Powdered Sugar;
Butter Cookies; Chenin Blanc or Malvasia Bianca

This party follows the same pattern as the four dinner menus on the preceding pages. But in this case, the emphasis is on the wines. The intent of the party is two-fold: to offer a limited sampling

of wines, and to reveal the character of each wine more clearly by serving it with a complementary food. You combine the wine and food along the lines of a several-course dinner, and here again, as for the previous menus, the courses are arranged at separate stations, ready for self-service. The size of the group can be as small as a dozen persons, or you can serve two or three times that number with surprisingly little difference in effort.

Allow the same quantities of food as you would for a sit-down meal, and about half a bottle of wine and one glass for each person. Between courses, each guest swirls a few drops of the new wine in his glass to rinse it.

Prepare cooked dishes ahead. When necessary, keep them warm or reheat to serve; use your chafing dishes, candle warmers, or electric warming trays. All the foods we suggest can be eaten with the fingers. You can make improvised wine coolers by covering paper paint buckets with self-adhesive plastic or spray-paint.

You can serve the exact four courses listed in the menu above, or make use of any of the alternate choices that follow.

FISH COURSE

Semillon served with smoked salmon and cucumber on buttered dark bread (also good: cold poached salmon). *Alternates:* Pinot Chardonnay with raw oysters on half shells. Johannisberg Riesling with cooked shrimp on ice or cold chunks of cooked lobster in shells to dip in bubbling butter and eat on sliced French bread. Sylvaner with hot scallops to spear from chafing dish. Serve these wines chilled.

MEAT COURSE

Cabernet Sauvignon and beef chunks braised tender in the same wine to eat on sliced French bread, or small chunks of broiled steak to spear. *Alternates:* Gamay with lamb stew simmered in Gamay. Grignolino with hot, meat-topped pizza, cut in small pieces. Ruby Cabernet, hot pork link sausages, and tiny corn muffins. Serve wines at room temperature.

CHEESE COURSE

Barbera with water crackers and Fontina, Gorgonzola, Provolone, and Reblochon cheeses, or any one or two of these cheeses. *Alternates:* Zinfandel with bread sticks and Asiago, Fontinella, Samsoe (or as many as you like). Pinot Noir with unsalted crackers, toasted almonds, and all or a choice of these: Brie, Camembert, Le Beau Pasteur (French process cheese)—or omit nuts and offer Gorgonzola, Mycella, or Roquefort. Petite Sirah with plain wafers and Caerphilly. Serve wines at room temperature.

DESSERT COURSE

Chilled Chenin Blanc (a fruity one) or Malvasia Bianca (12 per cent), and butter cookies with strawberries to dip in powdered sugar (or you could serve Pink Champagne or Sparkling Burgundy). *Alternates:* Chilled Haut (sweet) Sauterne with un-iced pound cake, and strawberries or nuts in shells (or serve chilled Brut or Extra Dry Champagne, or room-temperature Tawny or Ruby Port).

All-Appetizer Buffet

SWEET FRENCH BREAD   GARBANZO SESAME SPREAD

MEATBALLS OREGANO   CHEESE-FILLED DIAMONDS

MARINATED SHRIMP AND ARTICHOKES   STUFFED CLAMS

SKEWERED DOLMAS, OLIVES, AND EGGPLANT

PUMPKIN SEEDS   KASSERI AND FETA CHEESES

CANTALOUPE AND STRAWBERRIES

BAKLAVA   HALVAH   TURKISH COFFEE

The Greeks, with their zest for living, have a well developed custom of socializing with wine and mezé (meh-*zeh*, meaning "a little something to whet the appetite"). Mezé, in various degrees of complexity, is always offered at the colorful *tavernas* and at family holiday gatherings. As the spontaneous dancing and talk continue, the appetizers are so numerous that eventually they become the meal.

This party captures the merriment of a mezé party. The plan will handle two dozen guests for a non-stop, appetizer-through-dessert buffet. The foods are authentically Greek with a nod or two to the Turks. These Near Eastern dishes have the prize asset of being able to sit awhile outdoors without losing their flavor.

Greek specialty markets and international delicatessens carry many of the foods. Here you can buy *fila* (paper-thin dough), cheeses, olives, *tahini* (ground sesame seeds), *baklava,* and *halvah* (sesame seed candy). You can buy canned stuffed grape leaves and stuffed baby eggplant for the *dolmas* (sometimes spelled *dolmathes* or *dolmades)* or make your own following the recipes on pages 130 and 131. Set out pumpkin seeds (allow ½ lb.) and chunks of kasseri and feta cheeses (1½ pounds of each).

To best complement the food, we suggest serving Greek wines or oúzo, the potent aniseed-flavored liqueur. Domestic California red and white *retsinas* (with their pitch-pine flavoring) are surprisingly inexpensive, yet compare favorably with Greek resinated wines. Among Greek non-resinated wines, look for Hymettus (dry white), Roditys (rosé), or Kokineli (red). Set out the beverages in an iced container, letting them double as both aperitif and something to sip throughout the evening. Guests may take oúzo neat, diluted with cold water (it then turns milky white), or chilled with ice cubes.

GARBANZO SESAME SPREAD
(Humus Tahini)

    2 cans (1 lb. each) garbanzo beans, drained
    ⅔ cup lemon juice
    ⅔ cup tahini (ground sesame seeds)
    2 cloves garlic, minced
    ½ teaspoon salt
      Dry black Greek olives or California
        ripe olives for garnish
      Greek bread (Kouloura) or sweet
        French bread

Place beans in a blender with lemon juice, tahini, garlic, and salt; cover and blend well. (You may prepare this in two batches for easier handling.) Chill, covered, or freeze.

When ready to serve (thaw if frozen), mound on a plate, shaping into a cone with a spatula. Garnish with a cluster of dry black Greek olives or California ripe olives. Spread on slices of doughnut-shaped Greek bread or any sweet French bread. Makes about 1 quart spread.

(continued)

MEATBALLS OREGANO
(Keftethakia)

6 slices white bread
1 cup milk
1 cup finely chopped onion
2 tablespoons butter
4 pounds ground beef chuck
¾ cup finely chopped parsley
4 egg yolks
4 teaspoons salt
¼ teaspoon pepper
¾ cup red wine vinegar
1 teaspoon oregano

Crumble bread and soak in milk 5 minutes; beat with a fork until mushy. Sauté onion in butter until golden. In a large mixing bowl, place ground beef chuck, parsley, egg yolks, the milk mixture, sautéed onions, salt, and pepper. Thoroughly mix with your hands. Shape into 1¼-inch balls and place on two 10 by 15-inch baking pans. Bake at 450° for 15 minutes, or until meatballs are browned and slightly pink in the center.

Meanwhile bring the vinegar and oregano to a boil and let simmer 10 minutes; pour half the mixture over hot meatballs in each pan, scraping up the pan juices. Serve immediately or leave in pan and chill, covered, or freeze. To serve later (thaw if frozen), heat in 375° oven for 15 minutes. Serve warm. Makes about 6 dozen.

SKEWERED DOLMAS, OLIVES, EGGPLANT

1 jar (about 1 lb.) stuffed small eggplants
2 cans (about 13 oz. each) dolmas
4 dozen large Greek black olives or pitted
   California ripe olives
Parsley sprigs

On 9-inch-long wooden skewers (you'll need about 2 dozen), alternate on each stick a dolma, olive, eggplant, olive, and dolma. Poke into a large flower "frog" and stuff the metal base with parsley springs. Place on a small plate. Makes about 2 dozen skewered relishes.

CHEESE-FILLED DIAMONDS
(Bourekakia)

1 large package (8 oz.) cream cheese
½ pound feta cheese
1 pint large curd cottage cheese
3 egg yolks
2 tablespoons minced parsley
½ pound butter
24 sheets fila dough (about ⅔ of a 1-lb.
   package)

In a mixing bowl place cream cheese, feta cheese, cottage cheese, egg yolks, and parsley; cream until smoothly blended.

Melt the ½ pound butter in a small saucepan. Lay out three sheets of fila (keep remaining fila covered with clear plastic film). Brush one sheet lightly with melted butter using a wide pastry brush, lay on another sheet, brush with butter, top with the third sheet, and brush with butter. (It is not necessary to completely coat sheets with butter; just moisten them in four long streaks.)

Spoon a ½-inch-wide ribbon of cheese mixture along a lengthwise side of the dough, 1½ inches in from the bottom edge and the two sides. Fold ends and bottom edge over filling. Roll up loosely in jelly-roll fashion and place seam side down on an ungreased baking sheet. Repeat, making seven more rolls and placing them about 1 inch apart; you'll need two baking sheets.

Bake in a 375° oven for 15 minutes, or until puffed and lightly browned. Let cool 15 minutes, then slice through each roll on the diagonal about 2¼ inches apart, making diamond-shaped pieces. Serve at once or cool on pans and chill, covered (or freeze). To serve later, let thaw if frozen. Heat until crisp in a 375° oven for 15 minutes. Makes 4 dozen.

STUFFED CLAMS
(Kidonia Yemista)

½ cup olive oil
1½ cups uncooked short grain (or pearl) rice
2 medium-sized onions, finely chopped
½ cup pine nuts
3 cans (7½ oz. each) minced clams
½ cup tomato sauce
½ teaspoon each dill weed and allspice
⅓ cup currants
Lemon wedges

Heat olive oil in a large frying pan; add rice, onions, and pine nuts. Sauté, stirring, until nuts turn golden. Remove from heat. Thoroughly drain and measure liquid from clams (if needed, add enough water to make 1½ cups liquid) and pour over rice mixture. Add tomato sauce, dill weed, allspice, and currants. Cover and let stand 30 minutes.

Bring to a boil, reduce heat to low, and let simmer precisely 12 minutes. Remove from heat and let stand (without removing cover) for 10 minutes. Add clams and stir lightly with a fork. Let cool slightly, then spoon into small shells, such as clam, mussel, or scallop shells (or mound in a bowl). Chill, or freeze, well wrapped. Serve cold (thaw if frozen) with lemon wedges. Fills 4 dozen shells.

MARINATED SHRIMP AND ARTICHOKES
(Garides me Anginares Marinata)

4 jars (6 oz. each) marinated artichoke
  hearts
½ cup lemon juice
½ teaspoon tarragon
5 pounds large cooked shrimp (about
  15 to a pound), peeled and deveined
2½ cups cherry tomatoes

Drain marinade from artichoke hearts into a bowl. Stir in lemon juice and tarragon. Add shrimp, stir lightly to coat, cover and chill. To serve, arrange shrimp down the center of a platter; place marinated artichoke hearts on one side and cherry tomatoes on the other side. Spoon marinade over shrimp. Makes about 24 appetizer-size servings.

THE DESSERT TABLE

For a change of pace and to encourage mingling of guests, set up dessert in another part of the garden or by a pool.

You can make Turkish coffee, following directions on container, over a small brazier or hibachi on the spot. Also serve regular coffee, for those who prefer it, brewed in the kitchen. Offer an abundance of fresh strawberries with stems (about 2 quarts), and 4 or 5 cantaloupes, cut into a flower shape (cut each cantaloupe into six wedges from top but do not cut through bottom; remove seeds; separate slightly at top and fill center with the strawberries).

If it's available, buy chocolate-marbled halvah with nuts (about 2 pounds) and offer honey-soaked baklava.

Picnic for a Crowd

ICED COOKED SHRIMP   MAYONNAISE
TOMATO GAZPACHO WITH AVOCADO
LIME WEDGES   LIQUID HOT-PEPPER SEASONING
ASIAGO OR HARD JACK CHEESE   CRUSTY ROLLS
DRY WHITE WINE   FRUIT JUICES
WARM DANISH PASTRY
COFFEE WITH WHIPPED CREAM

A nearby public park with tables, plenty of space, and a few of the basic comforts can provide the setting for an easy-to-manage picnic for a large group, possibly one in which several families participate and share the work.

For a tablecloth, take along a piece of colorful oilcloth; it is sturdy and wipes clean, and in today's interesting designs, it gives a fresh look to the picnic table. You'll need a bag of crushed ice, from home or purchased from a vending machine. Mound the shrimp in it; chill the wine and fruit juices in it; add some to each bowl of soup when it is served. Carry the soup to the picnic in a wide-mouth jug.

Serve the shrimp on paper plates, and the soup in paper bowls with spoons; provide plenty of paper napkins. Buy cheese in a large wedge; take a knife to cut it in chunks. Heat frozen Danish pastries at home according to package directions, then wrap right in the pans with foil and towels, and pack in an insulated bag. Keep bag closed to hold heat. Swirl cream topping from a pressurized can into cups of coffee.

TOMATO GAZPACHO WITH AVOCADO

Here's a simple recipe for Gazpacho that can be doubled or tripled, as you wish, to serve any number of people.

½ cucumber, peeled
½ mild red or white onion, peeled
½ avocado, peeled
½ teaspoon crumbled oregano
3 tablespoons olive oil or salad oil
2 tablespoons wine vinegar
4 cups canned tomato juice
2 limes, cut in wedges
  Liquid hot-pepper seasoning

Cut off a few slices of cucumber and onion; save for garnish. Chop the rest of the cucumber and onion in small pieces. Slice or chop the avocado. Put onion, cucumber, avocado, oregano, oil, and vinegar in the picnic jug. Pour in the tomato juice. Top with cucumber and onion slices; chill.

To serve, ladle into bowls, adding a little ice to each serving. Let each person add lime juice and hot-pepper seasoning to taste. Serves 6.

Danish Party Fish

POACHED LOBSTER TAILS

BAKED FISH MOLD

OVEN-POACHED SOLE ROLLS

FRIED SOLE FILLETS

HOLLANDAISE SAUCE   SHERRY CREAM SAUCE

CREAMED MUSHROOMS IN PATTY SHELLS

POTATOES, RICE, OR PASTA (OPTIONAL)

GREEN SALAD

ASSORTED FRUITS AND CHEESES

A handsome platter of fish in variety is an ideal main course to serve buffet style to a small crowd of 10 or 12 or a large crowd of up to 30. The idea comes from Denmark, where "Party Fish" is often the main course for a family gathering. The Party Fish Platter also lends itself beautifully to a gourmet club gathering, to which each person brings a part of the menu assembled in advance and cooks it at the last minute.

Although the platter looks imposing and elaborate, it is easy to plan, cook, and serve. Several hours in advance, you can assemble the fish mold, the rolled fillets and the fillets to be fried, thaw the lobster, and refrigerate all until time to cook and serve. The mold and the poached fish rolls cook at the same time in the oven while you fry the fish fillets and quickly cook the lobster.

Bake frozen patty shells in advance or buy them from your bakery, and cook the mushrooms ahead, reheating them before serving. If you wish, add to the menu a starch dish of potatoes, rice, or pasta. Dessert can be an assortment of fruits and cheeses.

You'll need a large platter or tray, preferably one that can be heated or kept warm, about 24 to 30 inches in diameter or 18 by 36 inches if it is oblong. If you use a wooden platter, you may wish to line it with foil before using.

Arrange the baked fish mold on the platter first and surround it with poached sole rolls, poached lobster tails, and fried sole fillets. Put any extra fish on a tray, cover, and keep warm in a very low oven to refill the platter later, as needed. Serve the patty shells filled with creamed mushrooms on the platter with the fish or on another platter. Garnish the platter generously with parsley. Have ready a large plate of lemon wedges. Serve Hollandaise Sauce and Sherry Cream Sauce in separate bowls to spoon over individual servings.

The amounts given here are planned for a party of 10 to 12. If you serve up to 20, double the amounts given for poached and fried fish, but make just one mold. For 30 people, make two of the molds and triple the amount of fried and poached fish.

POACHED LOBSTER TAILS

Buy 4 frozen lobster tails, about 2 or 2¼ pounds, and thaw; split lengthwise. In a 2-quart pan, combine 1 cup *each* dry white wine and boiling water and 1½ teaspoons salt. Bring to a boil and drop in the lobster tails; reduce heat and simmer for 10 minutes or until shells turn pink and flesh becomes opaque white. Remove lobster tails from the liquid, drain; arrange on fish platter. Serve with lemon wedges and Hollandaise Sauce. (See recipe on page 203).

(continued)

BAKED FISH MOLD

**1 pound each boneless cod and flounder
(or sole) fillets
4 egg whites (reserve egg yolks for the
Hollandaise Sauce)
2 teaspoons salt
⅛ teaspoon white pepper
Dash allspice
2 cups whipping cream
Butter
3 tablespoons very finely ground almonds or
fine dry bread crumbs
Hollandaise Sauce or Sherry Cream Sauce
(recipes follow)**

Chop fish as fine as possible. Working with a small amount of the fish at a time, whirl in blender until smooth, adding egg whites to the entire amount. Or put fish through food chopper with the finest blade several times or until fish is a smooth purée. Turn into large bowl of electric mixer; add salt, white pepper, allspice, and cream. Beat at low speed for 20 minutes, mixing ingredients well to make a very smooth, thick, paste-like mixture.

Butter a 1 to 1½-quart mold very well and dust with almonds or bread crumbs. Turn fish mixture into mold. (You can do this much ahead, cover, and refrigerate until ready to cook.)

Place mold in a pan with 1 inch of hot water and bake in a 325° oven for 35 to 45 minutes or until knife inserted into the mold comes out clean. Do not overcook. Unmold and arrange on serving platter. Cut in slices to serve, and spoon over Hollandaise Sauce or Sherry Cream Sauce (recipes follow). Makes about a dozen 1-inch-thick slices, or about two dozen ½-inch slices.

OVEN-POACHED SOLE ROLLS

If you are serving 10, buy 8 medium-sized sole or flounder fillets. Split the fillets lengthwise to make two oval pieces, one larger than the other. Use the smaller piece for the flounder rolls and reserve the larger one for the fried sole fillets (recipe follows).

**8 sole fillets
2 teaspoons salt
4 teaspoons butter
Parsley
1 cup each dry white wine and boiling water
3 whole black peppers
1 tablespoon lemon juice**

Pound fillets with a smooth mallet to flatten slightly so they will be easier to roll. Sprinkle with ½ teaspoon of the salt. Put ½ teaspoon butter and a sprig of parsley in center of each piece of fish and roll up; secure with toothpicks. Arrange in a lightly greased casserole about 12 by 9 inches. (You can do this much ahead, cover, and refrigerate until cooking time.)

To cook, combine wine, boiling water, the remaining 1½ teaspoons salt, peppers, and 3 sprigs of parsley; pour over the fish rolls. Cover tightly with foil and bake in a 325° oven for 35 minutes or until fish flakes when probed with a fork. Remove fish rolls from the liquid (discard liquid) and arrange on the platter with the fish mold. Sprinkle with lemon juice. Serve with Hollandaise Sauce.

FRIED SOLE FILLETS

Use the 8 larger sole or flounder fillets from the preceding recipe to make these fried sole fillets.

    8 sole fillets
    1 cup milk
    1 cup flour
    1 teaspoon salt
    ½ teaspoon pepper
    3 eggs, slightly beaten
    2 cups fine dry bread crumbs
    3 tablespoons butter
    1 tablespoon lemon juice
      Lemon wedges
      Hollandaise Sauce (recipe follows)

Dip each piece of fish first in the milk, then in a mixture of the flour, salt, and pepper, and then in egg; drain briefly, then dip in the bread crumbs. Place on a tray lined with waxed paper, ready for frying. (You can do this much, cover with foil or plastic wrap, and refrigerate until ready to cook.)

Melt butter in a frying pan over medium heat and fry the crumb-coated fillets quickly until golden brown on each side, cooking about 4 to 5 minutes in all. Arrange on platter with the poached fish. Sprinkle with lemon juice. Serve with lemon wedges or Hollandaise Sauce.

HOLLANDAISE SAUCE

    4 egg yolks
    2 tablespoons lemon juice
    1 cup (½ lb.) butter
    4 teaspoons hot water
    ½ teaspoon salt
      Dash cayenne pepper
    1 teaspoon prepared Swedish or Dijon-style
      mustard

Combine egg yolks and lemon juice in blender. Melt butter and heat it until it bubbles—don't brown. Add the hot water to the egg and lemon juice, turn blender on high speed, and immediately pour in the hot butter in a slow, steady stream. Turn off blender, add the salt, cayenne, and mustard; whirl until blended, about 30 seconds. Makes about 2 cups.

SHERRY CREAM SAUCE

    2 tablespoons butter or margarine
    2 tablespoons flour
    1 cup half-and-half (light cream)
      Salt and pepper to taste
    1 cup cooked lobster or crab meat
    2 tablespoons Sherry

Melt butter in a small pan; stir in the flour until smooth and bubbly. Remove from heat and gradually stir in the half-and-half; cook, stirring, until thickened and smooth. Season with the salt and pepper; cover and keep on lowest heat until serving time. Just before serving, stir in the lobster or crab meat and the Sherry. Makes about 2 cups sauce.

CREAMED MUSHROOMS IN PATTY SHELLS

    12 patty shells or 2 packages (10 oz. each)
        frozen patty shells
     1 pound mushrooms
     3 tablespoons butter or margarine
     1 cup half-and-half (light cream)
    ½ teaspoon salt
       Pinch of tarragon

If you buy patty shells from your bakery, simply reheat them just before serving; if you bake frozen patty shells, follow directions on the package. Wash the mushrooms well and chop fine. Melt the butter in a 2-quart pan, add the mushrooms, and cook, stirring, over medium heat, until the mushrooms are heated through. Add the cream, salt, and tarragon; simmer, uncovered, for 15 minutes, stirring occasionally. Cover and let stand over low heat until serving time. Spoon the hot mushroom sauce into the patty shells just before serving. Makes 12 servings.

Index